THE BODLEY HEAD
MAX BEERBOHM

THE BODLEY HEAD

MAX
BEERBOHM

EDITED AND WITH
AN INTRODUCTION BY
DAVID CECIL

THE BODLEY HEAD
LONDON   SYDNEY
TORONTO

This selection © The Bodley Head 1970
Introduction © David Cecil 1970
ISBN 0 370 01335 2
Printed and bound in Great Britain for
The Bodley Head Ltd
9 Bow Street, London WC2
by William Clowes & Sons Ltd, Beccles
Set in Linotype Plantin
First published in this edition 1970

CONTENTS

[*see over*

INTRODUCTION

'THE INCOMPARABLE MAX', Shaw called him. The phrase has stuck. Indeed it is apt; from the first Max's work was too individual profitably to be compared with that of anyone else. Not that it was always the same. Max the impertinent exquisite of the 1890s changed gradually into Max the mature and subtle humorist of the 1920s. His style altered along with his spirit: the florid Rococo of the essay on 'Dandies and Dandies' sobered and refined itself into the classic Chippendale of the essay on 'Going Out for a Walk'. All the same the difference between the two is far less than their likeness. From the beginning to the end of his career Max's work is homogeneous; an expression of the same personality and the same attitude towards his art.

This is that of the entertainer. From the start of his career Max thought it the first duty of an artist to be true to the nature of his talent and to refrain from writing on subjects that did not inspire it. 'It is curious', he writes, 'how often an artist is ignorant of his own true bent. How many charming talents have been spoiled by the desire to do "important" work. Some are born to juggle with golden balls, some are born to lift heavy weights.' He was not ignorant of his own bent. He knew he was a juggler and he devised his work accordingly. Though as capable as anyone of serious views and deep feelings he recognised that these did not stir his artistic impulse: so that very rarely does he allow them to appear openly in his work. Deliberately he writes not to disturb or to instruct but to please: and more particularly to amuse.

For—and this is the second distinguishing characteristic of his work—his genius was a comic genius. The aspects of experience that stimulated him to create were the aspects

that made him smile or laugh: the balls he juggled with
were jokes: the Max Beerbohm entertainment is a comic
entertainment. But it is one of a special and superior kind,
for it is the expression of a special and superior man. Max
was very intelligent, with a sharp, searching intelligence,
continually at work noticing and concluding. Half his jokes
are also penetrating comments on human nature. Well-
informed comments too! Max liked to make out that he
was imperfectly educated. In fact every page he wrote
reveals him as the heir to an ancient culture which has
furnished his mind, enriched his imagination and refined
his taste, disclosing itself in his every casual allusion and
in the unobtrusive, graceful confidence of his tone of voice.
Finally culture and intelligence alike are strengthened by
the fact that they are under the direction of a shrewd judgment. Unlike some intelligent people Max was extremely
sensible. He surveyed the world with a realistic gaze that
made him as impervious to nonsense as Dr Johnson himself, however much it was accepted by respectable or fashionable opinion. Listen to him talking about the opponents
of woman's suffrage in the 90s:

Two or three years ago, other ladies, anxious to vote, came
forward and have gone around literally shrieking; and the
result is that already their desire is treated as a matter of
practical politics, and a quite urgent one at that. What a
pretty light all this throws—does it not?—on a world
governed by the animals which distinguish themselves from
the other animals by taking 'reasonable animals' as their
label! And yet the light does not seem to have enlightened the
brilliantly reasonable animals which write for the press. In-
variably, solemnly, at every fresh 'raid' or other escapade of the
suffragist ladies, those newspapers which are friendly to the
cause itself announce that 'this has put back the clock of
female suffrage by at least twenty years'. Bless their hearts!
The clock must now, by their computation, have been put
back 'at least' twelve centuries.

Or commenting on the gospel of Marinetti, the prophet of
the Futurist movement in art:

With the best will in the world, I fail to be frightened by Marinetti and his doctrines. . . . When he asks why we 'poison ourselves' by 'a daily walk through the museums', I assure him that his metaphor has no relation to fact. There are a few pedants who walk daily in museums; but even they don't poison themselves; on the contrary, they find there the food that best agrees with them. There is a vast mass of humanity which never sets foot in a museum. There are the artists who go now and again, and profit by the inspiration. It must be a very feeble talent that dares not, for fear of being overwhelmed and atrophied, contemplate the achievements of the past. No talent, however strong, can dispense with that inspiration. But how on earth is anyone going to draw any inspiration from the Future? Let us spell it with a capital letter, by all means. But don't let us expect it to give us anything in return. It can't, poor thing; for the very good reason that it doesn't yet exist, save as a dry abstract term.

The past and present—there are two useful and delightful things. I am sorry, Marinetti, but I'm afraid there is no future for the Future.

Anti-suffragists were old-fashioned; the Futurists were *avant-garde*. Max was as unimpressed by the one as by the other. His formidable good sense made him formidably independent. Even the great brains of his time could not stampede him into accepting their views against his better judgment.

Take them seriously? Ah no! If they happen to be artists expressing themselves through some art-form, through poems or novels, let us delight in their concentration, the narrowness that enables them to express just what they can feel, just what they can understand, so much more forcibly than if they had a sense of proportion and a little of the modesty that comes of wisdom. Our Ibsens and D'Annunzios and Bernard Shaws and Gorkis—let us harken to them and revel in them. But let us mix up all their 'messages' together, and strike an average, and not suppose even then that we are appreciably one whit nearer to the truth of things.

Sceptical about 'messages', Max, as this quotation shows, never questioned the value of art. Indeed the impulse be-

hind the work, in so far as it was not comic, was aesthetic.
The Beerbohm entertainment set out to entertain by its
beauty as well as by its fun. Max grew up during the
period of the Aesthetic Movement; and though he laughed
at it—as at most things—he shared its views. For him, art
was the most important and most precious of human activi-
ties: and the distinguishing mark of a work of art was its
beauty. Even a caricature, he thought, should aim at beauty
—'beauty to be achieved by the perfect adjustment of
means to ends'. Max's feeling for beauty, apparent in his
unsleeping sense of form, also showed itself in his taste.
This was in keeping with the general character of his
genius. Though he could recognise grand or primitive
types of beauty, he preferred it light, delicate, elegant;
beauty in its humbler, gayer manifestation as prettiness.
Mingled with his sense of fun, this sense of beauty often
incarnated itself in the form of graceful extravagant fantasy, the fantasy of wicked 'Lord George Hell' converted
to a saintly life by wearing a saintly wax mask, of the
busts of the Roman Emperors outside the Sheldonian
Theatre at Oxford bursting out in sweat at the sight of beautiful, fatal Zuleika Dobson. Yet—and this is one of the
things that gives Max's work its unique flavour—his fantasy is always disciplined by his intelligence and his good
sense. It is never silly: its charm comes largely from the
fact that it is seen against an unwavering standard of
realism and reason. The behaviour of the busts may be
fantastic, but not the Oxford scene in which it takes place:
Lord George Hell's conversion is described with a conscious, self-mocking affectation of manner which makes it
quite clear that the reader must not take it too solemnly.
Whatever clouds of fantasy may encircle Max's head his
feet were always firmly on the ground.

The effect of this contrast running through his work is
ironical. Irony is its most continuous and consistent characteristic; an irony at once delicate and ruthless, from which
nothing is altogether protected, not even the author himself. Ruthless but not savage: Max could be made angry –

by brutality or vulgarity – but very seldom does he reveal this in his creative works. His artistic sense told him that ill-temper was out of place in an entertainment, especially in an entertainment that aspired to be pretty as well as comic. His ruthlessness gains its particular flavour from the fact that it is also good-tempered. On the other hand it is not so good-tempered as to lose its edge. Max's irony is never that sort of 'kindly' irony that softens and sentimentalises. His artistic sense tells him that softness, as much as savagery, would destroy the clear bright atmosphere needed for his entertainment to make its effect.

The Max Beerbohm entertainment takes various forms. First of all there are the parodies. Here Max is a supreme master. He manages to parody his victim's sense as much as he does his style. Henry James, once questioned about his next work, replied, pointing to Max Beerbohm: 'Ask that young man. He knows me better than I know myself.' Reading the James parody in this selection, one sees what he means. If Henry James had chosen to write about two children waking up to find their stockings on Christmas morning this is what he would have said. And this almost is how he would have said it. The exaggeration of style needed to make parody amusing is all the more effective because it is so very slight. Sometimes Max hardly seems to exaggerate at all. 'If Euclid was alive to-day (and I daresay he is) . . .' Is this a phrase of Chesterton's or a phrase from Max's parody of Chesterton? Once again the likeness is of sense as well as of style. The sentence is an illuminating critical comment on Chesterton's whole mode of thought. So is the parody on James a profound and friendly criticism of James, so is the parody of Kipling a profound but devastating criticism of Kipling.

Max's entertainment took two other forms. The first is the occasional essay. Of these there are four volumes: *The Works of Max Beerbohm, More, Yet Again* and the last and best, *And Even Now*. Max's essays are what may be called 'pure' essays; that is to say they are vehicles not for instruction or confession but designed simply to fulfil his creative impulse, which is to amuse. If he does make a serious point in them, it is in a playful tone; any imaginative moment takes the form of a playful flight of fancy. For the rest they are deliberate exhibitions of personality. This personality is not a self-portrait. Max the essayist is not the same as Max the man, but rather a fictitious figure made up of those particular elements in his composition that he judged would enhance his entertainment. He isolates some of his own qualities—his humour, his fancy, his wit, his taste in style—and uses them as material from which by means of an elaborate process of arrangement and staging he creates the protagonist in his one-man show.

Such a type of essay is hard to write successfully, as can be realised by reading the essays of Max's imitators. On the one hand to keep the tone so consistently light is to run the risk of making the whole thing seem flimsy; on the other hand the writer who consciously exploits his personality easily appears an exhibitionist all too obviously anxious to show off his charm. Max walks the tightrope between these dangers with confidence and ease. His essays do not seem flimsy because they are not built of flimsy materials; they are the product of too lively an intelligence, too observant an eye. Such pieces as those on 'The Naming of Streets' or 'Hosts and Guests' are packed with enough fresh ideas and insights into human nature to furnish forth fifty average 'serious' writers. If the reader fails to notice this, it is only because Max's tone is so carefree and throw-away.

Intelligence saves his essays from flimsiness; good sense saves them from self-admiring exhibitionism. No doubt Max is showing off; it is the function of the entertainer to show off. But he is far too sensible to be unaware of this fact and far too humorous not to be amused by it. In the essay entitled 'Going Out for a Walk' he describes vividly how bored he has been by a fellow walker; but the climax of the piece is his unexpected revelation that he knows the fellow walker is likely to have found him equally boring. It is a secret of his strength that he is one of the very few writers whose irony is so impartial as to include himself.

Along with his 'pure' essays we may consider Max's critical pieces, mostly drawn from his work as the dramatic critic of the *Saturday Review*. He wrote these reluctantly as a means of livelihood; and they do show his limitations. One cannot call them failures; they are too clever and too accomplished. But the critical mode, except in the form of parody, did not stimulate him. Criticism is not primarily a comedian's mode. Max knew it. 'My whole position is uncomfortable,' he remarked. 'I have a satiric temperament; when I am laughing at anyone I am generally rather amusing but when I am praising anyone I am always dull.' Here he goes too far; he did not know how to be dull. It is true, however, that only now and again in these criticisms does he seem vitally and unmistakably himself, and that is when he leaves off talking about a play to follow some comic or whimsical train of thought suggested by it, or to re-create with affectionate amusement some personality which has appealed to his fancy, like Irving or Dan Leno; when in fact he stops being a critic and reverts to being an entertainer.

The last category in his entertainment consists of his stories. These in their turn subdivide into two types. First come his two fables, *The Dreadful Dragon of Hay Hill* and *The Happy Hypocrite*. *The Dreadful Dragon of Hay Hill* is not included in this book; even more than his play reviews it exposes Max's limitations. Written after the First World War, it is designed to illustrate his conviction, taught him by the war, that mankind is incurably, congenitally quarrelsome. This is a bleak conviction and, for all that Max writes in his usual playful tone, it is a bleak tale. As such it does not suit his talent, for bleakness involves the eclipse of that good-humour which is an essential condition of his inspiration. At the same time he lacks the harsh force to drive his story's harsh moral home. Max cannot divest himself of his usual easy urbanity. This blunts the cutting edge of his attack on humanity. *The*

Happy Hypocrite also points a moral, namely that by wearing a mask of goodness you may become good; for, as
Max said: 'I hold that Candour is good only when it reveals
good actions or good sentiments, and that when it reveals
evil, itself is evil.' Here for once he is talking seriously.
And wisely too; these principles, put into practice, are a
good deal more likely to lead a man to live a satisfactory
life than are all the hot gospels preached by the prophets
of romanticisim, from Shelley down to D. H. Lawrence.
The Happy Hypocrite is charming as well as wise; with a
fresh youthful charm that makes it impossible to omit it
from any selection of its author's best work. Its only fault
is that its charm and its wisdom do not completely har-
monise. The mock-nursery-tale mode in which Max has
chosen to tell his story is a little too childish to carry
the weight of its mature moral.

There is no such fault in the second group of his stories,
Zuleika Dobson and *Seven Men and Two Others*. These,
along with his best parodies, are his masterpieces. They are
best described as satiric fantasies and owe their peculiar
flavour, even more than his other works, to the fact that
they are a blend; on the one hand of humour and prettiness, on the other of fact and fancy. Most of them involve
extravagant flights of fancy; yet each is founded on
Max's personal experience of the real world and each derives substantial interest from the fact that it is sedulously
true to it. Fantasy is at its prettiest and boldest in *Zuleika
Dobson*. This tells how the most beautiful woman in the
world arrived in what was then the exclusively male world
of Oxford; how all the undergraduates fell in love with her
and how they drowned themselves for her sake at the close
of the boat races. This preposterous idea is exploited to its
full preposterousness. No note of serious feeling checks
the foaming flood of high spirits on which the tale sweeps
along. It is consistently and audaciously heartless. Yet the
fun is not 'sick'; there is no question of the author taking
an equivocal pleasure in pain. Our pleasure in it is unquali-
fied by the smallest hint of horror or perversity. With all

this, it is truthful too; the truest picture of Oxford in fiction. Dons and students and Rhodes scholars, Eights Week, Balliol concerts, exclusive dining clubs—every characteristic phase and fact of University life is described with an extraordinary, perceptive insight. Finally it is written in a style which is a masterpiece of sustained virtuosity, a parody of aesthetic fine writing which is even finer than the manner which it mocks. As a blend of comedy and prettiness *Zuleika Dobson* has no equal in English literature but *The Rape of the Lock*.

Seven Men and Two Others, written in the full maturity of its author's spirit and manner, is an even subtler triumph. It is the most autobiographical of his works in that he appears himself in each piece and also in that each relates to a phase of his own experience. Of the stories from it selected here, 'Enoch Soames' is about the London of the Decadent Nineties, 'Argallo and Ledgett' is set in the literary world of the Edwardian age, ' "Savonarola" Brown' recalls Max's life as a dramatic critic, 'James Pethel' is set in the Dieppe where he spent his youthful holidays. I have chosen these pieces for this collection partly because they are my favourites and partly because they are the most variously representative of his genius. 'Enoch Soames' shows Max the satirist at his keenest. It is at once the truest and most amusing portrait that we have of the world of *The Yellow Book*. Equally true, equally comic, is the portrait of the Edwardian literary world in 'Argallo and Ledgett'. In ' "Savonarola" Brown' we get Max's gift for exuberant fun at its most infectious. Like Buckingham's *Rehearsal* and Sheridan's *Critic* it is a skit on pseudo-poetic tragedy. It is more laughable than either; and it rises at moments to be a parody not just of pseudo-tragedy but of Shakespeare himself.

'James Pethel' differs from the other pieces in the volume in that it is not, like them, a fantasy, but rather a straight-forward realistic portrait of character, only differing from other portraits of the same kind in that it is conceived consistently in a comedy vein. It is a brilliantly convincing portrait, made substantial and alive by touch after touch of exact delicate observation of men and manners. But all through it maintains the comedy mood. It is noteworthy that though the story ends, as it should, with Pethel's death, this is mentioned as occurring painlessly and many years after Max's last meeting with him. Thus without falsification the smiling amenity of the entertainment is unbroken.

Two pieces in this selection do not fit into the categories I have named: 'William and Mary' and 'No. 2. The Pines'. In form they resemble the stories in *Seven Men*; narratives about characters, related by Max in person, mainly in an ironic tone. But the intention behind them is different. 'William and Mary', written late in Max's career, is his only attempt at 'serious' fiction. It ends sadly, and its dominant sentiment is a restrained pathos. Its irony is tender rather than satiric and the whole scene is bathed in a minor key which comes from the sense, bred in its author's heart by his advancing years, of the fleetingness of human life, the frailty of human happiness. The story does not leave a painful impression. Max still is out to please his readers, but this time by evoking agreeable tears rather than agreeable laughter. Yet he is not sentimental in the bad sense of that word. For the flow of tears is under the control of a vigilant sense of truth and a fastidious art. 'William and Mary' is an example of how, if it is disciplined by discretion and style, indulgence in tender feelings can result in a charming work of art; and in one which genuinely moves the reader. In it Max's appreciation of reality did not desert him. He does not make too much of his emotion. His gracefully expressed sadness is sincere.

In 'No. 2. The Pines' he adapts his fictional method to fact and uses it to give a portrait of the poet Swinburne in his later years. Max liked and admired Swinburne; but in this portrait his affection does not blind him or make him over-respectful. The portait has a Boswell-like detailed vividness.

It is also exquisitely amusing. Memorable as the portrait

of a famous writer, it is even more memorable as one more aspect of the Max Beerbohm comic entertainment. For in the end it is to Max's comedy one returns when attempting to analyse his achievement. It is its central pervading characteristic and that which gives him his place in literature. A distinguished place: Max is not a giant of the art of letters but still less is he one of its dwarfs—except to those who rate the comic element in human existence as of minor importance. For me, his work is the finest, richest expression of the spirit of comedy in all twentieth-century English literature, and the most varied, ranging, as it does, from the subtle satire of 'Enoch Soames' to the extravagant fantasy of *Zuleika Dobson*, from the ironic moralising of *The Happy Hypocrite* to the ironic pathos of 'William and Mary', from the psychological comedy of 'James Pethel' to the sheer rollicking fun of '"How Shall I Word It?"' It shines equally in a sustained passage of comic eloquence like the Duke of Dorset's proposal to Zuleika and in a concentrated epigrammatic phrase, as when Max says of the fashionable sages of his period: 'It distresses me, this failure to keep pace with the leaders of thought, as they pass into oblivion.'

It is in this variety of his humour that he surpasses his contemporaries. Others may rival him in one vein or other; Wilde in wit, for instance, or Firbank in the fantastic absurd. Max alone triumphs equally in every field. And two are all his own: parody and the comedy of human character as exhibited in himself. In this last his humour strikes deepest—though with how light a touch!

In the course of my long residence in London, I did entertain friends. But the memory of those occasions is not dear to me—especially not the memory of those that were in the more distinguished restaurants. Somewhere in the back of my brain, while I tried to lead the conversation brightly, was always the haunting fear that I had not brought enough money in my pocket. I never let this fear master me. I never said to anyone 'Will you have a liqueur?'—always 'What liqueur will you have?' But I postponed as far as possible the evil moment of asking for the bill. When I had, in the

proper casual tone (I hope and believe), at length asked for it,
I wished always it were not brought to me *folded* on a plate,
as though the amount were so hideously high that I alone must
be privy to it. So soon as it was laid beside me, I wanted to
know the worst at once. But I pretended to be so occupied in
talk that I was unaware of the bill's presence; and I was careful to be always in the middle of a sentence when I raised the
upper fold and took my not (I hope) frozen glance. In point
of fact, the amount was always much less than I had feared.
Pessimism does win us great happy moments.

It is impossible surely to be more finely, more enduringly
amusing than this. Max may be only a juggler; but the
balls he juggled with are of pure gold, and likely to be
shining brightly long after most of the heavy weights lifted
by his graver contemporaries have grown rusty and dull.

DAVID CECIL

March 1970

THE
HAPPY
HYPOCRITE

[1897]

NONE, IT IS SAID, of all who revelled with the Regent, was half so wicked as Lord George Hell. I will not trouble my little readers with a long recital of his great naughtiness. But it were well they should know that he was greedy, destructive, and disobedient. I am afraid there is no doubt that he often sat up at Cariton House until long after bedtime, playing at games, and that he generally ate and drank far more than was good for him. His fondness for fine clothes was such that he used to dress on week-days quite as gorgeously as good people dress on Sundays. He was thirty-five years old and a great grief to his parents.

And the worst of it was that he set such a bad example to others. Never, never did he try to conceal his wrongdoing; so that, in time, every one knew how horrid he was. In fact, I think he was proud of being horrid. Captain Tarleton, in his account of *Contemporary Bucks*, suggested that his Lordship's great Candour was a virtue and should incline us to forgive some of his abominable faults. But, painful as it is to me to dissent from any opinion expressed by one who is now dead, I hold that Candour is good only when it reveals good actions or good sentiments, and that when it reveals evil, itself is evil, even also.

Lord George Hell did, at last, atone for all his faults, in a way that was never revealed to the world during his lifetime. The reason of his strange and sudden disappearance from that social sphere in which he had so long moved, and never moved again, I will unfold. My little readers will then, I think, acknowledge that any angry judgment they may have passed upon him must be reconsidered and, maybe, withdrawn. I will leave his Lordship in their hands. But my plea for him will not be based upon that Candour of his, which some of his friends so much admired. There were, yes! some so weak and so wayward as to think it a fine thing to have an historic title and no scruples. 'Here comes George Hell,' they would say. 'How wicked my Lord is looking!' *Noblesse oblige*, you see, and so an aristocrat should be very careful of his good name. Anonymous naughtiness does little harm.

It is pleasant to record that many persons were inobnoxious to the magic of his title and disapproved of him so strongly that, whenever he entered a room where they happened to be, they would make straight for the door and watch him very severely through the keyhole. Every morning, when he strolled up Piccadilly, they crossed over to the other side in a compact body, leaving him to the companionship of his bad companions on that which is still called the 'shady' side. Lord George— $\sigma\chi\acute{\epsilon}\tau\lambda\iota os$ —was quite indifferent to this demonstration. Indeed, he seemed wholly hardened, and when ladies gathered up their skirts as they passed him, he would lightly appraise their ankles.

I am glad I never saw his Lordship. They say he was rather like Caligula, with a dash of Sir John Falstaff, and that sometimes on wintry mornings in St James's Street young children would hush their prattle and cling in disconsolate terror to their nurses' skirts, as they saw him come (that vast and fearful gentleman!) with the east wind ruffling the rotund surface of his beaver, ruffling the fur about his neck and wrists, and striking the purple complexion of his cheeks to a still deeper purple. 'King Bogey' they called him in the nurseries. In the hours when they too were naughty, their nurses would predict his advent down the chimney or from the linen-press, and then they always 'behaved'. So that, you see, even the unrighteous are a power for good, in the hands of nurses.

It is true that his Lordship was a non-smoker—a negative virtue, certainly, and due, even that, I fear, to the fashion of the day—but there the list of his good qualities comes to an abrupt conclusion. He loved with an insatiable love the town and the pleasures of the town, whilst the

ennobling influences of our English lakes were quite unknown to him. He used to boast that he had not seen a
buttercup for twenty years, and once he called the country
'a Fool's Paradise'. London was the only place marked on
the map of his mind. London gave him all he wished for.
Is it not extraordinary to think that he had never spent a
happy day nor a day of any kind in Follard Chase, that
desirable mansion in Herts, which he had won from Sir
Follard Follard, by a chuck of the dice, at Boodle's, on his
seventeenth birthday? Always cynical and unkind, he had
refused to give the broken baronet his 'revenge'. Always
unkind and insolent, he had offered to install him in the
lodge—an offer which was, after a little hesitation, accepted. 'On my soul, the man's place is a sinecure,' Lord
George would say; 'he never has to open the gate to me.'*
So rust had covered the great iron gates of Follard Chase,
and moss had covered its paths. The deer browsed upon
its terraces. There were only wild flowers anywhere. Deep
down among the weeds and water-lilies of the little stone-
rimmed pond he had looked down upon, lay the marble
faun, as he had fallen.

Of all the sins of his Lordship's life surely not one was
more wanton than his neglect of Follard Chase. Some
whispered (nor did he ever trouble to deny) that he had
won it by foul means, by loaded dice. Indeed no card-
player in St James's cheated more persistently than he. As
he was rich and had no wife and family to support, and as
his luck was always capital, I can offer no excuse for his
conduct. At Carlton House, in the presence of many
bishops and ministers, he once dunned the Regent most
arrogantly for 5000 guineas out of which he had cheated
him some months before, and went so far as to declare
that he would not leave the house till he got it; whereupon His Royal Highness, with that unfailing tact for
which he was ever famous, invited him to stay there as a
guest; which, in fact, Lord George did, for several months.

* *Lord Coleraine's Correspondence*, p. 101.

After this, we can hardly be surprised when we read that he 'seldom sat down to the fashionable game of Limbo with less than four, and sometimes with *as many as seven* aces up his sleeve.'* We can only wonder that he was tolerated at all.

At Garble's, that nightly resort of titled rips and roysterers, he usually spent the early hours of his evenings. Round the illuminated garden, with La Gambogi, the dancer, on his arm, and a Bacchic retinue at his heels, he would amble leisurely, clad in Georgian costume, which was not then, of course, fancy dress, as it is now.† Now and again, in the midst of his noisy talk, he would crack a joke of the period, or break into a sentimental ballad, dance a little, or pick a quarrel. When he tired of such fooling, he would proceed to his box in the tiny alfresco theatre and patronise the jugglers, pugilists, play-actors, and whatever eccentric persons happened to be performing there.

The stars were splendid and the moon as beautiful as a great camelia, one night in May, as his Lordship laid his arms upon the cushioned ledge of his box and watched the antics of the Merry Dwarf, a little, curly-headed creature, whose *début* it was. Certainly Garble had found a novelty. Lord George led the applause, and the Dwarf finished his frisking with a pretty song about lovers. Nor was this all. Feats of archery were to follow. In a moment the Dwarf reappeared with a small, gilded bow in his hand and a quiverful of arrows slung at his shoulder. Hither and thither he shot these vibrant arrows, very precisely, several into the bark of the acacias that grew about the overt stage, several into the fluted columns of the boxes, two or three to the stars. The audience was delighted. '*Bravo!*

* *Contemporary Bucks*, vol. i, p. 73.

† It would seem, however, that, on special occasions, his Lordship indulged in odd costumes. 'I have seen him', says Captain Tarleton (vol. i, p. 69), 'attired as a French clown, as a sailor, or in the crimson hose of a Sicilian grandee—*peu beau spectacle*. He never disguised his face, whatever his costume, however.'

Bravo Sagittaro!' murmured Lord George, in the language of La Gambogi, who was at his side. Finally, the waxen figure of a man was carried on by an assistant and propped against the trunk of a tree. A scarf was tied across the eyes of the Merry Dwarf, who stood in a remote corner of the stage. *Bravo* indeed! For the shaft had pierced the waxen figure through the heart, or just where the heart would have been if the figure had been human and not waxen.

Lord George called for port and champagne and beckoned the bowing homuncule to his box, that he might compliment him on his skill and pledge him in a bumper of the grape.

'On my soul, you have a genius for the bow,' his Lordship cried with florid condescension. 'Come and sit by me; but first let me present you to my divine companion the Signora Gambogi—Virgo and Sagittarius, egad! You may have met on the Zodiac.'

'Indeed, I met the Signora many years ago,' the Dwarf replied, with a low bow. 'But not on the Zodiac, and the Signora perhaps forgets me.'

At this speech the Signora flushed angrily, for she was indeed no longer young, and the Dwarf had a childish face. She thought he mocked her; her eyes flashed. Lord George's twinkled rather maliciously.

'Great is the experience of youth,' he laughed. 'Pray, are you stricken with more than twenty summers?'

'With more than I can count,' said the Dwarf. 'To the health of your Lordship!' and he drained his long glass of wine. Lord George replenished it, and asked by what means or miracle he had acquired his mastery of the bow.

'By long practice,' the little thing rejoined; 'long practice on human creatures.' And he nodded his curls mysteriously.

'On my heart, you are a dangerous box-mate.'

'Your Lordship is certainly a good target.'

Little liking this joke at his bulk, which really rivalled the Regent's, Lord George turned brusquely in his chair and fixed his eyes upon the stage. This time it was the Gambogi who laughed.

A new operette, *The Fair Captive of Samarcand*, was
being enacted, and the frequenters of Garble's were all
curious to behold the *débutante*, Jenny Mere, who was said
to be both pretty and talented. These predictions were
surely fufilled, when the captive peeped from the window
of her wooden turret. She looked so pale under her blue
turban. Her eyes were dark with fear; her parted lips did
not seem capable of speech. 'Is it that she is frightened of
us?' the audience wondered. 'Or of the flashing scimitar
of Aphoschaz, the cruel father who holds her captive?' So
they gave her loud applause, and when at length she
jumped down, to be caught in the arms of her gallant
lover, Nissarah, and, throwing aside her Eastern draperies,
did a simple dance in the convention of Columbine, their
delight was quite unbounded. She was very young and did
not dance very well, it is true, but they forgave her that.
And when she turned in the dance and saw her father with
his scimitar, their hearts beat swiftly for her. Nor were all
eyes tearless when she pleaded with him for her life.

Strangely absorbed, quite callous of his two companions,
Lord George gazed over the footlights. He seemed as one
who is in a trance. Of a sudden, something shot sharp into
his heart. In pain he sprang to his feet and, as he turned,
he seemed to see a winged and laughing child, in whose
hand was a bow, fly swiftly away into the darkness. At his
side was the Dwarf's chair. It was empty. Only La Gambogi was with him, and her dark face was like the face of
a fury.

Presently he sank back into his chair, holding one hand
to his heart, that still throbbed from the strange trans-
fixion. He breathed very painfully and seemed scarce conscious of his surroundings. But La Gambogi knew he
would pay no more homage to her now, for that the love
of Jenny Mere had come into his heart.

When the operette was over, his love-sick Lordship
snatched up his cloak and went away without one word to
the lady at his side. Rudely he brushed aside Count Karoloff and Mr FitzClarence, with whom he had arranged to

play hazard. Of his comrades, his cynicism, his reckless scorn—of all the material of his existence—he was oblivious now. He had no time for penitence or diffident delay. He only knew that he must kneel at the feet of Jenny Mere and ask her to be his wife.

'Miss Mere', said Garble, 'is in her room, resuming her ordinary attire. If your Lordship deign to await the conclusion of her humble toilet, it shall be my privilege to present her to your Lordship. Even now, indeed, I hear her footfall on the stair.'

Lord George uncovered his head and with one hand nervously smoothed his rebellious wig.

'Miss Mere, come hither,' said Garble. 'This is my Lord George Hell, that you have pleased, whom by your poor efforts this night will for ever be the prime gratification of your passage through the roseate realms of art.'

Little Miss Mere, who had never seen a lord, except in fancy or in dreams, curtseyed shyly and hung her head. With a loud crash, Lord George fell on his knees. The manager was greatly surprised, the girl greatly embarrassed. Yet neither of them laughed, for sincerity dignified his posture and sent eloquence from his lips.

'Miss Mere,' he cried, 'give ear, I pray you, to my poor words, nor spurn me in misprision from the pedestal of your Beauty, Genius, and Virtue. All too conscious, alas! of my presumption in the same, I yet abase myself before you as a suitor for your adorable Hand. I grope under the shadow of your raven Locks. I am dazzled in the light of those translucent Orbs, your Eyes. In the intolerable Whirlwind of your Fame I faint and am afraid.'

'Sir——' the girl began, simply.

'Say "My Lord",' said Garble solemnly.

'My Lord, I thank you for your words. They are beautiful. But indeed, indeed, I can never be your bride.'

Lord George hid his face in his hands.

'Child,' said Mr Garble, 'let not the sun rise ere you have retracted those wicked words.'

'My wealth, my rank, my irremediable love for you, I throw them at your feet,' Lord George cried piteously. 'I would wait an hour, a week, a lustre, even a decade, did you but bid me hope!'

'I can never be your wife,' she said, slowly. 'I can never be the wife of any man whose face is not saintly. Your face, my Lord, mirrors, it may be, true love for me, but it is even as a mirror long tarnished by the reflexion of this world's vanity. It is even as a tarnished mirror. Do not kneel to me, for I am poor and humble. I was not made for such impetuous wooing. Kneel, if you please, to some greater, gayer lady. As for my love, it is my own, nor can it be ever torn from me, but given, as true love must needs be given, freely. Ah, rise from your knees. That man, whose face is wonderful as are the faces of the saints, to him I will give my true love.'

Miss Mere, though visibly affected, had spoken this speech with a gesture and elocution so superb, that Mr Garble could not help applauding, deeply though he regretted her attitude towards his honoured patron. As for Lord George, he was immobile as a stricken oak. With a sweet look of pity, Miss Mere went her way, and Mr Garble, with some solicitude, helped his Lordship to rise from his knees. Out into the night, without a word, his Lordship went. Above him the stars were still splendid. They seemed to mock the festoons of little lamps, dim now and guttering, in the garden of Garble's. What should he do? No thoughts came; only his heart burnt hotly. He stood on the brim of Garble's lake, shallow and artificial as his past life had been. Two swans slept on its surface. The moon shone strangely upon their white, twisted necks. Should he drown himself? There was no one in the garden to prevent him, and in the morning they would find him floating there, one of the noblest of love's victims. The garden would be closed in the evening. There would be no performance in the little theatre. It might be that Jenny Mere would mourn him. 'Life is a prison, without bars,' he murmured, as he walked away.

All night long he strode, knowing not whither, through the mysterious streets and squares of London. The watchmen, to whom his figure was familiar, gripped their staves at his approach, for they had old reason to fear his wild and riotous habits. He did not heed them. Through that dim conflict between darkness and day, which is ever waged silently over our sleep, Lord George strode on in the deep absorption of his love and of his despair. At dawn he found himself on the outskirts of a little wood in Kensington. A rabbit rushed past him through the dew. Birds were fluttering in the branches. The leaves were tremulous with the presage of day, and the air was full of the sweet scent of hyacinths.

How cool the country was! It seemed to cool the feverish maladies of his soul and consecrate his love. In the fair light of the dawn he began to shape the means of winning Jenny Mere, that he had conceived in the desperate hours of the night. Soon an old woodman passed by, and, with rough courtesy, showed him the path that would lead him quickest to the town. He was loth to leave the wood. With Jenny, he thought, he would live always in the country. And he picked a posy of wild flowers for her.

His *rentrée* into the still silent town strengthened his Arcadian resolves. He, who had seen the town so often in its hours of sleep, had never noticed how sinister its whole aspect was. In its narrow streets the white houses rose on either side of him like cliffs of chalk. He hurried swiftly along the unswept pavement. How had he loved this city of evil secrets?

At last he came to St James's Square, to the hateful door of his own house. Shadows lay like memories in every corner of the dim hall. Through the window of his room, a sunbeam slanted across his smooth white bed, and fell ghastly on the ashen grate.

II

IT WAS A BRIGHT morning in Old Bond Street, and fat
little Mr Aeneas, the fashionable mask-maker, was sunning
himself at the door of his shop. His window was lined as
usual with all kinds of masks—beautiful masks with pink
cheeks, and absurd masks with protuberant chins; curious
πρόσωπα copied from old tragic models; masks of paper
for children, of fine silk for ladies, and of leather for working men; bearded or beardless, gilded or waxen (most of
them, indeed, were waxen), big or little masks. And in the
middle of this vain galaxy hung the presentment of a
Cyclops' face, carved cunningly of gold, with a great
sapphire in its brow.

The sun gleamed brightly on the window and on the
bald head and varnished shoes of fat little Mr Aeneas. It
was too early for any customers to come, and Mr Aeneas
seemed to be greatly enjoying his leisure in the fresh air.
He smiled complacently as he stood there, and well he
might, for he was a great artist and was patronised by
several crowned heads and not a few of the nobility. Only
the evening before, Mr Brummell had come into his shop
and ordered a light summer mask, wishing to evade for a
time the jealous vigilance of Lady Otterton. It pleased Mr
Aeneas to think that his art made him the recipient of so
many high secrets. He smiled as he thought of the titled
spendthrifts who, at this moment, *perdus* behind his
masterpieces, passed unscathed among their creditors. He
was the secular confessor of his day, always able to give
absolution. A unique position!

The street was as quiet as a village street. At an open
window over the way, a handsome lady, wrapped in a
muslin *peignoir*, sat sipping her cup of chocolate. It was
La Signora Gambogi, and Mr Aeneas made her many
elaborate bows. This morning, however, her thoughts

seemed far away, and she did not notice the little man's polite efforts. Nettled at her negligence, Mr Aeneas was on the point of retiring into his shop, when he saw Lord George Hell hastening up the street, with a posy of flowers in his hand.

'His Lordship is up betimes!' he said to himself. 'An early visit to La Signora, I suppose.'

Not so, however. His Lordship came straight towards the mask shop. Once he glanced up at La Signora's window and looked deeply annoyed when he saw her sitting there. He came quickly into the shop.

'I want the mask of a saint,' he said.

'Mask of a saint, my Lord? Certainly!' said Mr Aeneas, briskly. 'With or without halo? His Grace the Bishop of St Aldred's always wears his with a halo. Your Lordship does not wish for a halo? Certainly! If your Lordship will allow me to take his measurement——'

'I must have the mask to-day,' Lord George said. 'Have you none ready-made?'

'Ah I see. Required for immediate wear,' murmured Mr Aeneas, dubiously. 'You see, your Lordship takes a rather large size.' And he looked at the floor.

'Julius!' he cried suddenly to his assistant, who was putting the finishing touches to a mask of Barbarossa which the young king of Zürremburg was to wear at his coronation the following week. 'Julius! Do you remember the saint's mask we made for Mr Ripsby, a couple of years ago?'

'Yes, sir,' said the boy. 'It's stored upstairs.'

'I thought so,' replied Mr Aeneas. 'Mr Ripsby only had it on hire. Step upstairs, Julius, and bring it down. I fancy it is just what your Lordship would wish. Spiritual, yet handsome.'

'Is it a mask that is even as a mirror of true love?' Lord George asked, gravely.

'It was made precisely as such,' the mask-maker answered. 'In fact it was made for Mr Ripsby to wear at his silver wedding, and was very highly praised by the relatives of Mrs Ripsby. Will your Lordship step into my little room?'

So Mr Aeneas led the way to his parlour behind the shop. He was elated by the distinguished acquisition to his *clientèle*, for hitherto Lord George had never patronised his business. He bustled round his parlour and insisted that his Lordship should take a chair and a pinch from his snuff-box, while the saint's mask was being found.

Lord George's eyes travelled along the rows of framed letters from great personages, which lined the walls. He did not see them though, for he was calculating the chances that La Gambogi had not observed him as he entered the mask-shop. He had come down so early that he had thought she would still be abed. That sinister old proverb, *La jalouse se lève de bonne heure*, rose in his memory. His eye fell unconsciously on a large, round mask made of dull silver, with the features of a human face traced over its surface in faint filigree.

'Your Lordship wonders what mask that is?' chirped Mr Aeneas tapping the thing with one of his little finger-nails.

'What is that mask?' Lord George murmured, absently.

'I ought not to divulge, my Lord,' said the mask-maker. 'But I know your Lordship would respect a professional secret, a secret of which I am pardonably proud. This', he said, 'is a mask for the sun-god, Apollo, whom heaven bless!'

'You astound me,' said Lord George.

'Of no less a person, I do assure you. When Jupiter, his father, made him lord of the day, Apollo craved that he might sometimes see the doings of mankind in the hours of night-time. Jupiter granted so reasonable a request, and when next Apollo had passed over the sky and hidden in the sea, and darkness had fallen on all the world, he raised his head above the waters that he might watch the doings of mankind in the hours of night-time. But,' Mr Aeneas added, with a smile, 'his bright countenance made light all the darkness. Men rose from their couches or from their

revels, wondering that day was so soon come, and went
to their work. And Apollo sank weeping into the sea.
'Surely,' he cried, 'it is a bitter thing that I alone, of all
the gods, may not watch the world in the hours of night-
time. For in those hours, as I am told, men are even as
gods are. They spill the wine and are wreathed with roses.
Their daughters dance in the light of torches. They laugh
to the sound of flutes. On their long couches they lie down
at last, and sleep comes to kiss their eyelids. None of these
things I see. Wherefore the brightness of my beauty is
even as a curse to me, and I would put it from me.' And as
he wept, Vulcan said to him, 'I am not the least cunning
of the gods, not the least pitiful. Do not weep, for I will
give you that which shall end your sorrow. Nor need you
put from you the brightness of your beauty.' And Vulcan
made a mask of dull silver and fastened it across his
brother's face. And that night, thus masked, the sun-god
rose from the sea and watched the doings of mankind in
the night-time. Nor any longer were men abashed by his
bright beauty, for it was hidden by the mask of silver.
Those whom he had so often seen haggard over their daily
tasks, he saw feasting now and wreathed with red roses.
He heard them laugh to the sound of flutes, as their daughters danced in the red light of torches. And when at length
they lay down upon their soft couches and sleep kissed
their eyelids, he sank back into the sea and hid his mask
under a little rock in the bed of the sea. Nor have men
ever known that Apollo watches them often in the night-
time, but fancied it to be some pale goddess.'

'I myself have always thought it was Diana,' said Lord
George Hell.

'An error, my Lord!' said Mr Aeneas, with a smile.
'Ecce signum!' And he tapped the mask of dull silver.

'Strange!' said his Lordship. 'And pray how comes it
that Apollo has ordered of *you* this new mask?'

'He has always worn twelve new masks every year, inasmuch as no mask can endure for many nights the near
brightness of his face, before which even a mask of the

best and purest silver soon tarnishes and wears away. Centuries ago, Vulcan tired of making so very many masks. And so Apollo sent Mercury down to Athens, to the shop of Phoron, a Phœnician mask-maker of great skill. Phoron made Apollo's masks for many years, and every month Mercury came to his shop for a new one. When Phoron died, another artist was chosen, and, when *he* died, another, and so on through all the ages of the world. Conceive, my Lord, my pride and pleasure when Mercury flew into my shop, one night last year, and made me Apollo's warrant-holder. It is the highest privilege that any mask-maker can desire. And when I die,' said Mr Aeneas, with some emotion, 'Mercury will confer my post upon another.'

'And do they pay you for your labour?' Lord George asked.

Mr Aeneas drew himself up to his full height, such as it was. 'In Olympus, my Lord,' he said, 'they have no currency. For any mask-maker, so high a privilege is its own reward. Yet the sun-god is generous. He shines more brightly into my shop than into any other. Nor does he suffer his rays to melt any waxen mask made by me, until its wearer doff it and it be done with.'

At this moment Julius came in with the Ripsby mask. 'I must ask your Lordship's pardon for having kept you so long,' pleaded Mr Aeneas. 'But I have a large store of old masks and they are imperfectly catalogued.'

It certainly was a beautiful mask, with its smooth pink cheeks and devotional brows. It was made of the finest wax. Lord George took it gingerly in his hands and tried it on his face. It fitted *à merveille*.

'Is the expression exactly as your Lordship would wish?' asked Mr Aeneas.

Lord George laid it on the table and studied it intently. 'I wish it were more as a perfect mirror of true love,' he said at length. 'It is too calm, too contemplative.'

'Easily remedied!' said Mr Aeneas. Selecting a fine pencil, he deftly drew the eyebrows closer to each other. With a brush steeped in some scarlet pigment, he put a fuller curve upon the lips. And behold! it was the mask of a saint who loves dearly. Lord George's heart throbbed with pleasure.

'And for how long does your Lordship wish to wear it?' asked Mr Aeneas.

'I must wear it until I die,' replied Lord George.

'Kindly be seated then, I pray,' rejoined the little man. 'For I must apply the mask with great care. Julius, you will assist me!'

So, while Julius heated the inner side of the waxen mask over a little lamp, Mr Aeneas stood over Lord George gently smearing his features with some sweet-scented pomade. Then he took the mask and powdered its inner side, quite soft and warm now, with a fluffy puff. 'Keep quite still, for one instant,' he said, and clapped the mask firmly on his Lordship's upturned face. So soon as he was sure of its perfect adhesion, he took from his assistant's hand a silver file and a little wooden spatula, with which he proceeded to pare down the edge of the mask, where it joined the neck and ears. At length, all traces of the 'join' were obliterated. It remained only to arrange the curls of the lordly wig over the waxen brow.

The disguise was done. When Lord George looked through the eyelets of his mask into the mirror that was placed in his hand, he saw a face that was saintly, itself a mirror of true love. How wonderful it was! He felt his past was a dream. He felt he was a new man indeed. His voice went strangely through the mask's parted lips, as he thanked Mr Aeneas.

'Proud to have served your Lordship,' said that little worthy, pocketing his fee of fifty guineas, while he bowed his customer out.

When he reached the street, Lord George nearly uttered a curse through those sainted lips of his. For there, right in his way, stood La Gambogi, with a small pink parasol. She laid her hand upon his sleeve and called him softly by his name. He passed her by without a word. Again she confronted him.

'I cannot let go so handsome a lover,' she laughed, 'even though he spurn me! Do not spurn me, George. Give me your posy of wild flowers. Why, you never looked so lovingly at me in all your life!'

'Madam,' said Lord George, sternly, 'I have not the honour to know you.' And he passed on.

The lady gazed after her lost lover with the blackest hatred in her eyes. Presently she beckoned across the road to a certain spy.

And the spy followed him.

III

LORD GEORGE, GREATLY AGITATED, had turned into Piccadilly. It was horrible to have met this garish embodiment of his past on the very threshold of his fair future. The mask-maker's elevating talk about the gods, followed by the initiative ceremony of his saintly mask, had driven all discordant memories from his love-thoughts of Jenny Mere. And then to be met by La Gambogi! It might be that, after his stern words, she would not seek to cross his path again. Surely she would not seek to mar his sacred love. Yet, he knew her dark Italian nature, her passion of revenge. What was the line in Virgil? *Spretaeque*—something. Who knew but that somehow, sooner or later, she might come between him and his love?

He was about to pass Lord Barrymore's mansion. Count Karoloff and Mr FitzClarence were lounging in one of the lower windows. Would they know him behind his mask? Thank God! they did not. They merely laughed as he went by, and Mr FitzClarence cried in a mocking voice, 'Sing us a hymn, Mr Whatever-your-saint's-name is!' The mask, then, at least, was perfect. Jenny Mere would not know him. He need fear no one but La Gambogi. But would not she betray his secret? He sighed.

That night he was going to visit Garble's and to declare his love to the little actress. He never doubted that she would love him for his saintly face. Had she not said, 'That man whose face is wonderful as are the faces of the saints, to him I will give my true love'? She could not say now that his face was as a tarnished mirror of love. She would smile on him. She would be his bride. But would La Gambogi be at Garble's?

The operette would not be over before ten that night. The clock in Hyde Park Gate told him it was not yet ten—ten of the morning. Twelve whole hours to wait before he could fall at Jenny's feet! 'I cannot spend that time in this place of memories,' he thought. So he hailed a yellow cabriolet and bade the jarvey drive him out to the village of Kensington.

When they came to the little wood where he had been but a few hours ago, Lord George dismissed the jarvey. The sun, that had risen as he stood there thinking of Jenny, shone down on his altered face, but, though it shone very fiercely, it did not melt his waxen features. The old woodman, who had shown him his way, passed by under a load of faggots and did not know him. He wandered among the trees. It was a lovely wood.

Presently he came to the bank of that tiny stream, the Ken, which still flowed there in those days. On the moss of its bank he lay down and let its water ripple over his hand. Some bright pebble glistened under the surface, and, as he peered down at it, he saw in the stream the reflection of his mask. A great shame filled him that he should so cheat the girl he loved. Behind that fair mask there would still be the evil face that had repelled her. Could he be so base as to decoy her into love of that most ingenious deception? He was filled with a great pity for her, with a hatred of himself. And yet, he argued, was the mask indeed a mean trick? Surely it was a secret symbol of his true repentance and of his true love. His face was evil, because his life had been evil. He had seen a gracious girl, and of a sudden his very soul had changed. His face alone was the same as it had been. It was not just that his face should be evil still.

There was a faint sound of someone sighing. Lord George looked up, and there, on the further bank, stood Jenny Mere, watching him. As their eyes met, she blushed and hung her head. She looked like nothing but a tall child as she stood there with her straight limp frock of lilac cotton and her sunburnt straw bonnet. He dared not speak; he could only gaze at her.

Suddenly there perched astride the bough of a tree, at her side, that winged and laughing child in whose hand was a bow. Before Lord George could warn her, an arrow had flashed down and vanished in her heart, and Cupid had flown away.

No cry of pain did she utter, but stretched out her arms to her lover, with a glad smile. He leapt quite lightly over the little stream and knelt at her feet. It seemed more fitting that he should kneel before the gracious thing he was unworthy of. But she, knowing only that his face was as the face of a great saint, bent over him and touched him with her hand.

'Surely,' she said, 'you are that good man for whom I have waited. Therefore do not kneel to me, but rise and suffer me to kiss your hand. For my love of you is lowly, and my heart is all yours.'

But he answered, looking up into her fond eyes, 'Nay, you are a queen, and I must needs kneel in your presence.'

But she shook her head wistfully, and she knelt down, also, in her tremulous ecstasy, before him. And as they knelt, the one to the other, the tears came into her eyes, and he kissed her. Though the lips that he pressed to her lips were only waxen, he thrilled with happiness, in that mimic kiss. He held her close to him in his arms, and they were silent in the sacredness of their love.

From his breast he took the posy of wild flowers that he had gathered.

'They are for you,' he whispered. 'I gathered them for you hours ago, in this wood. See! They are not withered.'

But she was perplexed by his words and said to him, blushing, 'How was it for me that you gathered them, though you had never seen me?'

'I gathered them for you,' he answered, 'knowing I should soon see you. How was it that you, who had never seen me, yet waited for me?'

'I waited, knowing I should see you at last.' And she kissed the posy and put it at her breast.

And they rose from their knees and went into the wood, walking hand in hand. As they went, he asked the names of the flowers that grew under their feet. 'These are primroses,' she would say. 'Did you not know? And these are ladies'-feet, and these forget-me-nots. And that white flower, climbing up the trunk of the trees and trailing down so prettily from the branches, is called Astyanax. These little yellow things are buttercups. Did you not know?' And she laughed.

'I know the names of none of the flowers,' he said.

She looked up into his face and said timidly, 'Is it worldly and wrong of me to have loved the flowers? Ought I to have thought more of those higher things that are unseen?'

His heart smote him. He could not answer her simplicity.

'Surely the flowers are good, and did you not gather this posy for me?' she pleaded. 'But if you do not love them, I must not. And I will try to forget their names. For I must try to be like you in all things.'

'Love the flowers always,' he said. 'And teach me to love them.'

So she told him all about the flowers, how some grew very slowly and others bloomed in a night; how clever the convolvulus was at climbing, and how shy violets were, and why honeycups had folded petals. She told him of the birds, too, that sang in the wood, how she knew them all by their voices. 'That is a chaffinch singing. Listen!' she said. And she tried to imitate its note, that her lover might remember. All the birds, according to

her, were good, except the cuckoo, and whenever she
heard him sing she would stop her ears, lest she should
forgive him for robbing the nests. 'Every day,' she said,
'I have come to the wood, because I was lonely, and it
seemed to pity me. But now I have you. And it is glad!'

She clung closer to his arm, and he kissed her. She
pushed back her straw bonnet, so that it dangled from
her neck by its ribands, and laid her little head against
his shoulder. For a while he forgot his treachery to her,
thinking only of his love and her love. Suddenly she said
to him, 'Will you try not to be angry with me, if I tell
you something? It is something that will seem dreadful to
you.'

'*Pauvrette*,' he answered, 'you cannot have anything
very dreadful to tell.'

'I am very poor,' she said, 'and every night I dance in
a theatre. It is the only thing I can do to earn my bread.
Do you despise me because I dance?' She looked up
shyly at him and saw that his face was full of love for her
and not angry.

'Do you like dancing?' he asked.

'I hate it,' she answered, quickly. 'I hate it indeed. Yet
—to-night, alas! I must dance again in the theatre.'

'You need never dance again,' said her lover. 'I am
rich and I will pay them to release you. You shall dance
only for me. Sweetheart, it cannot be much more than
noon. Let us go into the town, while there is time, and
you shall be made my bride, and I your bridegroom, this
very day. Why should you and I be lonely?'

'I do not know,' she said.

So they walked back through the wood, taking a narrow path which Jenny said would lead them quickest to
the village. And, as they went, they came to a tiny cottage,
with a garden that was full of flowers. The old woodman
was leaning over its paling, and he nodded to them as
they passed.

'I often used to envy the woodman,' said Jenny, 'living
in that dear little cottage.'

'Let us live there, then,' said Lord George. And he went back and asked the old man if he were not unhappy, living there alone.

''Tis a poor life here for me,' the old man answered. 'No folk come to the wood, except little children, now and again, to play, or lovers like you. But they seldom notice me. And in winter I am alone with Jack Frost! Old men love merrier company than that. Oh! I shall die in the snow with my faggots on my back. A poor life here!'

'I will give you gold for your cottage and whatever is in it, and then you can go and live happily in the town,' Lord George said. And he took from his coat a note for two hundred guineas, and held it across the palings.

'Lovers are poor foolish derry-docks,' the old man muttered. 'But I thank you kindly, Sir. This little sum will keep me cosy, as long as I last. Come into the cottage as soon as can be. It's a lonely place and does my heart good to depart from it.'

'We are going to be married this afternoon, in the town,' said Lord George. 'We will come straight back to our home.'

'May you be happy,' replied the woodman. 'You'll find me gone when you come.'

And the lovers thanked him and went their way.

'Are you very rich?' Jenny asked. 'Ought you to have bought the cottage for that great price?'

'Would you love me as much if I were quite poor, little Jenny?' he asked her, after a pause.

'I did not know you were rich when I saw you across the stream,' she said.

And in his heart Lord George made a good resolve. He would put away from him all his worldly possessions. All the money that he had won at the clubs, fairly or foully, all that hideous accretion of gold guineas, he would distribute among the comrades he had impoverished. As he walked, with the sweet and trustful girl at his side, the vague record of his infamy assailed him, and a look of pain shot behind his smooth mask. He would atone. He would shun no sacrifice that might cleanse his soul. All his fortune he would put from him. Follard Chase he would give back to Sir Follard. He would sell his house in St James's Square. He would keep some little part of his patrimony, enough for him in the wood with Jenny, but no more.

'I shall be quite poor, Jenny!' he said.

And they talked of the things that lovers love to talk of, how happy they would be together and how economical. As they were passing Herbert's pastry shop, which, as my little readers know, still stands in Kensington, Jenny looked up rather wistfully into her lover's ascetic face.

'Should you think me greedy,' she asked him, 'if I wanted a bun? They have beautiful buns here!'

Buns! The simple word started latent memories of his childhood. Jenny was only a child after all. Buns! He had forgotten what they were like. And as they looked at the piles of variegated cakes in the window, he said to her, 'Which are buns, Jenny? I should like to have one, too.'

'I am almost afraid of you,' she said. 'You must despise me so. Are you so good that you deny yourself all the vanity and pleasure that most people love? It is wonderful not to know what buns are! The round, brown, shiny cakes, with little raisins in them, are buns.'

So he bought two beautiful buns, and they sat together in the shop, eating them. Jenny bit hers rather diffidently, but was reassured when he said that they must have buns very often in the cottage. Yes! he, the famous toper and *gourmet* of St James's, relished this homely fare, as it passed through the insensible lips of his mask to the palate. He seemed to rise, from the consumption of his bun, a better man.

But there was no time to lose now. It was already past two o'clock. So he got a chaise from the inn opposite the pastry-shop, and they were swiftly driven to Doctors' Commons. There he purchased a special licence. When the clerk asked him to write his name upon it, he hesitated. What name should he assume? Under a mask he had wooed this girl, under an unreal name he must make her his bride. He loathed himself for a trickster. He had vilely stolen from her the love she would not give him. Even now, should he not confess himself the man whose face had frightened her, and go his way? And yet, surely, it was not just that he, whose soul was transfigured, should bear his old name. Surely George Hell was dead, and his name had died with him. So he dipped a pen in the ink and wrote 'George Heaven', for want of a better name. And Jenny wrote 'Jenny Mere' beneath it.

An hour later they were married according to the simple rites of a dear little registry-office in Covent Garden.

And in the cool evening they went home.

IV

IN THE COTTAGE THAT had been the woodman's they had a wonderful honeymoon. No king and queen in any palace of gold were happier than they. For them their tiny cottage was a palace, and the flowers that filled the garden were their courtiers. Long and careless and full of kisses were the days of their reign.

Sometimes, indeed, strange dreams troubled Lord George's sleep. Once he dreamed that he stood knocking and knocking at the great door of a castle. It was a bitter night. The frost enveloped him. No one came. Presently he heard a footstep in the hall beyond, and a pair of frightened eyes peered at him through the grill. Jenny was scanning his face. She would not open to him. With tears and wild words he besought her, but she would not open to him. Then, very stealthily he crept round the castle and found a small casement in the wall. It was open. He climbed swiftly, quietly, through it. In the darkness of the room someone ran to him and kissed him gladly. It was Jenny. With a cry of joy and shame he awoke. By his side lay Jenny, sleeping like a little child.

After all, what was a dream to him? It could not mar the reality of his daily happiness. He cherished his true penitence for the evil he had done in the past. The past! That was indeed the only unreal thing that lingered in his life. Every day its substance dwindled, grew fainter yet, as he lived his rustic honeymoon. Had he not utterly put it from him? Had he not, a few hours after his marriage, written to his lawyer, declaring solemnly that he, Lord George Hell, had forsworn the world, that he was where no man would find him, that he desired all his worldly goods to be distributed, thus and thus, among these and those of his companions? By this testament he had verily atoned for the wrong he had done, had made himself dead indeed to the world.

No address had he written upon his document. Though its injunctions were final and binding, it could betray no clue of his hiding-place. For the rest, no one would care to seek him out. He, who had done no good to human creature, would pass unmourned out of memory. The clubs, doubtless, would laugh and puzzle over his strange recantations, envious of whomever he had enriched. They would say 'twas a good riddance of a rogue, and soon forget him.* But she, whose prime patron he had been, who

* I would refer my little readers once more to the pages of *Contemporary Bucks*, where Captain Tarleton speculates upon the sudden disappearance of Lord George Hell and describes its effect on the town. 'Not even the shrewdest', says he, 'even gave a guess that would throw a ray of revealing light on the *disparition* of this profligate man. It was supposed that he carried off with him a little dancer from Garble's, at which *haunt of pleasantry* he was certainly on the night he vanished, and whither the young lady never returned again. Garble declared he had been compensated for her perfidy, but that he was sure she had not succumbed to his Lordship, having in fact rejected him soundly. Did his Lordship, say the cronies, take his life—and hers? *Il n'y a pas d'épreuve.* The *most astonishing* matter is that the runaway should have written out a complete will, restoring all money he had won at cards, etc. etc.

had loved him in her vile fashion, La Gambogi, would she forget him easily, like the rest? As the sweet days went by, her spectre, also, grew fainter and less formidable. She knew his mask indeed, but how should she find him in the cottage near Kensington? *Devia dulcedo latebrarum!* He was safe-hidden with his bride. As for the Italian, she might search and search—or had forgotten him, in the arms of another lover.

Yes! Few and faint became the blemishes of his honeymoon. At first he had felt that his waxen mask, though it had been the means of his happiness, was rather a barrier 'twixt him and his bride. Though it was sweet to kiss her through it, to look at her through it with loving eyes, yet there were times when it incommoded him with its mockery. Could he put it from him! Yet that, of course, could not be. He must wear it all his life. And so, as days went by, he grew reconciled to his mask. No longer did he feel it jarring on his face. It seemed to become a very part of him, and, for all its rigid material, it did forsooth express the one emotion that filled him, true love. The face for whose sake Jenny gave him her heart could not but be dear to this George Heaven, also.

Every day chastened him with its joy. They lived a very simple life, he and Jenny. They rose betimes, like the birds, for whose goodness they both had so sincere a love. Bread and honey and little strawberries were their

---

This certainly corroborates the opinion that he was seized with a sudden repentance and fled over the seas to a foreign monastery, where he died at last in *religious silence*. That's as it may, but many a spendthrift found his pockets clinking with guineas, a not unpleasant sound, I declare. The Regent himself was benefited by the odd will, and old Sir Follard Follard found himself once more in the ancestral home he had forfeited. As for Lord George's mansion in St James's Square, that was sold with all its appurtenances, and the money fetched by the sale, no bagatelle, was given to various good objects, according to my Lord's stated wishes. Well, many of us blessed his name—we had cursed it often enough. Peace to his ashes, in whatever urn they may be resting, on the billows of whatever ocean they float!'

morning fare, and in the evening they had seed-cake and
dewberry wine. Jenny herself made the wine, and her
husband drank it, in strict moderation, never more than
two glasses. He thought it tasted far better than the
Regent's cherry brandy, or the Tokay at Brooks's. Of
these treasured topes he had, indeed, nearly forgotten the
taste. The wine made from wild berries by his little bride
was august enough for his palate. Sometimes, after they
had dined thus, he would play the flute to her upon the
moonlit lawn, or tell her of the great daisy-chain he was
going to make for her on the morrow, or sit silently by her
side, listening to the nightingale, till bedtime. So admirably simple were their days.

V

ONE MORNING, AS HE was helping Jenny to water the
flowers, he said to her suddenly, 'Sweetheart, we had forgotten!'

'What was there we should forget?' asked Jenny, looking up from her task.

''Tis the mensiversary of our wedding,' her husband
answered gravely. 'We must not let it pass without some
celebration.'

'No indeed,' she said, 'we must not. What shall we do?'

Between them they decided upon an unusual feast.
They would go into the village and buy a bag of beautiful
buns and eat them in the afternoon. So soon, then, as all
the flowers were watered, they set forth to Herbert's
shop, bought the buns and returned home in very high
spirits, George bearing a paper bag that held no less than
twelve of the wholesome delicacies. Under the plane-tree
on the lawn Jenny sat her down, and George stretched
himself at her feet. They were loth to enjoy their feast too
soon. They dallied in childish anticipation. On the little
rustic table Jenny built up the buns, one above another,

till they looked like a tall pagoda. When, very gingerly, she had crowned the structure with the twelfth bun, her husband looking on with admiration, she clapped her hands and danced about it. She laughed so loudly (for, though she was only sixteen years old, she had a great sense of humour) that the table shook, and alas! the pagoda tottered and fell to the lawn. Swift as a kitten, Jenny chased the buns, as they rolled, hither and thither, over the grass, catching them deftly with her hand. Then she came back, flushed and merry under her tumbled hair, with her arm full of buns. She began to put them back in the paper bag.

'Dear husband,' she said, looking down to him, 'why do not you too smile at my folly? Your grave face rebukes me. Smile, or I shall think I vex you. Please smile a little.'

But the mask could not smile, of course. It was made for a mirror of true love, and it was grave and immobile. 'I am very much amused, dear,' he said, 'at the fall of the buns, but my lips will not curve to a smile. Love of you has bound them in spell.'

'But I can laugh, though I love you. I do not understand.' And she wondered. He took her hand in his and stroked it gently, wishing it were possible to smile. Some day, perhaps, she would tire of this monotonous gravity, this rigid sweetness. It was not strange that she should long for a little facial expression. They sat silently.

'Jenny, what is it?' he whispered suddenly. For Jenny, with wide-open eyes, was gazing over his head, across the lawn, 'Why do you look frightened?'

'There is a strange woman smiling at me across the palings,' she said. 'I do not know her.'

Her husband's heart sank. Somehow, he dared not turn his head to the intruder.

'She is nodding to me,' said Jenny. 'I think she is foreign, for she has an evil face.'

'Do not notice her,' he whispered. 'Does she look evil?'

'Very evil and very dark. She has a pink parasol. Her teeth are like ivory.'

'Do not notice her. Think! It is the mensiversary of our wedding, dear!'

'I wish she would not smile at me. Her eyes are like bright blots of ink.'

'Let us eat our beautiful buns!'

'Oh, she is coming in!' George heard the latch of the gate jar. 'Forbid her to come in!' whispered Jenny. 'I am afraid!' He heard the jar of heels on the gravel path. Yet he dared not turn. Only he clasped Jenny's hand more tightly, as he waited for the voice. It was La Gambogi's.

'Pray, pray, pardon me! I could not mistake the back of so old a friend.'

With the courage of despair, George turned and faced the woman.

'Even', she smiled, 'though his face has changed marvellously.'

'Madam,' he said, rising to his full height and stepping between her and his bride, 'begone, I command you, from this garden. I do not see what good is to be served by the renewal of our acquaintance.'

'Acquaintance!' murmured La Gambogi, with an arch of her beetle-brows. 'Surely we were friends, rather, nor is my esteem for you so dead that I would crave estrangement.'

'Madam,' rejoined Lord George, with a tremor in his voice, 'you see me happy, living very peacefully with my bride——'

'To whom, I beseech you, old friend, present me.'

'I would not,' he said hotly, 'desecrate her sweet name by speaking it with so infamous a name as yours.'

'Your choler hurts me, old friend,' said La Gambogi, sinking composedly upon the garden-seat and smoothing the silk of her skirts.

'Jenny,' said George, 'then do you retire, pending this lady's departure, to the cottage.' But Jenny clung to his arm. 'I were less frightened at your side,' she whispered. 'Do not send me away!'

'Suffer her pretty presence,' said La Gambogi. 'Indeed

I am come this long way from the heart of the town, that I may see her, no less than you, George. My wish is only to befriend her. Why should she not set you a mannerly example, giving me welcome? Come and sit by me, little bride, for I have things to tell you. Though you reject my friendship, give me, at least, the slight courtesy of audience. I will not detain you over-long, will be gone very soon. Are you expecting guests, George? *On dirait une masque champêtre!*' She eyed the couple critically. 'Your wife's mask', she said, 'is even better than yours.'

'What does she mean?' whispered Jenny. 'Oh, send her away!'

'Serpent,' was all George could say, 'crawl from our Eden, ere you poison with your venom its fairest denizen.'

La Gambogi rose. 'Even *my* pride', she cried passionately, 'knows certain bounds. I have been forbearing, but even in *my* zeal for friendship I will not be called "serpent". I will indeed be gone from this rude place. Yet, ere I go, there is a boon I will deign to beg. Show me, oh, show me but once again, the dear face I have so often caressed, the lips that were dear to me!'

George started back.

'What does she mean?' whispered Jenny.

'In memory of our old friendship,' continued La Gambogi, 'grant me this piteous favour. Show me your own face but for one instant, and I vow that I will never again remind you that I live. Intercede for me, little bride. Bid him unmask for me. You have more authority over him than I. Doff his mask with your own uxorious fingers.'

'What does she mean?' was the refrain of poor Jenny.

'If', said George, gazing sternly at his traitress, 'you do not go now, of your own will, I must drive you, man though I am, violently from the garden.'

'Doff your mask and I am gone.'

George made a step of menace towards her.

'False saint!' she shrieked, 'then *I* will unmask you.'

Like a panther she sprang upon him and clawed at his waxen cheeks. Jenny fell back, mute with terror. Vainly

did George try to free himself from his assailant, who
writhed round and round him, clawing, clawing at what
Jenny fancied to be his face. With a wild cry, Jenny
fell upon the furious creature and tried, with all her
childish strength, to release her dear one. The combatives
swayed to and fro, a revulsive trinity. There was a loud
pop, as though some great cork had been withdrawn, and
La Gambogi recoiled. She had torn away the mask. It lay
before her upon the lawn, upturned to the sky.

George stood motionless. La Gambogi stared up into
his face, and her dark flush died swiftly away. For there,
staring back at her, was the man she had unmasked, but
lo! his face was even as his mask had been. Line for line,
feature for feature, it was the same. 'Twas a saint's face.

'Madame,' he said, in the calm voice of despair, 'your
cheek may well blanch, when you regard the ruin you
have brought upon me. Nevertheless do I pardon you.
The gods have avenged, through you, the imposture I
wrought upon one who was dear to me. For that un-
pardonable sin I am punished. As for my poor bride,
whose love I stole by the means of that waxen semblance,
of her I cannot ask pardon. Ah, Jenny, Jenny, do not look
at me. Turn your eyes from the foul reality that I dis-
sembled.' He shuddered and hid his face in his hands.
'Do not look at me. I will go from the garden. Nor will
I ever curse you with the odious spectacle of my face.
Forget me, forget me.'

But, as he turned to go, Jenny laid her hands upon his
wrists and besought him that he would look at her. 'For
indeed,' she said, 'I am bewildered by your strange words.
Why did you woo me under a mask? And why do you
imagine I could love you less dearly, seeing your own
face?'

He looked into her eyes. On their violet surface he saw
the tiny reflection of his own face. He was filled with joy
and wonder.

'Surely,' said Jenny, 'your face is even dearer to me,
even fairer, than the semblance that hid it and deceived

me. I am not angry. 'Twas well that you veiled from me the full glory of your face, for indeed I was not worthy to behold it too soon. But I am your wife now. Let me look always at your own face. Let the time of my probation be over. Kiss me with your own lips.'

So he took her in his arms, as though she had been a little child, and kissed her with his own lips. She put her arms round his neck, and he was happier than he had ever been. They were alone in the garden now. Nor lay the mask any longer upon the lawn, for the sun had melted it.

From

SEVEN MEN
AND TWO OTHERS

Enoch Soames
[1912]

James Pethel
[1912]

'*Savonarola*' *Brown*
[1917]

*Felix Argallo
and Walter Ledgett*
[1927]

ENOCH SOAMES

WHEN A BOOK ABOUT the literature of the eighteen-nineties was given by Mr Holbrook Jackson to the world, I looked eagerly in the index for SOAMES, ENOCH. I had feared he would not be there. He was not there. But everybody else was. Many writers whom I had quite forgotten, or remembered but faintly, lived again for me, they and their work, in Mr Holbrook Jackson's pages. The book was as thorough as it was brilliantly written. And thus the omission found by me was an all the deadlier record of poor Soames' failure to impress himself on his decade.

I daresay I am the only person who noticed the omission. Soames had failed so piteously as all that! Nor is there a counterpoise in the thought that if he had had some measure of success he might have passed, like those others, out of my mind, to return only at the historian's beck. It is true that had his gifts, such as they were, been acknowledged in his lifetime, he would never have made the bargain I saw him make—that strange bargain whose results have kept him always in the foreground of my memory. But it is from those very results that the full piteousness of him glares out.

Not my compassion, however, impels me to write of him. For his sake, poor fellow, I should be inclined to keep my pen out of the ink. It is ill to deride the dead. And how can I write about Enoch Soames without making him ridiculous? Or rather, how am I to hush up the horrid fact that he *was* ridiculous? I shall not be able to do that. Yet, sooner or later, write about him I must. You will see, in due course, that I have no option. And I may as well get the thing done now.

In the Summer Term of '93 a bolt from the blue flashed
down on Oxford. It drove deep, it hurtlingly embedded
itself in the soil. Dons and undergraduates stood around,
rather pale, discussing nothing but it. Whence came it,
this meteorite? From Paris. Its name? Will Rothenstein.
Its aim? To do a series of twenty-four portraits in litho-
graph. These were to be published from the Bodley Head,
London. The matter was urgent. Already the Warden of
A, and the Master of B, and the Regius Professor of C,
had meekly 'sat'. Dignified and doddering old men, who
had never consented to sit to any one, could not with-
stand this dynamic little stranger. He did not sue: he
invited; he did not invite: he commanded. He was twenty-
one years old. He wore spectacles that flashed more than
any other pair ever seen. He was a wit. He was brimful of
ideas. He knew Whistler. He knew Edmond de Goncourt.
He knew everyone in Paris. He knew them all by heart.
He was Paris in Oxford. It was whispered that, so soon as
he had polished off his selection of dons, he was going to
include a few undergraduates. It was a proud day for me
when I—I—was included. I liked Rothenstein not less than
I feared him; and there arose between us a friendship
that has grown ever warmer, and been more and more
valued by me, with every passing year.

At the end of Term he settled in—or rather, meteor-
itically into—London. It was to him I owed my first
knowledge of that forever enchanting little world-in-itself,
Chelsea, and my first acquaintance with Walter Sickert
and other august elders who dwelt there. It was Rothenstein that took me to see, in Cambridge Street, Pimlico, a
young man whose drawings were already famous among
the few—Aubrey Beardsley, by name. With Rothenstein
I paid my first visit to the Bodley Head. By him I was
inducted into another haunt of intellect and daring, the
domino room of the Café Royal.

There, on that October evening—there, in that exuberant vista of gilding and crimson velvet set amidst all those
opposing mirrors and upholding caryatids, with fumes of

tobacco ever rising to the painted and pagan ceiling, and with the hum of presumably cynical conversation broken into so sharply now and again by the clatter of dominoes shuffled on marble tables, I drew a deep breath, and 'This indeed,' said I to myself, 'is life!'

It was the hour before dinner. We drank vermouth. Those who knew Rothenstein were pointing him out to those who knew him only by name. Men were constantly coming in through the swing-doors and wandering slowly up and down in search of vacant tables, or of tables occupied by friends. One of these rovers interested me because I was sure he wanted to catch Rothenstein's eye. He had twice passed our table, with a hesitating look; but Rothenstein, in the thick of a disquisition on Puvis de Chavannes, had not seen him. He was a stooping, shambling person, rather tall, very pale, with longish and brownish hair. He had a thin vague beard—or rather, he had a chin on which a large number of hairs weakly curled and clustered to cover its retreat. He was an odd-looking person; but in the 'nineties odd apparitions were more frequent, I think, than they are now. The young writers of that era—and I was sure this man was a writer—strove earnestly to be distinct in aspect. This man had striven unsuccessfully. He wore a soft black hat of clerical kind but of Bohemian intention, and a grey waterproof cape which, perhaps because it was waterproof, failed to be romantic. I decided that 'dim' was the *mot juste* for him. I had already essayed to write, and was immensely keen on the *mot juste*, that Holy Grail of the period.

The dim man was now again approaching our table, and this time he made up his mind to pause in front of it. 'You don't remember me,' he said in a toneless voice.

Rothenstein brightly focussed him. 'Yes, I do,' he replied after a moment, with pride rather than effusion— pride in a retentive memory. 'Edwin Soames.'

'Enoch Soames,' said Enoch.

'Enoch Soames,' repeated Rothenstein in a tone implying that it was enough to have hit on the surname. 'We met in Paris two or three times when you were living there. We met at the Café Groche.'

'And I came to your studio once.'

'Oh yes; I was sorry I was out.'

'But you were in. You showed me some of your paint-ings, you know. . . . I hear you're in Chelsea now.'

'Yes.'

I almost wondered that Mr Soames did not, after this monosyllable, pass along. He stood patiently there, rather like a dumb animal, rather like a donkey looking over a gate. A sad figure, his. It occurred to me that 'hungry' was perhaps the *mot juste* for him; but—hungry for what? He looked as if he had little appetite for anything. I was sorry for him; and Rothenstein, though he had not invited him to Chelsea, did ask him to sit down and have some-thing to drink.

Seated, he was more self-assertive. He flung back the wings of his cape with a gesture which—had not those wings been waterproof—might have seemed to hurl de-fiance at things in general. And he ordered an absinthe. '*Je me tiens toujours fidèle*', he told Rothenstein, '*à la sorcière glauque.*'

'It is bad for you,' said Rothenstein drily.

'Nothing is bad for one,' answered Soames. '*Dans ce monde il n'y a ni de bien ni de mal.*'

'Nothing good and nothing bad? How do you mean?'

'I explained it all in the preface to *Negations*.'

'*Negations*?'

'Yes; I gave you a copy of it.'

'Oh yes, of course. But did you explain—for instance —that there was no such thing as bad or good grammar?'

'N-no,' said Soames. 'Of course in Art there is the good and the evil. But in Life—no.' He was rolling a cigarette. He had weak white hands, not well washed, and with finger-tips much stained by nicotine. 'In Life there are illusions of good and evil, but'—his voice trailed away to a murmur in which the words 'vieux jeu' and 'rococo' were faintly audible. I think he felt he was not doing himself justice, and feared that Rothenstein was going to point out fallacies. Anyway, he cleared his throat and said, '*Parlons d'autre chose.*'

It occurs to you that he was a fool? It didn't to me. I was young, and had not the clarity of judgment that Rothenstein already had. Soames was quite five or six years older than either of us. Also, he had written a book.

It was wonderful to have written a book.

If Rothenstein had not been there, I should have revered Soames. Even as it was, I respected him. And I was very near indeed to reverence when he said he had another book coming out soon. I asked if I might ask what kind of book it was to be.

'My poems,' he answered. Rothenstein asked if this was to be the title of the book. The poet meditated on this suggestion, but said he rather thought of giving the book no title at all. 'If a book is good in itself——' he murmured, waving his cigarette.

Rothenstein objected that absence of title might be bad for the sale of a book. 'If,' he urged, 'I went into a book-seller's and said simply "Have you got?" or "Have you a copy of?" how would they know what I wanted?'

'Oh, of course I should have my name on the cover,' Soames answered earnestly. 'And I rather want', he added, looking hard at Rothenstein, 'to have a drawing of myself as frontispiece.' Rothenstein admitted that this was a capital idea, and mentioned that he was going into the country and would be there for some time. He then looked at his watch, exclaimed at the hour, paid the waiter, and went away with me to dinner. Soames remained at his post of fidelity to the glaucous witch.

'Why were you so determined not to draw him?' I asked.

'Draw him? Him? How can one draw a man who doesn't exist?'

'He is dim,' I admitted. But my *mot juste* fell flat. Rothenstein repeated that Soames was non-existent.

Still, Soames had written a book. I asked if Rothenstein

had read *Negations*. He said he had looked into it, 'but,'
he added crisply, 'I don't profess to know anything about
writing.' A reservation very characteristic of the period!
Painters would not then allow that any one outside their
own order had a right to any opinion about painting. This
law (graven on the tablets brought down by Whistler from
the summit of Fujiyama) imposed certain limitations. If
other arts than painting were not utterly unintelligible to
all but the men who practised them, the law tottered—the
Monroe Doctrine, as it were, did not hold good. Therefore
no painter would offer an opinion of a book without warning you at any rate that his opinion was worthless. No one
is a better judge of literature than Rothenstein; but it
wouldn't have done to tell him so in those days; and I
knew that I must form an unaided judgment on *Negations*.

Not to buy a book of which I had met the author face to
face would have been for me in those days an impossible
act of self-denial. When I returned to Oxford for the
Christmas Term I had duly secured *Negations*. I used to
keep it lying carelessly on the table in my room, and whenever a friend took it up and asked what it was about I
would say 'Oh, it's rather a remarkable book. It's by a man
whom I know.' Just 'what it was about' I never was able to
say. Head or tail was just what I hadn't made of that slim
green volume. I found in the preface no clue to the exiguous labyrinth of contents, and in that labyrinth nothing to
explain the preface.

Lean near to life. Lean very near—nearer.

*Life is web, and therein nor warp nor woof is, but web
only.*

*It is for this I am Catholick in church and in thought,
yet do let swift Mood weave there what the shuttle of
Mood wills.*

These were the opening phrases of the preface, but
those which followed were less easy to understand. Then
came 'Stark: A *Conte*', about a midinette who, so far as

I could gather, murdered, or was about to murder, a mannequin. It seemed to me like a story by Catule Mendès in which the translator had either skipped or cut out every alternate sentence. Next, a dialogue between Pan and St Ursula—lacking, I rather felt, in 'snap'. Next, some aphorisms (entitled ἀφορίσματα). Throughout, in fact, there was a great variety of form; and the forms had evidently been wrought with much care. It was rather the substance that eluded me. Was there, I wondered, any substance at all? It did now occur to me: suppose Enoch Soames was a fool! Up cropped a rival hypothesis: suppose *I* was! I inclined to give Soames the benefit of the doubt. I had read *L'Après-midi d'un Faune* without extracting a glimmer of meaning. Yet Mallarmé—of course—was a Master. How was I to know that Soames wasn't another? There was a sort of music in his prose, not indeed arresting, but perhaps, I thought, haunting, and laden perhaps with meanings as deep as Mallarmé's own. I awaited his poems with an open mind.

And I looked forward to them with positive impatience after I had had a second meeting with him. This was on an evening in January. Going into the aforesaid domino room, I passed a table at which sat a pale man with an open book before him. He looked from his book to me, and I looked back over my shoulder with a vague sense that I ought to have recognised him. I returned to pay my respects. After exchanging a few words, I said with a glance to the open book, 'I see I am interrupting you,' and was about to pass on, but 'I prefer', Soames replied in his toneless voice, 'to be interrupted,' and I obeyed his gesture that I should sit down.

I asked him if he often read here. 'Yes; things of this kind I read here,' he answered, indicating the title of his book—*The Poems of Shelley*.

'Anything that you really'—and I was going to say 'admire?' But I cautiously left my sentence unfinished, and was glad that I had done so, for he said, with unwonted emphasis, 'Anything second-rate.'

I had read little of Shelley, but 'Of course,' I murmured, 'he's very uneven.'

'I should have thought evenness was just what was wrong with him. A deadly evenness. That's why I read him here. The noise of this place breaks the rhythm. He's tolerable here.' Soames took up the book and glanced through the pages. He laughed. Soames' laugh was a short, single and mirthless sound from the throat, unaccompanied by any movement of the face or brightening of the eyes. 'What a period!' he uttered, laying the book down. And 'What a country!' he added.

I asked rather nervously if he didn't think Keats had more or less held his own against the drawbacks of time and place. He admitted that there were 'passages in Keats', but did not specify them. Of 'the older men', as he called them, he seemed to like only Milton. 'Milton', he said, 'wasn't sentimental.' Also, 'Milton had a dark insight.' And again, 'I can always read Milton in the reading-room.'

'The reading-room?'

'Of the British Museum. I go there every day.'

'You do? I've only been there once. I'm afraid I found it rather a depressing place. It—it seemed to sap one's vitality.'

'It does. That's why I go there. The lower one's vitality, the more sensitive one is to great art. I live near the Museum. I have rooms in Dyott Street.'

'And you go round to the reading-room to read Milton?'

'Usually Milton.' He looked at me. 'It was Milton', he certificatively added, 'who converted me to Diabolism.'

'Diabolism? Oh yes? Really?' said I, with that vague discomfort and that intense desire to be polite which one feels when a man speaks of his own religion. 'You—worship the Devil?'

Soames shook his head. 'It's not exactly worship,' he qualified, sipping his absinthe. 'It's more a matter of trusting and encouraging.'

'Ah, yes. . . . But I had rather gathered from the preface to *Negations* that you were a—a Catholic.'

'*Je l'étais à cette époque.* Perhaps I still am. Yes, I'm a Catholic Diabolist.'

This profession he made in an almost cursory tone. I could see that what was upmost in his mind was the fact that I had read *Negations.* His pale eyes had for the first time gleamed. I felt as one who is about to be examined, *viva voce,* on the very subject in which he is shakiest. I hastily asked him how soon his poems were to be published. 'Next week,' he told me.

'And are they to be published without a title?'

'No, I found a title, at last. But I shan't tell you what it is,' as though I had been so impertinent as to inquire. 'I am not sure that it wholly satisfies me. But it is the best I can find. It does suggest something of the quality of the poems. . . . Strange growths, natural and wild; yet exquisite,' he added, 'and many-hued, and full of poisons.'

I asked him what he thought of Baudelaire. He uttered the snort that was his laugh, and 'Baudelaire', he said, 'was a *bourgeois malgré lui.*' France had had only one poet: Villon; 'and two-thirds of Villon were sheer journalism.' Verlaine was 'an *épicier malgré lui.*' Altogether, rather to my surprise, he rated French literature lower than English. There were 'passages' in Villiers de l'Isle-Adam. But 'I', he summed up, 'owe nothing to France.' He nodded at me. 'You'll see,' he predicted.

I did not, when the time came, quite see that. I thought the author of *Fungoids* did—unconsciously, no doubt— owe something to the young Parisian decadents, or to the young English ones who owed something to *them.* I still think so. The little book—bought by me in Oxford—lies before me as I write. Its pale grey buckram cover and silver lettering have not worn well. Nor have its contents. Through these, with a melancholy interest, I have again been looking. They are not much. But at the time of their publication I had a vague suspicion that they *might* be. I suppose it's my capacity for faith, not poor Soames' work, that is weaker than it once was. . . .

To a Young Woman

Thou art, who has not been!
    Pale tunes irresolute
    And traceries of old sounds
    Blown from a rotted flute
Mingle with noise of cymbals rouged with rust,
Nor not strange forms and epicene
    Lie bleeding in the dust,
      Being wounded with wounds.
      For this it is
    That is thy counterpart
      Of age-long mockeries
    Thou has not been nor art!

There seemed to me a certain inconsistency as between the first and last lines of this. I tried, with bent brows, to resolve the discord. But I did not take my failure as wholly incompatible with a meaning in Soames' mind. Might it not rather indicate the depth of his meaning? As for the craftsmanship, 'rouged with rust' seemed to me a fine stroke, and 'nor not' instead of 'and' had a curious felicity. I wondered who the Young Woman was, and what she had made of it all. I sadly suspect that Soames could not have made more of it than she. Yet, even now, if one doesn't try to make any sense at all of the poem, and reads it just for the sound, there is a certain grace of cadence. Soames was an artist—in so far as he was anything, poor fellow!

It seemed to me, when first I read *Fungoids*, that, oddly enough, the Diabolistic side of him was the best. Diabolism seemed to be a cheerful, even a wholesome, influence in his life.

Nocturne

Round and round the shutter'd Square
I stroll'd with the Devil's arm in mine.
No sound but the scrape of his hoofs was there
And the ring of his laughter and mine.
    We had drunk black wine.

I scream'd 'I will race you, Master!'
'What matter,' he shriek'd, 'to-night
Which of us runs the faster?
There is nothing to fear to-night
  In the foul moon's light!'

Then I look'd him in the eyes,
And I laugh'd full shrill at the lie he told
And the gnawing fear he would fain disguise.
It was true, what I'd time and again been told:
  He was old—old.

There was, I felt, quite a swing about that first stanza—a joyous and rollicking note of comradeship. The second was slightly hysterical perhaps. But I liked the third: it was so bracingly unorthodox, even according to the tenets of Soames' peculiar sect in the faith. Not much 'trusting and encouraging' here! Soames triumphantly exposing the Devil as a liar, and laughing 'full shrill', cut a quite heartening figure, I thought—then! Now, in the light of what befell, none of his poems depresses me so much as 'Nocturne'.

I looked out for what the metropolitan reviewers would have to say. They seemed to fall into two classes: those who had little to say and those who had nothing. The second class was the larger, and the words of the first were cold; insomuch that

Strikes a note of modernity throughout. . . . These tripping numbers—*Preston Telegraph.*

was the sole lure offered in advertisements by Soames' publisher. I had hoped that when next I met the poet I could congratulate him on having made a stir; for I fancied he was not so sure of his intrinsic greatness as he seemed. I was but able to say, rather coarsely, when next I did see him, that I hoped *Fungoids* was 'selling splendidly'. He looked at me across his glass of absinthe and asked if I had bought a copy. His publisher had told him that three had been sold. I laughed, as at a jest.

'You don't suppose I *care*, do you?' he said, with something like a snarl. I disclaimed the notion. He added that he was not a tradesman. I said mildly that I wasn't, either, and murmured that an artist who gave truly new and great things to the world had always to wait long for recognition. He said he cared not a sou for recognition. I agreed that the act of creation was its own reward.

His moroseness might have alienated me if I had regarded myself as a nobody. But ah! hadn't both John Lane and Aubrey Beardsley suggested that I should write an essay for the great new venture that was afoot—*The Yellow Book*? And hadn't Henry Harland, as editor, accepted my essay? And wasn't it to be in the very first number? At Oxford I was still *in statu pupillari*. In London I regarded myself as very much indeed a graduate now— one whom no Soames could ruffle. Partly to show off, partly in sheer good-will, I told Soames he ought to contribute to *The Yellow Book*. He uttered from the throat a sound of scorn for that publication.

Nevertheless, I did, a day or two later, tentatively ask Harland if he knew anything of the work of a man called Enoch Soames. Harland paused in the midst of his characteristic stride around the room, threw up his hands towards the ceiling, and groaned aloud: he had often met 'that absurd creature' in Paris, and this very morning had received some poems in manuscript from him.

'Has he *no* talent?' he asked.

'He has an income. He's all right.' Harland was the most joyous of men and most generous of critics, and he hated to talk of anything about which he couldn't be enthusiastic. So I dropped the subject of Soames. The news that Soames had an income did take the edge off solicitude. I learned afterwards that he was the son of an unsuccessful and deceased bookseller in Preston, but had inherited an annuity of £300 from a married aunt, and had no surviving relatives of any kind. Materially, then, he was 'all right'. But there was still a spiritual pathos about him, sharpened for me now by the possibility that even the praises of *The*

Preston Telegraph might not have been forthcoming had he not been the son of a Preston man. He had a sort of weak doggedness which I could not but admire. Neither he nor his work received the slightest encouragement; but he persisted in behaving as a personage: always he kept his dingy little flag flying. Wherever congregated the *jeunes féroces* of the arts, in whatever Soho restaurant they had just discovered, in whatever music-hall they were most frequenting, there was Soames in the midst of them, or rather on the fringe of them, a dim but inevitable figure. He never sought to propitiate his fellow-writers, never bated a jot of his arrogance about his own work or of his contempt of theirs. To the painters he was respectful, even humble; but for the poets and prosaists of *The Yellow Book*, and later of *The Savoy*, he had never a word but of scorn. He wasn't resented. It didn't occur to anybody that he or his Catholic Diabolism mattered. When, in the autumn of '96, he brought out (at his own expense, this time) a third book, his last book, nobody said a word for or against it. I meant, but forgot, to buy it. I never saw it, and am ashamed to say I don't even remember what it was called. But I did, at the time of its publication, say to Rothenstein that I thought poor old Soames was really a rather tragic figure, and that I believed he would literally die for want of recognition. Rothenstein scoffed. He said I was trying to get credit for a kind heart which I didn't possess; and perhaps this was so. But at the private view of the New English Art Club, a few weeks later, I beheld a pastel portrait of 'Enoch Soames, Esq.'. It was very like him, and very like Rothenstein to have done it. Soames was standing near it, in his soft hat and his waterproof cape, all through the afternoon. Anybody who knew him would have recognised the portrait at a glance, but nobody who didn't know him would have recognised the portrait from its bystander: it 'existed' so much more than he; it was bound to. Also, it had not that expression of faint happiness which on this day was discernible, yes, in Soames' countenance. Fame had breathed on him. Twice

again in the course of the month I went to the New English, and on both occasions Soames himself was on view
there. Looking back, I regard the close of that exhibition as
having been virtually the close of his career. He had felt
the breath of Fame against his cheek—so late, for such a
little while; and at its withdrawal he gave in, gave up, gave
out. He, who had never looked strong or well, looked
ghastly now—a shadow of the shade he had once been. He
still frequented the domino room, but, having lost all wish
to excite curiosity, he no longer read books there. 'You
read only at the Museum now?' asked I, with attempted
cheerfulness. He said he never went there now. 'No absinthe there,' he muttered. It was the sort of thing that in
the old days he would have said for effect; but it carried
conviction now. Absinthe, erst but a point in the 'personality' he had striven so hard to build up, was solace
and necessity now. He no longer called it *la sorcière
glauque*. He had shed away all his French phrases. He
had become a plain, unvarnished, Preston man.

Failure, if it be a plain, unvarnished, complete failure,
and even though it be a squalid failure, has always a certain dignity. I avoided Soames because he made me feel
rather vulgar. John Lane had published, by this time, two
little books of mine, and they had had a pleasant little
success of esteem. I was a—slight but definite—'personality'. Frank Harris had engaged me to kick up my heels
in *The Saturday Review*, Alfred Harmsworth was letting
me do likewise in *The Daily Mail*. I was just what Soames
wasn't. And he shamed my gloss. Had I known that he
really and firmly believed in the greatness of what he as an
artist had achieved, I might not have shunned him. No
man who hasn't lost his vanity can be held to have altogether failed. Soames' dignity was an illusion of mine. One
day in the first week of June, 1897, that illusion went.
But on the evening of that day Soames went too.

I had been out most of the morning, and, as it was too
late to reach home in time for luncheon, I sought 'the
Vingtième'. This little place—Restaurant du Vingtième

Siècle, to give it its full title—had been discovered in '96 by the poets and prosaists, but had now been more or less abandoned in favour of some later find. I don't think it lived long enough to justify its name; but at that time it still was, in Greek Street, a few doors from Soho Square, and almost opposite to that house where, in the first years of the century, a little girl, and with her a boy named De Quincey, made nightly encampment in darkness and hunger among dust and rats and old legal parchments. The Vingtième was but a small whitewashed room, leading out into the street at one end and into a kitchen at the other. The proprietor and cook was a Frenchman, known to us as Monsieur Vingtième; the waiters were his two daughters, Rose and Berthe; and the food, according to faith, was good. The tables were so narrow, and were set so close together, that there was space for twelve of them, six jutting from either wall.

Only the two nearest to the door, as I went in, were occupied. On one side sat a tall, flashy, rather Mephistophelian man whom I had seen from time to time in the domino room and elsewhere. On the other side sat Soames. They made a queer contrast in that sunlit room—Soames sitting haggard in that hat and cape which nowhere at any season had I seen him doff, and this other, this keenly vital man, at sight of whom I more than ever wondered whether he were a diamond merchant, a conjurer, or the head of a private detective agency. I was sure Soames didn't want my company; but I asked, as it would have seemed brutal not to, whether I might join him, and took the chair opposite to his. He was smoking a cigarette, with an untasted salmi of something on his plate and a half-empty bottle of Sauterne before him; and he was quite silent. I said that the preparations for the Jubilee made London impossible. (I rather liked them, really.) I professed a wish to go right away till the whole thing was over. In vain did I attune myself to his gloom. He seemed not to hear me nor even to see me. I felt that his behaviour made me ridiculous in the eyes of the other man. The gangway between the two

rows of tables at the Vingtième was hardly more than two
feet wide (Rose and Berthe, in their ministrations, had
always to edge past each other, quarrelling in whispers as
they did so), and any one at the table abreast of yours was
practically at yours. I thought our neighbour was amused
at my failure to interest Soames, and so, as I could not
explain to him that my insistence was merely charitable,
I became silent. Without turning my head, I had him well
within my range of vision. I hoped I looked less vulgar
than he in contrast with Soames. I was sure he was not an
Englishman, but what *was* his nationality? Though his
jet-black hair was *en brosse*, I did not think he was French.
To Berthe, who waited on him, he spoke French fluently,
but with a hardly native idiom and accent. I gathered that
this was his first visit to the Vingtième; but Berthe was off-
hand in her manner to him: he had not made a good
impression. His eyes were handsome, but—like the
Vingtième's tables—too narrow and set too close together.
His nose was predatory, and the points of his moustache,
waxed up beyond his nostrils, gave a fixity to his smile.
Decidedly, he was sinister. And my sense of discomfort
in his presence was intensified by the scarlet waistcoat
which tightly, and so unseasonably in June, sheathed his
ample chest. This waistcoat wasn't wrong merely because
of the heat, either. It was somehow all wrong in itself. It
wouldn't have done on Christmas morning. It would have
struck a jarring note at the first night of 'Hernani'. I was
trying to account for its wrongness when Soames suddenly
and strangely broke silence. 'A hundred years hence!' he
murmured, as in a trance.

'We shall not be here!' I briskly but fatuously added.

'We shall not be here. No,' he droned, 'but the Museum
will still be just where it is. And the reading-room, just
where it is. And people will be able to go and read there.'
He inhaled sharply, and a spasm as of actual pain con-
torted his features.

I wondered what train of thought poor Soames had been

following. He did not enlighten me when he said, after a long pause, 'You think I haven't minded.'

'Minded what, Soames?'

'Neglect. Failure.'

'*Failure?*' I said heartily. 'Failure?' I repeated vaguely. 'Neglect—yes, perhaps; but that's quite another matter. Of course you haven't been—appreciated. But what then? Any artist who—who gives——' What I wanted to say was, 'Any artist who gives truly new and great things to the world has always to wait long for recognition'; but the flattery would not out: in the face of his misery, a misery so genuine and so unmasked, my lips would not say the words.

And then—he said them for me. I flushed. 'That's what you were going to say, isn't it?' he asked.

'How did you know?'

'It's what you said to me three years ago, when *Fungoids* was published.' I flushed the more. I need not have done so at all, for 'It's the only important thing I ever heard you say,' he continued. 'And I've never forgotten it. It's a true thing. It's a horrible truth. But—d'you remember what I answered? I said "I don't care a sou for recognition." And you believed me. You've gone on believing I'm above that sort of thing. You're shallow. What should *you* know of the feelings of a man like me? You imagine that a great artist's faith in himself and in the verdict of posterity is enough to keep him happy.... You've never guessed at the bitterness and loneliness, the'—his voice broke; but presently he resumed, speaking with a force that I had never known in him. 'Posterity! What use is it to *me*? A dead man doesn't know that people are visiting his grave—visiting his birthplace—putting up tablets to him—unveiling statues of him. A dead man can't read the books that are written about him. A hundred years hence! Think of it! If I could come back to life *then*—just for a few hours—and go to the reading-room, and *read*! Or better still: if I could be projected, now, at this moment, into that future, into that reading-room, just for this one afternoon! I'd sell myself body and soul to the devil, for that! Think of the pages and pages in the catalogue: "Soames, Enoch" endlessly—endless editions, commentaries, prolegomena, biographies'—but here he was interrupted by a sudden loud creak of the chair at the next table. Our neighbour had half risen from his place. He was leaning towards us, apologetically intrusive.

'Excuse—permit me,' he said softly. 'I have been unable not to hear. Might I take a liberty? In this little *restaurant-sans-façon*'—he spread wide his hands—'might I, as the phrase is, "cut in"?'

I could but signify our acquiescence. Berthe had appeared at the kitchen door, thinking the stranger wanted his bill. He waved her away with his cigar, and in another moment had seated himself beside me, commanding a full view of Soames.

'Though not an Englishman,' he explained, 'I know my London well, Mr Soames. Your name and fame—Mr Beerbohm's too—very known to me. Your point is: who am *I*?' He glanced quickly over his shoulder, and in a lowered voice said, 'I am the Devil.'

I couldn't help it: I laughed. I tried not to, I knew there was nothing to laugh at, my rudeness shamed me, but—I laughed with increasing volume. The Devil's quiet dignity, the surprise and disgust of his raised eyebrows, did but the more dissolve me. I rocked to and fro, I lay back aching. I behaved deplorably.

'I am a gentleman, and,' he said with intense emphasis, 'I thought I was in the company of *gentlemen*.'

'Don't!' I gasped faintly. 'Oh, don't!'

'Curious, *nicht wahr*?' I heard him say to Soames. 'There is a type of person to whom the very mention of my name is—oh-so-awfully-funny! In your theatres the dullest *comédien* needs only to say "The Devil!" and right away they give him "the loud laugh that speaks the vacant mind". Is it not so?'

I had now just breath enough to offer my apologies. He

accepted them, but coldly, and readdressed himself to Soames.

'I am a man of business,' he said, 'and always I would put things through "right now", as they say in the States. You are a poet. *Les affaires*—you detest them. So be it. But with me you will deal, eh? What you have said just now gives me furiously to hope.'

Soames had not moved, except to light a fresh cigarette. He sat crouched forward, with his elbows squared on the table, and his head just above the level of his hands, staring up at the Devil. 'Go on,' he nodded. I had no remnant of laughter in me now.

'It will be the more pleasant, our little deal,' the Devil went on, 'because you are—I mistake not?—a Diabolist.'

'A Catholic Diabolist,' said Soames.

The Devil accepted the reservation genially. 'You wish', he resumed, 'to visit now—this afternoon as-ever-is—the reading-room of the British Museum, yes? but of a hundred years hence, yes? *Parfaitement*. Time—an illusion. Past and future—they are as ever-present as the present, or at any rate only what you call "just-round-the-corner". I switch you on to any date. I project you—pouf! You wish to be in the reading-room just as it will be on the afternoon of June 3rd, 1997? You wish to find yourself standing in that room, just past the swing-doors, this very minute, yes? and to stay there till closing time? Am I right?'

Soames nodded.

The Devil looked at his watch. 'Ten past two,' he said, 'Closing time in summer same then as now: seven o'clock. That will give you almost five hours. At seven o'clock—pouf!—you find yourself again here, sitting at this table. I am dining to-night *dans le monde—dans le higlif*. That concludes my present visit to your great city. I come and fetch you here, Mr Soames, on my way home.'

'Home?' I echoed.

'Be it never so humble!' said the Devil lightly.

'All right,' said Soames.

'Soames!' I entreated. But my friend moved not a muscle.

The Devil had made as though to stretch forth his hand across the table and touch Soames' forearm; but he paused in his gesture.

'A hundred years hence, as now,' he smiled, 'no smoking allowed in the reading-room. You would better there-fore——'

Soames removed the cigarette from his mouth and dropped it into his glass of Sauterne.

'Soames!' again I cried. 'Can't you'—but the Devil had now stretched forth his hand across the table. He brought it slowly down on—the table-cloth. Soames' chair was empty. His cigarette floated sodden in his wine-glass. There was no other trace of him.

For a few moments the Devil let his hand rest where it lay, gazing at me out of the corners of his eyes, vulgarly triumphant.

A shudder shook me. With an effort I controlled myself and rose from my chair. 'Very clever,' I said condescend-ingly. 'But—*The Time Machine* is a delightful book, don't you think? So entirely original!'

'You are pleased to sneer,' said the Devil, who had also risen, 'but it is one thing to write about a not possible machine; it is a quite other thing to be a Supernatural Power.' All the same, I had scored.

Berthe had come forth at the sound of our rising. I explained to her that Mr Soames had been called away, and that both he and I would be dining here. It was not until I was out in the open air that I began to feel giddy. I have but the haziest recollection of what I did, where I wandered, in the glaring sunshine of that endless after-noon. I remember the sound of carpenters' hammers all along Piccadilly, and the bare chaotic look of the half-erected 'stands'. Was it in the Green Park, or in Kensing-ton Gardens, or *where* was it that I sat on a chair beneath a tree, trying to read an evening paper? There was a phrase in the leading article that went on repeating itself in my

fagged mind—'Little is hidden from this august Lady full
of the garnered wisdom of sixty years of Sovereignty.' I
remember wildly conceiving a letter (to reach Windsor by
express messenger told to await answer):

'MADAM,—Well knowing that your Majesty is full of
the garnered wisdom of sixty years of Sovereignty, I venture to ask your advice in the following delicate matter.
Mr Enoch Soames, whose poems you may or may not
know,' . . .

Was there *no* way of helping him—saving him? A bargain
was a bargain, and I was the last man to aid or abet any
one in wriggling out of a reasonable obligation. I wouldn't
have lifted a little finger to save Faust. But poor Soames!
—doomed to pay without respite an eternal price for
nothing but a fruitless search and a bitter disillusion-
ing. . . .

Odd and uncanny it seemed to me that he, Soames, in
the flesh, in the waterproof cape, was at this moment living
in the last decade of the next century, poring over books
not yet written, and seeing and seen by men not yet born.
Uncannier and odder still, that to-night and evermore he
would be in Hell. Assuredly, truth was stranger than fiction.

Endless that afternoon was. Almost I wished I had gone
with Soames—not indeed to stay in the reading-room, but
to sally forth for a brisk sight-seeing walk around a new
London. I wandered restlessly out of the Park I had sat in.
Vainly I tried to imagine myself an ardent tourist from the
eighteenth century. Intolerable was the strain of the slow-
passing and empty minutes. Long before seven o'clock I
was back at the Vingtième.

I sat there just where I had sat for luncheon. Air came
in listlessly through the open door behind me. Now and
again Rose or Berthe appeared for a moment. I told them
I would not order any dinner until Mr Soames came. A
hurdy-gurdy began to play, abruptly drowning the noise
of a quarrel between some Frenchmen further up the

street. Whenever the tune was changed I heard the quarrel
still raging. I had bought another evening paper on my
way. I unfolded it. My eyes gazed ever away from it to the
clock over the kitchen door. . . .

Five minutes, now, to the hour! I remembered that
clocks in restaurants are kept five minutes fast. I concentrated my eyes on the paper. I vowed I would not look
away from it again. I held it upright, at its full width,
close to my face, so that I had no view of anything but it.
. . . Rather a tremulous sheet? Only because of the
draught, I told myself.

My arms gradually became stiff; they ached; but I could
not drop them—now. I had a suspicion, I had a certainty.
Well, what then? . . . What else had I come for? Yet I
held tight that barrier of newspaper. Only the sound of
Berthe's brisk footstep from the kitchen enabled me, forced
me, to drop it, and to utter:

'What shall we have to eat, Soames?'

'*Il est souffrant, ce pauvre Monsieur Soames?*' asked
Berthe.

'He's only—tired.' I asked her to get some wine—Burgundy—and whatever food might be ready. Soames sat
crouched forward against the table, exactly as when last I
had seen him. It was as though he had never moved—he
who had moved so unimaginably far. Once or twice in the
afternoon it had for an instant occurred to me that perhaps
his journey was not to be fruitless—that perhaps we had
all been wrong in our estimate of the works of Enoch
Soames. That we had been horribly right was horribly
clear from the look of him. But 'Don't be discouraged,' I
falteringly said. 'Perhaps it's only that you—didn't leave
enough time. Two, three centuries hence, perhaps——'

'Yes,' his voice came. 'I've thought of that.'

'And now—now for the more immediate future! Where
are you going to hide? How would it be if you caught the
Paris express from Charing Cross? Almost an hour to
spare. Don't go on to Paris. Stop at Calais. Live in Calais.
He'd never think of looking for you in Calais.'

'It's like my luck', he said, 'to spend my last hours on earth with an ass.' But I was not offended. 'And a treacherous ass,' he strangely added, tossing across to me a crumpled bit of paper which he had been holding in his hand. I glanced at the writing on it—some sort of gibberish, apparently. I laid it impatiently aside.

'Come, Soames! pull yourself together! This isn't a mere matter of life and death. It's a question of eternal torment, mind you! You don't mean to say you're going to wait limply here till the Devil comes to fetch you?'

'I can't do anything else. I've no choice.'

'Come! This is "trusting and encouraging" with a vengeance! This is Diabolism run mad!' I filled his glass with wine. 'Surely, now that you've *seen* the brute——'

'It's no good abusing him.'

'You must admit there's nothing Miltonic about him, Soames.'

'I don't say he's not rather different from what I expected.'

'He's a vulgarian, he's a swell-mobsman, he's the sort of man who hangs about the corridors of trains going to the Riviera and steals ladies' jewel-cases. Imagine eternal torment presided over by *him*!'

'You don't suppose I look forward to it, do you?'

'Then why not slip quietly out of the way?'

Again and again I filled his glass, and always, mechanically, he emptied it; but the wine kindled no spark of enterprise in him. He did not eat, and I myself ate hardly at all. I did not in my heart believe that any dash for freedom could save him. The chase would be swift, the capture certain. But better anything than this passive, meek, miserable waiting. I told Soames that for the honour of the human race he ought to make some show of resistance. He asked what the human race had ever done for him. 'Besides,' he said, 'can't you understand that I'm in his power? You saw him touch me, didn't you? There's an end of it. I've no will. I'm sealed.'

I made a gesture of despair. He went on repeating the

word 'sealed'. I began to realise that the wine had clouded his brain. No wonder! Foodless he had gone into futurity, foodless he still was. I urged him to eat at any rate some bread. It was maddening to think that he, who had so much to tell, might tell nothing. 'How was it all,' I asked, 'yonder? Come! Tell me your adventures.'

'They'd make first-rate "copy", wouldn't they?'

'I'm awfully sorry for you, Soames, and I make all possible allowances; but what earthly right have you to insinuate that I should make "copy", as you call it, out of you?'

The poor fellow pressed his hands to his forehead. 'I don't know,' he said. 'I had some reason, I'm sure. . . . I'll try to remember.'

'That's right. Try to remember everything. Eat a little more bread. What did the reading-room look like?'

'Much as usual,' he at length muttered.

'Many people there?'

'Usual sort of number.'

'What did they look like?'

Soames tried to visualise them. 'They all,' he presently remembered, 'looked very like one another.'

My mind took a fearsome leap. 'All dressed in Jaeger?'

'Yes, I think so. Greyish-yellowish stuff.'

'A sort of uniform?' He nodded. 'With a number on it, perhaps?—a number on a large disc of metal sewn on to the left sleeve? DKF 78,910—that sort of thing?' It was even so. 'And all of them—men and women alike—looking very well-cared-for? very Utopian? and smelling rather strongly of carbolic? and all of them quite hairless?' I was right every time. Soames was only not sure whether the men and women were hairless or shorn. 'I hadn't time to look at them very closely,' he explained.

'No, of course not. But——'

'They stared at *me*, I can tell you. I attracted a great deal of attention.' At last he had done that! 'I think I rather scared them. They moved away whenever I came near. They followed me about at a distance, wherever I went. The men at the round desk in the middle seemed to have a sort of panic whenever I went to make inquiries.'

'What did you do when you arrived?'

Well, he had gone straight to the catalogue, of course—to the S volumes, and had stood long before SN-SOF, unable to take this volume out of the shelf, because his heart was beating so. . . . At first, he said, he wasn't disappointed—he only thought there was some new arrangement. He went to the middle desk and asked where the catalogue of *twentieth*-century books was kept. He gathered that there was still only one catalogue. Again he looked up his name, stared at the three little pasted slips he had known so well. Then he went and sat down for a long time. . . .

'And then,' he droned, 'I looked up the *Dictionary of National Biography* and some encyclopaedias. . . . I went back to the middle desk and asked what was the best modern book on late nineteenth-century literature. They told me Mr T. K. Nupton's book was considered the best. I looked it up in the catalogue and filled in a form for it. It was brought to me. My name wasn't in the index, but——Yes!' he said with a sudden change of tone. 'That's what I'd forgotten. Where's that bit of paper? Give it me back.'

I, too, had forgotten that cryptic screed. I found it fallen on the floor, and handed it to him.

He smoothed it out, nodding and smiling at me disagreeably. 'I found myself glancing through Nupton's book,' he resumed. 'Not very easy reading. Some sort of phonetic spelling. . . . All the modern books I saw were phonetic.'

'Then I don't want to hear any more, Soames, please.'

'The proper names seemed all to be spelt in the old way. But for that, I mightn't have noticed my own name.'

'Your own name? Really? Soames, I'm *very* glad.'

'And yours.'

'No!'

'I thought I should find you waiting here to-night. So I took the trouble to copy out the passage. Read it.'

I snatched the paper. Soames' handwriting was characteristically dim. It, and the noisome spelling, and my excitement, made me all the slower to grasp what T. K. Nupton was driving at.

The document lies before me at this moment. Strange that the words I here copy out for you were copied out for me by poor Soames just seventy-eight years hence. . . .

From p. 234 of 'Inglish Littracher 1890–1900', bi T. K. Nupton, published bi th Stait, 1992:

'Fr. egzarmpl, a riter ov th time, naimd Max Beerbohm, hoo woz stil alive in th twentieth senchri, rote a stauri in wich e pautraid an immajnari karrakter kauld "Enoch Soames"—a thurd-rait poit hoo beleevz imself a grate jeneus and maix a bargin with th Devvl in auder ter no wot posterriti thinx ov im! It is a sumwot labud sattire but not without vallu az showing hou seriusli the yung men ov th aiteen-ninetiz took themselvz. Nou that the littreri professhn has bin auganized az a department of publik servis, our riters hav found their levvl an hav lernt ter doo their duti without thort ov th morro. "Th laibrer iz werthi ov hiz hire", an that iz aul. Thank hevvn we hav no Enoch Soameses amung us to-dai!'

I found that by murmuring the words aloud (a device which I commend to my reader) I was able to master them, little by little. The clearer they became, the greater was my bewilderment, my distress and horror. The whole thing was a nightmare. Afar, the great grisly background of what was in store for the poor dear art of letters; here, at the table, fixing on me a gaze that made me hot all over, the poor fellow whom—whom evidently . . . but no: whatever down-grade my character might take in coming years, I should never be such a brute as to——

Again I examined the screed. 'Immajnari'—but here Soames was, no more imaginary, alas! than I. And 'labud' —what on earth was that? (To this day, I have never made out that word.) 'It's all very—baffling,' I at length stammered.

Soames said nothing, but cruelly did not cease to look at me.

'Are you sure,' I temporised, 'quite sure you copied the thing out correctly?'

'Quite.'

'Well, then it's this wretched Nupton who must have made—must be going to make—some idiotic mistake.... Look here, Soames! you know me better than to suppose that I ... After all, the name "Max Beerbohm" is not at all an uncommon one, and there must be several Enoch Soameses running around—or rather, "Enoch Soames" is a name that might occur to any one writing a story. And I don't write stories: I'm an essayist, an observer, a recorder.... I admit that it's an extraordinary coincidence. But you must see——'

'I see the whole thing,' said Soames quietly. And he added, with a touch of his old manner, but with more dignity than I had ever known in him, '*Parlons d'autre chose.*'

I accepted that suggestion very promptly. I returned straight to the more immediate future. I spent most of the long evening in renewed appeals to Soames to slip away and seek refuge somewhere. I remember saying at last that if indeed I was destined to write about him, the supposed 'stauri' had better have at least a happy ending. Soames repeated those last three words in a tone of intense scorn. 'In Life and in Art,' he said, 'all that matters is an *inevitable* ending.'

'But,' I urged, more hopefully than I felt, 'an ending that can be avoided *isn't* inevitable.'

'You aren't an artist,' he rasped. 'And you're so hopelessly not an artist that, so far from being able to imagine a thing and make it seem true, you're going to make even a true thing seem as if you'd made it up. You're a miserable bungler. And it's like my luck.'

I protested that the miserable bungler was not I—was not going to be I—but T. K. Nupton; and we had a rather heated argument, in the thick of which it suddenly seemed to me that Soames saw he was in the wrong: he had quite physically cowered. But I wondered why—and now I guessed with a cold throb just why—he stared so, past me. The bringer of that 'inevitable ending' filled the doorway.

I managed to turn in my chair and to say, not without a semblance of lightness, 'Aha, come in!' Dread was indeed rather blunted in me by his looking so absurdly like a villain in a melodrama. The sheen of his tilted hat and of his shirtfront, the repeated twists he was giving to his moustache, and most of all the magnificence of his sneer, gave token that he was there only to be foiled.

He was at our table in a stride. 'I am sorry', he sneered witheringly, 'to break up your pleasant party, but—'

'You don't: you complete it,' I assured him. 'Mr Soames and I want to have a little talk with you. Won't you sit? Mr Soames got nothing—frankly nothing—by his journey this afternoon. We don't wish to say that the whole thing was a swindle—a common swindle. On the contrary, we believe you meant well. But of course the bargain, such as it was, is off.'

The Devil gave no verbal answer. He merely looked at Soames and pointed with rigid forefinger to the door. Soames was wretchedly rising from his chair when, with a desperate quick gesture, I swept together two dinner-knives that were on the table, and laid their blades across each other. The Devil stepped sharp back against the table behind him, averting his face and shuddering.

'You are not superstitious!' he hissed.

'Not at all,' I smiled.

'Soames!' he said as to an underling, but without turning his face, 'put those knives straight!'

With an inhibitive gesture to my friend, 'Mr Soames', I said emphatically to the Devil, 'is a *Catholic* Diabolist'; but my poor friend did the Devil's bidding, not mine; and now, with his master's eyes again fixed on him, he arose, he shuffled past me. I tried to speak. It was he that spoke. 'Try,' was the prayer he threw back at me as the Devil pushed him roughly out through the door, '*try* to make them know that I did exist!'

In another instant I too was through that door. I stood staring all ways—up the street, across it, down it. There was moonlight and lamplight, but there was not Soames nor that other.

Dazed, I stood there. Dazed, I turned back, at length, into the little room; and I suppose I paid Berthe or Rose for my dinner and luncheon, and for Soames': I hope so, for I never went to the Vingtième again. Ever since that night I have avoided Greek Street altogether. And for years I did not set foot even in Soho Square, because on that same night it was there that I paced and loitered, long and long, with some such dull sense of hope as a man has in not straying far from the place where he has lost something. . . . 'Round and round the shutter'd Square'—that line came back to me on my lonely beat, and with it the whole stanza, ringing in my brain and bearing in on me how tragically different from the happy scene imagined by him was the poet's actual experience of that prince in whom of all princes we should put not our trust.

But—strange how the mind of an essayist, be it never so stricken, roves and ranges!—I remember pausing before a wide doorstep and wondering if perchance it was on this very one that the young De Quincey lay ill and faint while poor Ann flew as fast as her feet would carry her to Oxford Street, the 'stony-hearted stepmother' of them both, and came back bearing that 'glass of port wine and spices' but for which he might, so he thought, actually have died. Was this the very doorstep that the old De Quincey used to revisit in homage? I pondered Ann's fate, the cause of her sudden vanishing from the ken of her boy-friend; and presently I blamed myself for letting the past over-ride the present. Poor vanished Soames!

And for myself, too, I began to be troubled. What had I better do? Would there be a hue and cry—Mysterious Disappearance of an Author, and all that? He had last been seen lunching and dining in my company. Hadn't I better get a hansom and drive straight to Scotland Yard? . . . They would think I was a lunatic. After all, I reassured myself, London was a very large place, and one very dim figure might easily drop out of it unobserved—now especially, in the blinding glare of the near Jubilee. Better say nothing at all, I thought.

And I was right. Soames' disappearance made no stir at all. He was utterly forgotten before any one, so far as I am aware, noticed that he was no longer hanging around. Now and again some poet or prosaist may have said to another, 'What has become of that man Soames?' but I never heard any such question asked. The solicitor through whom he was paid his annuity may be presumed to have made inquiries, but no echo of these resounded. There was something rather ghastly to me in the general unconsciousness that Soames had existed, and more than once I caught myself wondering whether Nupton, that babe unborn, were going to be right in thinking him a figment of my brain.

In that extract from Nupton's repulsive book there is one point which perhaps puzzles you. How is it that the author, though I have here mentioned him by name and have quoted the exact words he is going to write, is not going to grasp the obvious corollary that I have invented nothing? The answer can be but this: Nupton will not have read the later passages of this memoir. Such lack of thoroughness is a serious fault in any one who undertakes to do scholar's work. And I hope these words will meet the eye of some contemporary rival to Nupton and be the undoing of Nupton.

I like to think that some time between 1992 and 1997 somebody will have looked up this memoir, and will have forced on the world his inevitable and startling conclusions. And I have reasons for believing that this will be so. You realise that the reading-room into which Soames was projected by the Devil was in all respects precisely as it will be on the afternoon of June 3rd, 1997. You realise, therefore, that on that afternoon, when it comes round, there the self-same crowd will be, and there Soames too will be, punctually, he and they doing precisely what they did before. Recall now Soames' account of the sensation he made. You may say that the mere difference of his costume was enough to make him sensational in that uniformed crowd. You wouldn't say so if you had ever seen him. I assure you that in no period could Soames be anything but dim. The fact that people are going to stare at him, and follow him around, and seem afraid of him, can be explained only on the hypothesis that they will somehow have been prepared for his ghostly visitation. They will have been awfully waiting to see whether he really would come. And when he does come the effect will of course be—awful.

An authentic, guaranteed, proven ghost, but—only a ghost, alas! Only that. In his first visit, Soames was a creature of flesh and blood, whereas the creatures into whose midst he was projected were but ghosts, I take it— solid, palpable, vocal, but unconscious and automatic ghosts, in a building that was itself an illusion. Next time, that building and those creatures will be real. It is of Soames that there will be but the semblance. I wish I could think him destined to revisit the world actually, physically, consciously. I wish he had this one brief escape, this one small treat, to look forward to. I never forget him for long. He is where he is, and forever. The more rigid moralists among you may say he has only himself to blame. For my part, I think he has been very hardly used. It is well that vanity should be chastened; and Enoch Soames' vanity was, I admit, above the average, and called for special treatment. But there was no need for vindictiveness. You say he contracted to pay the price he is paying; yes; but I maintain that he was induced to do so by fraud. Well-informed in all things, the Devil must have known that my friend would gain nothing by his visit to futurity. The whole thing was a very shabby trick. The more I think of it, the more detestable the Devil seems to me.

Of him I have caught sight several times, here and there, since that day at the Vingtième. Only once, however, have I seen him at close quarters. This was in Paris. I was walking, one afternoon, along the Rue d'Antin, when I saw him advancing from the opposite direction—over-dressed as

ever, and swinging an ebony cane, and altogether behaving
as though the whole pavement belonged to him. At thought
of Enoch Soames and the myriads of other sufferers eternally in this brute's dominion, a great cold wrath filled me,
and I drew myself up to my full height. But—well, one is
so used to nodding and smiling in the street to anybody
one knows, that the action becomes almost independent of
oneself: to prevent it requires a very sharp effort and great
presence of mind. I was miserably aware, as I passed the
Devil, that I nodded and smiled to him. And my shame
was the deeper and hotter because he, if you please, stared
straight at me with the utmost haughtiness.

To be cut—deliberately cut—by *him*! I was, I still am,
furious at having had that happen to me.

JAMES PETHEL

THOUGH SEVEN YEARS HAVE gone by since the day
when last I saw him, and though that day was but the
morrow of my first meeting with him, I was shocked when
I saw in my newspaper this morning the announcement
of his sudden death.

I had formed, in the dim past, the habit of spending
August in Dieppe. The place was less popular then than
it is now. Some pleasant English people shared it with
some pleasant French people. We used rather to resent
the race-week—the third week of the month—as an intrusion of our privacy. We sneered as we read in the Paris
edition of the *New York Herald* the names of the
intruders. We disliked the nightly crush in the baccarat
room of the Casino, and the croupiers' obvious excitement at the high play. I made a point of avoiding that
room during that week, for the especial reason that the

sight of serious, habitual gamblers has always filled me with a depression bordering on disgust. Most of the men, by some subtle stress of their ruling passion, have grown so monstrously fat, and most of the women so harrowingly thin. The rest of the women seem to be marked out for apoplexy, and the rest of the men to be wasting away. One feels that anything thrown at them would be either embedded or shattered, and looks vainly among them for a person furnished with the normal amount of flesh. Monsters they are, all of them, to the eye (though I believe that many of them have excellent moral qualities in private life); but, just as in an American town one goes sooner or later—goes against one's finer judgment, but somehow goes—into the dime-museum, so, year by year, in Dieppe's race-week, there would be always one evening when I drifted into the baccarat room. It was on such an evening that I first saw the man whose memory I here celebrate. My gaze was held by him for the very reason that he would have passed unnoticed elsewhere. He was conspicuous, not in virtue of the mere fact that he was taking the bank at the principal table, but because there was nothing at all odd about him.

Between his lips was a cigar of moderate size. Everything about him, except the amount of money he had been winning, seemed moderate. Just as he was neither fat nor thin, so had his face neither that extreme pallor nor that extreme redness which belongs to the faces of seasoned gamblers: it was just a clear pink. And his eyes had neither the unnatural brightness nor the unnatural dullness of the eyes around him: they were ordinarily clear eyes, of an ordinary grey. His very age was moderate: a putative thirty-six, not more. ('Not less', I would have said in those days.) He assumed no air of nonchalance. He did not deal out the cards as though they bored him. But he had no look of grim concentration. I noticed that the removal of his cigar from his mouth made never the least difference to his face, for he kept his lips pursed out as steadily as ever when he was not smoking. And this constant pursing of his lips seemed to denote just a pensive interest.

His bank was nearly done now. There were but a few cards left. Opposite to him was a welter of parti-coloured counters which the croupier had not yet had time to sort out and add to the rouleaux already made; there were also a fair accumulation of notes and several little stacks of gold. In all, not less than five hundred pounds, certainly. Happy banker! How easily had he won in a few minutes more than I, with utmost pains, could earn in many months! I wished I were he. His lucre seemed to insult me personally. I disliked him. And yet I hoped he would not take another bank. I hoped he would have the good sense to pocket his winnings and go home. Deliberately to risk the loss of all those riches would intensify the insult to myself.

'Messieurs, la banque est aux enchères!' There was some brisk bidding, while the croupier tore open and shuffled the two new packs. But it was as I feared: the gentleman whom I resented kept his place.

'Messieurs, la banque est faite. Quinze mille francs à la banque. Messieurs, les cartes passent! Messieurs, les cartes passent!'

Turning to go, I encountered a friend—one of the race-weekers, but in a sense a friend.

'Going to play?' I asked.

'Not while Jimmy Pethel's taking the bank,' he answered, with a laugh.

'Is that the man's name?'

'Yes. Don't you know him? I thought every one knew old Jimmy Pethel.'

I asked what there was so wonderful about 'old Jimmy Pethel' that every one should be supposed to know him.

'Oh, he's a great character. Has extraordinary luck. Always.'

I do not think my friend was versed in the pretty theory that good luck is the unconscious wisdom of them who in previous incarnations have been consciously wise.

He was a member of the Stock Exchange, and I smiled as at a certain quaintness in his remark. I asked in what ways besides luck the 'great character' was manifested. Oh, well, Pethel had made a huge 'scoop' on the Stock Exchange when he was only twenty-three, and very soon doubled that, and doubled it again; then retired. He wasn't more than thirty-five now. And? Oh, well, he was a regular all-round sportsman—had gone after big game all over the world and had a good many narrow shaves. Great steeple-chaser, too. Rather settled down now. Lived in Leicestershire mostly. Had a big place there. Hunted five times a week. Still did an occasional flutter, though. Cleared eighty thousand in Mexicans last February. Wife had been a barmaid at Cambridge. Married her when he was nineteen. Thing seemed to have turned out quite well. Altogether, a great character.

Possibly, thought I. But my cursory friend, accustomed to quick transactions and to things accepted 'on the nod', had not proved his case to my slower, more literary intelligence. It was to him, however, that I owed, some minutes later, a chance of testing his opinion. At the cry of *'Messieurs, la banque est aux enchères'* we looked round and saw that the subject of our talk was preparing to rise from his place. 'Now one can punt!' said Grierson (this was my friend's name), and turned to the bureau at which counters are for sale. 'If old Jimmy Pethel punts,' he added, 'I shall just follow his luck.' But this lodestar was not to be. While my friend was buying counters, and I wondering whether I too would buy some, Pethel himself came up to the bureau. With his lips no longer pursed, he had lost his air of gravity, and looked younger. Behind him was an attendant bearing a big wooden bowl—that plain but romantic bowl supplied by the establishment to a banker whose gains are too great to be pocketed. He and Grierson greeted each other. He said he had arrived in Dieppe this afternoon— was here for a day or two. We were introduced. He spoke to me with some *empressement*, saying he was a 'very

great admirer' of my work. I no longer disliked him.
Grierson, armed with counters, had now darted away to
secure a place that had just been vacated. Pethel, with a
wave of his hand towards the tables, said, 'I suppose
you never condescend to this sort of thing?'

'Well——' I smiled indulgently.

'Awful waste of time,' he admitted.

I glanced down at the splendid mess of counters and
gold and notes that were now becoming, under the swift
fingers of the little man at the bureau, an orderly array.
I did not say aloud that it pleased me to be, and to be
seen, talking, on terms of equality, to a man who had
won so much. I did not say how wonderful it seemed to
me that he, whom I had watched just now with awe
and with aversion, had all the while been a great admirer
of my work. I did but say (again indulgently) that I supposed baccarat to be as good a way of wasting time as
another.

'Ah, but you despise us all the same!' He added that
he always envied men who had resources within themselves. I laughed lightly, to imply that it *was* very pleasant
to have such resources, but that I didn't want to boast.
And indeed, I had never, I vow, felt flimsier than when
the little man at the bureau, naming a fabulous sum,
asked its owner whether he would take the main part
in notes of mille francs? cinq mille? dix mille? quoi?
Had it been mine, I should have asked to have it all in
five-franc pieces. Pethel took it in the most compendious
form and crumpled in into a pocket. I asked if he were
going to play any more to-night.

'Oh, later on,' he said. 'I want to get a little sea-air
into my lungs now'; and he asked with a sort of breezy
diffidence if I would go with him. I was glad to do so.
It flashed across my mind that yonder on the terrace he
might suddenly blurt out, 'I say, look here, don't think
me awfully impertinent, but this money's no earthly use
to me: I do wish you'd accept it, as a very small return
for all the pleasure your work has given me, and . . .

There! PLEASE! Not another word!'—all with such candour, delicacy, and genuine zeal that I should be unable to refuse. But I must not raise false hopes in my reader. Nothing of the sort happened. Nothing of that sort ever does happen.

We were not long on the terrace. It was not a night on which you could stroll and talk: there was a wind against which you had to stagger, holding your hat on tightly and shouting such remarks as might occur to you. Against that wind acquaintance could make no headway. Yet I see now that despite that wind—or rather because of it—I ought really to have known Pethel a little better than I did when we presently sat down together inside the café of the Casino. There had been a point in our walk, or our stagger, when we paused to lean over the parapet, looking down at the black and driven sea. And Pethel had shouted that it would be great fun to be out in a sailing-boat to-night and that at one time he had been very fond of sailing.

As we took our seats in the café, he looked around him with boyish interest and pleasure. Then, squaring his arms on the little table, he asked me what I would drink. I protested that I was the host—a position which he, with the quick courtesy of the very rich, yielded to me at once. I feared he would ask for champagne, and was gladdened by his demand for water. 'Apollinaris? St Galmier? Or what?' I asked. He preferred plain water. I felt bound to warn him that such water was never 'safe' in these places. He said he had often heard that, but would risk it. I remonstrated, but he was firm. *'Alors,'* I told the waiter, *'pour Monsieur un verre d'eau fraîche, et pour moi un demi blonde.'* Pethel asked me to tell him who every one was. I told him no one was any one in particular, and suggested that we should talk about ourselves. 'You mean', he laughed, 'that you want to know who the devil I am?' I assured him that I had often heard of him. At this he was unaffectedly pleased. 'But,' I added, 'it's always more interesting to hear a man talked about by himself.' And indeed, since he had *not* handed his winnings over to me, I did hope he would at any rate give me some glimpses into that 'great character' of his. Full though his life had been, he seemed but like a rather clever schoolboy out on a holiday. I wanted to know more.

'That beer does look good,' he admitted when the waiter came back. I asked him to change his mind. But he shook his head, raised to his lips the tumbler of water that had been placed before him, and meditatively drank a deep draught. 'I never', he then said, 'touch alcohol of any sort.' He looked solemn; but all men do look solemn when they speak of their own habits, whether positive or negative, and no matter how trivial; and so (though I had really no warrant for not supposing him a reclaimed drunkard) I dared ask him for what reason he abstained.

'When I say I *never* touch alcohol,' he said hastily, in a tone as of self-defence, 'I mean that I don't touch it often—or at any rate—well, I never touch it when I'm *gambling*, you know. It—it takes the edge off.'

His tone did make me suspicious. For a moment I wondered whether he had married the barmaid rather for what she symbolised than for what in herself she was. But no, surely not: he had been only nineteen years old. Nor in any way had he now—this steady, brisk, clear-eyed fellow—the aspect of one who had since fallen. 'The edge off the excitement?' I asked.

'Rather! Of course that sort of excitement seems awfully stupid to *you*. But—no use denying it—I do like a bit of a flutter—just occasionally, you know. And one has to be in trim for it. Suppose a man sat down dead drunk to a game of chance, what fun would it be for him? None. And it's only a question of degree. Soothe yourself ever so little with alcohol, and you don't get *quite* the full sensation of gambling. You do lose just a little something of the proper tremors before a coup, the proper throes during a coup, the proper thrill of joy or anguish after a coup. . . . You're bound to, you know,' he added, purposely making this bathos when he saw me smiling at the heights to which he had risen.

'And to-night,' I asked, remembering his prosaically pensive demeanour in taking the bank, 'were you feeling these throes and thrills to the utmost?'

He nodded.

'And you'll feel them again to-night?'

'I hope so.'

'I wonder you can stay away.'

'Oh, one gets a bit deadened after an hour or so. One needs to be freshened up. So long as I don't bore you——'

I laughed, and held out my cigarette-case. 'I rather wonder you smoke,' I murmured, after giving him a light. 'Nicotine's a sort of drug. Doesn't it soothe you? Don't you lose just a little something of the tremors and things?'

He looked at me gravely. 'By jove,' he ejaculated, 'I never thought of that. Perhaps you're right. 'Pon my word, I must think that over.'

I wondered whether he were secretly laughing at me. Here was a man to whom (so I conceived, with an effort of the imagination) the loss or gain of a few hundred pounds could not matter. I told him I had spoken in jest. 'To give up tobacco might', I said, 'intensify the pleasant agonies of a gambler staking his little all. But in your case—well, frankly, I don't see where the pleasant agonies come in.'

'You mean because I'm beastly rich?'

'Rich,' I amended.

'All depends on what you call rich. Besides, I'm not the sort of fellow who's content with 3 per cent. A couple of months ago—I tell you this in confidence—I risked practically all I had, in an Argentine deal.'

'And lost it?'

'No, as a matter of fact I made rather a good thing out of it. I did rather well last February, too. But there's no knowing the future. A few errors of judgment—a war

here, a revolution there, a big strike somewhere else, and
—' He blew a jet of smoke from his lips, and looked at
me as at one whom he could trust to feel for him in a
crash already come.

My sympathy lagged, and I stuck to the point of my
inquiry. 'Meanwhile,' I suggested, 'and all the more because you aren't merely a rich man, but also an active
taker of big risks, how can these tiny little baccarat risks
give you so much emotion?'

'There you rather have me,' he laughed. 'I've often
wondered at that myself. I suppose', he puzzled it out,
'I do a good lot of make-believe. While I'm playing a
game like this game to-night, I *imagine* the stakes are
huge, and I *imagine* I haven't another penny in the
world.'

'Ah! So that with you it's always a life-and-death
affair?'

He looked away. 'Oh, no, I don't say that.'

'Stupid phrase,' I admitted. 'But,' there was yet one
point I would put to him, 'if you have extraordinary
luck—always—'

'There's no such thing as luck.'

'No, strictly, I suppose, there isn't. But if in point of
fact you always do win, then—well, surely, perfect luck
driveth out fear?'

'Who ever said I always won?' he asked sharply.

I waved my hands and said, 'Oh, you have the reputation, you know, for extraordinary luck.'

'That isn't the same thing as always winning. Besides,
I *haven't* extraordinary luck—never *have* had. Good
heavens,' he exclaimed, 'if I thought I had any more
chance of winning than of losing, I'd—I'd—'

'Never again set foot in that baccarat room to-night,'
I soothingly suggested.

'Oh, baccarat be blowed! I wasn't thinking of baccarat. I was thinking of—oh, lots of things; baccarat
included, yes.'

'What things?' I ventured to ask.

'What things?' He pushed back his chair, and 'Look here,' he said with a laugh, 'don't pretend I haven't been boring your head off with all this talk about myself. You've been too patient. I'm off. Shall I see you to-morrow? Perhaps you'd lunch with us to-morrow? It would be a great pleasure for my wife. We're at the Hôtel Royal.'

I said I should be most happy, and called the waiter; at sight of whom my friend said he had talked himself thirsty, and asked for another glass of water. He mentioned that he had brought his car over with him: his little daughter (by the news of whose existence I felt idiotically surprised) was very keen on motoring, and they were all three start-ing the day after to-morrow for 'a spin through France'. Afterwards, they were going to Switzerland, 'for some climbing'. Did I care about motoring? If so, we might go for a spin after luncheon, to Rouen or somewhere? He drank his glass of water, and, linking a friendly arm in mine, passed out with me into the corridor. He asked what I was writing now, and said that he looked to me to 'do something big, one of these days', and that he was sure I had it 'in' me. This remark (though of course I pre-tended to be pleased by it) irritated me very much. It was destined, as you shall see, to irritate me very much more in recollection.

Yet was I glad he had asked me to luncheon. Glad be-cause I liked him, glad because I dislike mysteries. Though you may think me very dense for not having thoroughly understood Pethel in the course of my first meeting with him, the fact is that I was only conscious, and that dimly, of something more in him than he had cared to reveal—some veil behind which perhaps lurked his right to the title so airily bestowed on him by Grierson. I assured my-self, as I walked home, that if veil there were I should to-morrow find an eyelet.

But one's intuition when it is off duty seems always so much more powerful an engine than it does on active service; and next day, at sight of Pethel awaiting me outside his hotel, I became less confident. His, thought I, was a face which, for all its animation, would tell nothing—nothing, at any rate, that mattered. It expressed well enough that he was pleased to see me; but for the rest, I was reminded, it had a sort of frank inscrutability. Besides, it was at all points so very usual a face—a face that couldn't (so I then thought), even if it had leave to, betray connexion with a 'great character'. It was a strong face, certainly. But so are yours and mine.

And very fresh it looked, though, as he confessed, Pethel had sat up in 'that beastly baccarat room' till 5 a.m. I asked, had he lost? Yes, he had lost steadily for four hours (proudly he laid stress on this), but in the end —well (he admitted), he had won it all back 'and a bit more'. 'By the way,' he murmured as we were about to enter the hall, 'don't ever happen to mention to my wife what I told you about that Argentine deal. She's always rather nervous about—investments. I don't tell her about them. She's rather a nervous woman altogether, I'm sorry to say.'

This did not square with my preconception of her. Slave that I am to traditional imagery, I had figured her as 'flaunting', as golden-haired, as haughty to most men but with a provocative smile across the shoulder for some. Nor indeed did her husband's words prevent me from the suspicion that my eyes deceived me when anon I was presented to a very pale small lady whose hair was rather white than grey. And the 'little daughter'! This prodigy's hair was as yet 'down', but looked as if it might be up at any moment: she was nearly as tall as her father, whom she very much resembled in face and figure and heartiness of handshake. Only after a rapid mental calculation could I account for her. 'I must warn you, she's in a great rage this morning,' said Pethel. 'Do try to soothe her.' She blushed, laughed, and bade her father not be so silly. I asked her the cause of her great rage. She said, 'He only means I was disappointed. And he was just as disappointed as I was. Weren't you, now, Father?'

'I suppose they meant well, Peggy,' he laughed.

'They were *quite* right,' said Mrs Pethel, evidently not for the first time.

'They', as I presently learned, were the authorities of the bathing establishment. Pethel had promised his daughter he would take her for a swim; but on their arrival at the bathing-cabins they were ruthlessly told that bathing was '*défendu à cause du mauvais temps*'. This embargo was our theme as we sat down to luncheon. Miss Peggy was of opinion that the French were cowards. I pleaded for them that even in English watering-places bathing was forbidden when the sea was *very* rough. She did not admit that the sea was very rough to-day. Besides, she appealed to me, what was the fun of swimming in absolutely calm water? I dared not say that this was the only sort of water I liked to swim in. 'They were *quite* right,' said Mrs Pethel yet again.

'Yes, but, darling Mother, you can't swim. Father and I are both splendid swimmers.'

To gloze over the mother's disability, I looked brightly at Pethel, as though in ardent recognition of his prowess among waves. With a movement of his head he indicated his daughter—indicated that there was no one like her in the whole world. I beamed agreement. Indeed, I did think her rather nice. If one liked the father (and I liked Pethel all the more in that capacity), one couldn't help liking the daughter: the two were so absurdly alike. Whenever he was looking at her (and it was seldom that he looked away from her) the effect, if you cared to be fantastic, was that of a very vain man before a mirror. It might have occurred to me that, if there were any mystery in him, I could solve it through her. But, in point of fact, I had forgotten all about that possible mystery. The amateur detective was lost in the sympathetic observer of a father's love. That Pethel did love his daughter I have never doubted. One passion is not less true because another predominates. No one who ever saw that father with that daughter could doubt that he loved her intensely. And this intensity gauges for me the strength of what else was in him.

Mrs Pethel's love, though less explicit, was not less evidently profound. But the maternal instinct is less attractive to an onlooker, because he takes it more for granted, than the paternal. What endeared poor Mrs Pethel to me was—well, the inevitability of the epithet I give her. She seemed, poor thing, so essentially out of it; and by 'it' is meant the glowing mutual affinity of husband and child. Not that she didn't, in her little way, assert herself during the meal. But she did so, I thought, with the knowledge that she didn't count, and never would count. I wondered how it was that she had, in that Cambridge bar-room long ago, counted for Pethel to the extent of matrimony. But from any such room she seemed so utterly remote that she might well be in all respects now an utterly changed woman. She did pre-eminently look as if much had by some means been taken out of her, with no compensatory process of putting in. Pethel looked so very young for his age, whereas she would have had to be quite old to look young for hers. I pitied her as one might a governess with two charges who were hopelessly out of hand. But a governess, I reflected, can always give notice. Love tied poor Mrs Pethel to her present situation.

As the three of them were to start next day on their tour through France, and as the four of us were to make a tour to Rouen this afternoon, the talk was much about motoring—a theme which Miss Peggy's enthusiasm made almost tolerable. I said to Mrs Pethel, with more good-will than truth, that I supposed she was 'very keen on it'. She replied that she was.

'But, darling Mother, you aren't. I believe you *hate* it. You're *always* asking Father to go slower. And what *is* the fun of just crawling along?'

'Oh, come, Peggy, we never crawl,' said her father.

'No, indeed,' said her mother, in a tone of which Pethel laughingly said it would put me off coming out with them this afternoon. I said, with an expert air to reassure Mrs

Pethel, that it wasn't fast driving, but only bad driving, that was a danger. 'There, Mother!' cried Peggy. 'Isn't that what we're always telling you?'

I felt that they were always either telling Mrs Pethel something or, as in the matter of that intended bath, not telling her something. It seemed to me possible that Peggy advised her father about his 'investments'. I wondered whether they had yet told Mrs Pethel of their intention to go on to Switzerland for some climbing.

Of his secretiveness for his wife's sake I had a touching little instance after luncheon. We had adjourned to have coffee in front of the hotel. The car was already in attendance, and Peggy had darted off to make her daily inspection of it. Pethel had given me a cigar, and his wife presently noticed that he himself was not smoking. He explained to her that he thought he had smoked too much lately, and that he was going to 'knock it off' for a while. I would not have smiled if he had met my eye. But his avoidance of it made me quite sure that he really had been 'thinking over' what I had said last night about nicotine and its possibly deleterious action on the gambling thrill.

Mrs Pethel saw the smile that I could not repress. I explained that I was wishing *I* could knock off tobacco, and envying her husband's strength of character. She smiled too, but wanly, with her eyes on him. 'Nobody has so much strength of character as *he* has,' she said.

'Nonsense!' he laughed. 'I'm the weakest of men.'

'Yes,' she said quietly. 'That's true, too, James.'

Again he laughed, but he flushed. I saw that Mrs Pethel also had faintly flushed; and I became horribly conscious of following suit. In the sudden glow and silence created by Mrs Pethel's paradox, I was grateful to the daughter for bouncing back into our midst and asking how soon we should be ready to start.

Pethel looked at his wife, who looked at me and rather strangely asked if I were sure I wanted to go with them. I protested that of course I did. Pethel asked her if *she*

really wanted to come: 'You see, dear, there was the run
yesterday from Calais. And to-morrow you'll be on the
road again, and all the days after.'

'Yes,' said Peggy, 'I'm *sure* you'd much rather stay at
home, darling Mother, and have a good rest.'

'Shall we go and put on our things, Peggy?' replied
Mrs Pethel, rising from her chair. She asked her husband
whether he were taking the chauffeur with him. He said
he thought not.

'Oh, hurrah!' cried Peggy. 'Then I can be on the front
seat!'

'No, dear,' said her mother. 'I am sure Mr Beerbohm
would like to be on the front seat.'

'You'd like to be with Mother, wouldn't you?' the girl
appealed. I replied with all possible emphasis that I should
like to be with Mrs Pethel. But presently, when the mother
and daughter reappeared in the guise of motorists, it became clear that my aspiration had been set aside. 'I am to
be with Mother,' said Peggy.

I was inwardly glad that Mrs Pethel could, after all,
assert herself to some purpose. Had I thought she disliked
me, I should have been hurt; but I was sure her desire
that I should not sit with her was due merely to a belief
that a person on the front seat was less safe in case of
accidents than a person behind. And of course I did not
expect her to prefer my life to her daughter's. Poor lady!
My heart was with her. As the car glided along the sea-
front and then under the Norman archway, through the
town and past the environs, I wished that her husband
inspired in her as much confidence as he did in me. For
me the sight of his clear, firm profile (he did not wear
motor-goggles) was an assurance in itself. From time to
time (for I too was ungoggled) I looked round to nod and
smile cheerfully at his wife. She always returned the nod,
but left the smile to be returned by the daughter.

Pethel, like the good driver he was, did not talk: just
drove. But he did, as we came out on to the Rouen road,
say that in France he always rather missed the British

police-traps. 'Not', he added, 'that I've ever fallen into one. But the chance that a policeman *may* at any moment dart out, and land you in a bit of a scrape, does rather add to the excitement, don't you think?' Though I answered in the tone of one to whom the chance of a police-trap is the very salt of life, I did not inwardly like the spirit of his remark. However, I dismissed it from my mind; and the sun was shining, and the wind had dropped: it was an ideal day for motoring; and the Norman landscape had never looked lovelier to me in its width of sober and silvery grace.

I presently felt that this landscape was not, after all, doing itself full justice. Was it not rushing rather too quickly past? 'James!' said a shrill, faint voice from behind; and gradually—'Oh, darling Mother, really!' protested another voice—the landscape slackened pace. But after a while, little by little, the landscape lost patience, forgot its good manners, and flew faster, and faster than before. The road rushed furiously beneath us, like a river in spate. Avenues of poplars flashed past us, every tree of them on either side hissing and swishing angrily in the draught we made. Motors going Rouen-wards seemed to be past as quickly as motors that bore down on us. Hardly had I espied in the landscape ahead a château or other object of interest before I was craning my neck round for a final glimpse of it as it faded on the backward horizon. An endless up-hill road was breasted and crested in a twinkling and transformed into a decline near the end of which our car lept straight across to the opposite ascent, and—'James!' again, and again by degrees the laws of Nature were re-established, but again by degrees revoked. I didn't doubt that speed in itself was no danger; but when the road was about to make a sharp curve why shouldn't Pethel, just as a matter of form, slow down slightly and sound a note or two of the hooter? Suppose another car were—well, that was all right: the road was clear. But at the next turning, when our car neither slackened nor hooted and *was*, for an instant, full on the

wrong side of the road, I had within me a contraction
which (at thought of what must have been if——) lasted
though all was well. Loth to betray fear, I hadn't turned
my face to Pethel. Eyes front! And how about that wagon
ahead, huge hay-wagon plodding with its back to us,
seeming to occupy whole road? Surely Pethel would
slacken, hoot? No. Imagine a needle threaded with one
swift gesture from afar. Even so was it that we shot, between wagon and road's edge, through; whereon, con-
fronting us within a few yards—inches now, but we
swerved—was a cart, a cart that incredibly we grazed not
as we rushed on, on. Now indeed had I turned my eyes
on Pethel's profile. And my eyes saw there that which
stilled, with a greater emotion, all fear and wonder in me.

I think that for the first instant, oddly, what I felt was
merely satisfaction, not hatred; for I all but asked him
whether by not smoking to-day he had got a keener edge
to his thrills. I understood him, and for an instant this
sufficed me. Those pursed-out lips, so queerly different
from the compressed lips of the normal motorist, and
seeming, as elsewhere last night, to denote no more than a
pensive interest, had told me suddenly all that I needed
to know about Pethel. Here, as there—and oh, ever so
much better here than there!—he could gratify the passion that was in him. No need of any 'make-believe' here!
I remembered the strange look he had given when I asked
if his gambling were always 'a life-and-death affair'. Here
was the real thing—the authentic game, for the highest
stakes! And here was I, a little extra-stake tossed on to
the board. He had vowed I had it 'in' me to do 'something
big'. Perhaps, though, there had been a touch of his make-
believe about that. . . . I am afraid it was not before my
thought about myself that my moral sense began to operate
and my hatred of Pethel set in. But I claim that I did see
myself as no more than a mere detail in his villainy. Nor,
in my just wrath for other sakes, was I without charity
even for him. I gave him due credit for risking his own
life—for having doubtless risked it, it and none other,

again and again in the course of his adventurous—and abstemious—life by field and flood. I was even rather touched by memory of his insistence last night on another glass of that water which just *might* give him typhoid; rather touched by memory of his unsaying that he 'never' touched alcohol—he who, in point of fact, had to be *always* gambling on something or other. I gave him due credit, too, for his devotion to his daughter. But his use of that devotion, his cold use of it to secure for himself the utmost thrill of gambling, did seem utterly abominable to me.

And it was even more for the mother than for the daughter that I was incensed. That daughter did not know him, did but innocently share his damnable love of chances. But that wife had for years known him at least as well as I knew him now. Here again, I gave him credit for wishing, though he didn't love her, to spare her what he could. That he didn't love her I presumed from his indubitable willingness not to stake her in this afternoon's game. That he never had loved her—had taken her, in his precocious youth, simply as a gigantic chance against him—was likely enough. So much the more credit to him for such consideration as he showed her; but little enough this was. He could wish to save her from being a looker-on at his game; but he could, he couldn't not, go on playing. Assuredly she was right in deeming him at once the strongest and the weakest of men. 'Rather a nervous woman'! I remembered an engraving that had hung in my room at Oxford—and in scores of other rooms there: a presentment by Sir Marcus (then Mr) Stone of a very pretty young person in a Gainsborough hat, seated beneath an ancestral elm, looking as though she were about to cry, and entitled 'A Gambler's Wife'. Mrs Pethel was not like that. Of her there were no engravings for undergraduate hearts to melt at. But there was one man, certainly, whose compassion was very much at her service. How was he going to help her?

I know not how many hair's-breadth escapes we may

have had while these thoughts passed through my brain.
I had closed my eyes. So preoccupied was I that, but for
the constant rush of air against my face I might, for aught
I knew, have been sitting ensconced in an arm-chair at
home. After a while, I was aware that this rush had abated;
I opened my eyes to the old familiar streets of Rouen. We
were to have tea at the Hôtel d'Angleterre. What was to be
my line of action? Should I take Pethel aside and say
'Swear to me, on your word of honour as a gentleman, that
you will never again touch the driving-gear (or whatever
you call it) of a motor-car. Otherwise I shall expose you
to the world. Meanwhile, we shall return to Dieppe by
train'? He might flush—for I knew him capable of flush-
ing—as he asked me to explain. And after? He would
laugh in my face. He would advise me not to go motoring
any more. He might even warn me not to go back to
Dieppe in one of those dangerous railway-trains. He might
even urge me to wait until a nice Bath chair had been sent
out for me from England. . . .

I heard a voice (mine, alas) saying brightly, 'Well, here
we are!' I helped the ladies to descend. Tea was ordered.
Pethel refused that stimulant and had a glass of water. I
had a liqueur brandy. It was evident to me that tea meant
much to Mrs Pethel. She looked stronger after her second
cup, and younger after her third. Still, it was my duty to
help her, if I could. While I talked and laughed, I did not
forget that. But—what on earth was I to do? I am no hero.
I hate to be ridiculous. I am inveterately averse from any
sort of fuss. Besides, how was I to be sure that my own
personal dread of the return-journey hadn't something to
do with my intention of tackling Pethel? I thought it had.
What this woman would dare daily because she was a
mother, could not I dare once? I reminded myself of
Pethel's reputation for invariable luck. I reminded myself
that he was an extraordinarily skilful driver. To that skill
and luck I would pin my faith. . . .

What I seem to myself, do you ask of me?

But I answered your question a few lines back. Enough that my faith was rewarded. We did reach Dieppe safely. I still marvel that we did.

That evening, in the vestibule of the Casino, Grierson came up to me: 'Seen Jimmy Pethel? He was asking for you. Wants to see you particularly. He's in the baccarat room, punting—winning hand over fist, of course. Said he'd seldom met a man he liked more than you. Great character, what?' One is always glad to be liked, and I plead guilty to a moment's gratification at the announcement that Pethel liked me. But I did not go and seek him in the baccarat room. A great character assuredly he was; but of a kind with which (very imperfect though I am, and no censor) I prefer not to associate.

Why he had particularly wanted to see me was made clear in a note sent by him to my room early next morning. He wondered if I could be induced to join them in their little tour. He hoped I wouldn't think it great cheek, his asking me. He thought it might rather amuse me to come. It would be a very great pleasure for his wife. He hoped I wouldn't say No. Would I send a line by bearer? They would be starting at 3 o'clock. He was mine sincerely.

It was not too late to tackle him, even now. Should I go round to his hotel? I hesitated and—well, I told you at the outset that my last meeting with him was on the morrow of my first. I forget what I wrote to him, but am sure the excuse that I made for myself was a good and graceful one, and that I sent my kindest regards to Mrs Pethel. She had not (I am sure of that, too) authorised her husband to say she would like me to come with them. Else would not the thought of her have haunted me so poignantly as for a long time it did. I do not know whether she is still alive. No mention is made of her in the obituary notice which woke these memories in me. This notice I will, however, transcribe, because (for all its crudeness of phraseology) it is rather interesting both as an echo and as an amplification. Its title is—'Death of Wealthy Aviator'. Its text is—'Widespread regret will be felt in Leicestershire at the tragic death of Mr James Pethel, who had long resided there and was very popular as an all-round sportsman. In recent years he had been much interested in aviation, and had become one of the most enthusiastic of amateur airmen. Yesterday afternoon he fell down dead quite suddenly as he was returning to his house, apparently in his usual health and spirits, after descending from a short flight which despite an extremely high wind he had made on his new biplane and on which he was accompanied by his married daughter and her infant son. It is not expected that an inquest will be necessary, as his physician, Dr Saunders, has certified death to be due to heart-disease, from which, it appears, the deceased gentleman had been suffering for some years. Dr Saunders adds that he had repeatedly warned deceased that any strain on the nervous system might prove fatal.'

Thus—for I presume that his ailment had its origin in his habits—James Pethel did not, despite that merely pensive look of his, live his life with impunity. And by reason of that life he died. As for the manner of his death, enough that he did die. Let not our hearts be vexed that his great luck was with him to the end.

'SAVONAROLA' BROWN

I LIKE TO REMEMBER that I was the first to call him so, for, though he always deprecated the nickname, in his heart he was pleased by it, I know, and encouraged to go on.

Quite apart from its significance, he had reason to welcome it. He had been unfortunate at the font. His parents, at the time of his birth, lived in Ladbroke Crescent, W. They must have been an extraordinarily unimaginative couple, for they could think of no better name for their

child than Ladbroke. This was all very well for him till he
went to school. But you can fancy the indignation and
delight of us boys at finding among us a new-comer, who,
on his own confession, had been named after a Crescent. I
don't know how it is nowadays, but thirty-five years ago,
certainly, schoolboys regarded the possession of *any* Christian name as rather unmanly. As we all had these encum-
brances, we had to wreak our scorn on any one who was
cumbered in a queer fashion. I myself, bearer of a Christian name adjudged eccentric though brief, had had much
to put up with in my first term. Brown's arrival, therefore,
at the beginning of my second term, was a good thing for
me, and I am afraid I was very prominent among his perse-
cutors. Trafalgar Brown, Tottenham Court Brown, Bond
Brown—what names did we little brutes *not* cull for him
from the London Directory? Except how miserable we
made his life, I do not remember much about him as he
was at that time, and the only important part of the little
else that I do recall is that already he showed a strong
sense for literature. For the majority of us Carthusians,
literature was bounded on the north by Whyte Melville, on
the south by Hawley Smart, on the east by the former, and
and on the west by the latter. Little Brown used to read
Harrison Ainsworth, Wilkie Collins, and other writers
whom we, had we assayed them, would have dismissed as
'deep'. It has been said by Mr Arthur Symons that 'all art
is a mode of escape'. The art of letters did not, however,
enable Brown to escape so far from us as he would have
wished. In my third term he did not reappear among us.
His parents had in some sort atoned. Unimaginative
though they were, it seems they could understand a tale
of woe laid before them circumstantially, and had engaged
a private tutor for their boy. Fifteen years elapsed before I
saw him again.

This was at the second night of some play. I was dramatic critic for the *Saturday Review*, and, weary of meeting the same lot of people over and over again at first
nights, had recently sent a circular to the managers asking

that I might have seats for second nights instead. I found that there existed as distinct and invariable a lot of second-nighters as of first-nighters. The second-nighters were less 'showy'; but then, they came rather to see than to be seen, and there was an air, that I liked, of earnestness and hope-fulness about them. I used to write a great deal about the future of the British drama, and they, for their part, used to think and talk a great deal about it. People who care about books and pictures find much to interest and please them in the present. It is only the students of the theatre who always fall back, or rather forward, on the future. Though second-nighters do come to see, they remain rather to hope and pray. I should have known anywhere, by the visionary look in his eyes, that Brown was a confirmed second-nighter.

What surprises me is that I knew he was Brown. It is true that he had not grown much in those fifteen years: his brow was still disproportionate to his body, and he looked young to have become 'confirmed' in any habit. But it is also true that not once in the past ten years, at any rate, had he flitted through my mind and poised on my conscience.

I hope that I and those other boys had long ago ceased from recurring to him in nightmares. Cordial though the hand was that I offered him, and highly civilised my whole demeanour, he seemed afraid that at any moment I might begin to dance around him, shooting out my lips at him and calling him Seven-Sisters Brown or something of that kind. It was only after constant meetings at second nights, and innumerable *entr'acte* talks about the future of the drama, that he began to trust me. In course of time we formed the habit of walking home together as far as Cum-berland Place, at which point our ways diverged. I gathered that he was still living with his parents, but he did not tell me where, for they had not, as I learned by reference to the Red Book, moved from Ladbroke Crescent.

I found his company restful rather than inspiring. His days were spent in clerkship at one of the smaller

Government Offices, his evenings—except when there was a second night—in reading and writing. He did not seem to know much, or to wish to know more, about life. Books and plays, first editions and second nights, were what he cared for. On matters of religion and ethics he was as little keen as he seemed to be on human character in the raw; so that (though I had already suspected him of writing, or meaning to write, a play) my eyebrows did rise when he told me he meant to write a play about Savonarola.

He made me understand, however, that it was rather the name than the man that had first attracted him. He said that the name was in itself a great incentive to blank-verse. He uttered it to me slowly, in a voice so much deeper than his usual voice, that I nearly laughed. For the actual bearer of the name he had no hero-worship, and said it was by a mere accident that he had chosen him as central figure. He had thought of writing a tragedy about Sardanapalus; but the volume of the 'Encyclopædia Britannica' in which he was going to look up the main facts about Sardanapalus happened to open at Savonarola. Hence a sudden and complete peripety in the student's mind. He told me he had read the Encyclopædia's article carefully, and had dipped into one or two of the books there mentioned as authorities. He seemed almost to wish he hadn't. 'Facts get in one's way so,' he complained. 'History is one thing, drama is another. Aristotle said drama was more philosophic than history because it showed us what men *would* do, not just what they *did*. I think that's so true, don't you? I want to show what Savonarola *would* have done if—' He paused.

'If what?'

'Well, that's just the point. I haven't settled that yet. When I've thought of a plot, I shall go straight ahead.'

I said that I supposed he intended his tragedy rather for the study than for the stage. This seemed to hurt him. I told him that what I meant was that managers always shied at anything without 'a strong feminine interest'. This seemed to worry him. I advised him not to think about managers. He promised that he would think only about Savonarola.

I know now that this promise was not exactly kept by him; and he may have felt slightly awkward when, some weeks later, he told me he had begun the play. 'I've hit on an initial idea,' he said, 'and that's enough to start with. I gave up my notion of inventing a plot in advance. I thought it would be a mistake. I don't want puppets on wires. I want Savonarola to work out his destiny in his own way. Now that I have the initial idea, what I've got to do is to make Savonarola *live*. I hope I shall be able to do this. Once he's alive, I shan't interfere with him. I shall just watch him. Won't it be interesting? He isn't alive yet. But there's plenty of time. You see, he doesn't come on at the rise of the curtain. A Friar and a Sacristan come on and talk about him. By the time they've finished, perhaps he'll be alive. But they won't have finished yet. Not that they're going to say very much. But I write slowly.'

I remember the mild thrill I had when, one evening, he took me aside and said in an undertone, 'Savonarola has come on. Alive!' For me the MS hereinafter printed has an interest that for you it cannot have, so a-bristle am I with memories of the meetings I had with its author throughout the nine years he took over it. He never saw me without reporting progress, or lack of progress. Just what was going on, or standing still, he did not divulge. After the entry of Savonarola, he never told me what characters were appearing. 'All sorts of people appear,' he would say rather helplessly. 'They insist. I can't prevent them.' I used to say it must be great fun to be a creative artist; but at this he always shook his head: 'I don't create. *They* do. Savonarola especially, of course. I just look on and record. I never know what's going to happen next.' He had the advantage of me in knowing at any rate what had happened last. But whenever I pled for a glimpse he would again shake his head:

'The thing *must* be judged as a whole. Wait till I've come to the end of the Fifth Act.'

So impatient did I grow that, as the years went by, I used rather to resent his presence at second nights. I felt he ought to be at his desk. His, I used to tell him, was the only drama whose future ought to concern him now. And in point of fact he had, I think, lost the true spirit of the second-nighter, and came rather to be seen than to see. He liked the knowledge that here and there in the auditorium, when he entered it, some one would be saying 'Who is that?' and receiving the answer 'Oh, don't you know? That's "Savonarola" Brown.' This sort of thing, however, did not make him cease to be the modest, unaffected fellow I had known. He always listened to the advice I used to offer him, though inwardly he must have chafed at it. Myself a fidgety and uninspired person, unable to begin a piece of writing before I know just how it shall end, I had always been afraid that sooner or later Brown would take some turning that led nowhither— would lose himself and come to grief. This fear crept into my gladness when, one evening in the spring of 1909, he told me he had finished the Fourth Act. Would he win out safely through the Fifth?

He himself was looking rather glum; and, as we walked away from the theatre, I said to him, 'I suppose you feel rather like Thackeray when he'd "killed the Colonel": you've got to kill the Monk.'

'Not quite that,' he answered. 'But of course he'll die very soon now. A couple of years or so. And it does seem rather sad. It's not merely that he's so full of life. He has been becoming much more *human* lately. At first I only respected him. Now I have a real affection for him.'

This was an interesting glimpse at last, but I turned from it to my besetting fear.

'Haven't you', I asked, 'any notion of *how* he is to die?'

Brown shook his head.

'But in a tragedy', I insisted, 'the catastrophe *must* be led up to, step by step. My dear Brown, the end of the hero *must* be logical and rational.'

'I don't see that,' he said, as we crossed Piccadilly

Circus. 'In actual life it isn't so. What is there to prevent
a motor-omnibus from knocking me over and killing me
at this moment?'

At that moment, by what has always seemed to me the
strangest of coincidences, and just the sort of thing that
playwrights ought to avoid, a motor-omnibus knocked
Brown over and killed him.

He had, as I afterwards learned, made a will in which
he appointed me his literary executor. Thus passed into
my hands the unfinished play by whose name he had become known to so many people.

I hate to say that I was disappointed in it, but I had
better confess quite frankly that, on the whole, I was.
Had Brown written it quickly and read it to me soon after
our first talk about it, it might in some ways have exceeded
my hopes. But he had become for me, by reason of that
quiet and unhasting devotion to his work while the years
came and went, a sort of a hero; and the very mystery
involving just what he was about had addicted me to those
ideas of magnificence which the unknown is said always
to foster.

Even so, however, I am not blind to the great merits of
the play as it stands. It is well that the writer of poetic
drama should be a dramatist and a poet. Here is a play
that abounds in striking situations, and I have searched it
vainly for one line that does not scan. What I nowhere
feel is that I have not elsewhere been thrilled or lulled by
the same kind of thing. I do not go so far as to say that
Brown inherited his parents' deplorable lack of imagination. But I do wish he had been less sensitive than he
was to impressions, or else had seen and read fewer poetic
dramas ancient and modern. Remembering that visionary
look in his eyes, remembering that he was as displeased as
I by the work of all living playwrights, and as dissatisfied
with the great efforts of the Elizabethans, I wonder that
he was not more immune from influences.

Also, I cannot but wish still that he had faltered in his

decision to make no scenario. There is much to be said for the theory that a dramatist should first vitalise his characters and then leave them unfettered; but I do feel that Brown's misused the confidence he reposed in them. The labour of so many years has somewhat the air of being a mere improvisation. Savonarola himself, after the First Act or so, strikes me as utterly inconsistent. It may be that he is just complex, like Hamlet. He does in the Fourth Act show traces of that Prince. I suppose this is why he struck Brown as having become 'more human'. To me he seems merely a poorer creature.

But enough of these reservations. In my anxiety for poor Brown's sake that you should not be disappointed, perhaps I have been carrying tactfulness too far and prejudicing you against that for which I specially want your favour. Here, without more ado, is——

'SAVONAROLA'

A Tragedy

By

L. BROWN

ACT I

SCENE: *A Room in the Monastery of San Marco, Florence.*
TIME: 1490, A.D. *A summer morning.*

Enter the SACRISTAN *and a* FRIAR.

SACR.
Savonarola looks more grim to-day
Than ever. Should I speak my mind, I'd say
That he was fashioning some new great scourge
To flay the backs of men.

FRI.

'Tis even so.
Brother Filippo saw him stand last night
In solitary vigil till the dawn
Lept o'er the Arno, and his face was such
As men may wear in Purgatory—nay,
E'en in the inmost core of Hell's own fires.

SACR.

I often wonder if some woman's face,
Seen at some rout in his old worldling days,
Haunts him e'en now, e'en here, and urges him
To fierier fury 'gainst the Florentines.

FRI.

Savonarola love-sick! Ha, ha, ha!
Love-sick? He, love-sick? 'Tis a goodly jest?
The *con*firm'd misogyn a ladies' man!
Thou must have eaten of some strange red herb
That takes the reason captive. I will swear
Savonarola never yet hath seen
A woman but he spurn'd her. Hist! He comes.

[*Enter* SAVONAROLA, *rapt in thought.*]

Give thee good morrow, Brother.

SACR.

And therewith
A multitude of morrows equal-good
Till thou, by Heaven's grace, hast wrought the work
Nearest thine heart.

SAV.

I thank thee, Brother, yet
I thank thee not, for that my thankfulness
(An such there be) gives thanks to Heav'n alone.

FRI. [*To* SACR.]

'Tis a right answer he hath given thee.
Had Sav'narola spoken less than thus,

Methinks me, the less Sav'narola he.
As when the snow lies on yon Apennines.
White as the hem of Mary Mother's robe,
And insusceptible to the sun's rays,
Being harder to the touch than temper'd steel,
E'en so this great gaunt monk white-visagèd
Upstands to Heaven and to Heav'n devotes
The scarpèd thoughts that crown the upper slopes
Of his abrupt and *aus*tere nature.

SACR.

Aye.

[*Enter* LUCREZIA BORGIA, ST FRANCIS OF ASSISI, *and*
LEONARDO DA VINCI. LUC. *is thickly veiled.*]

ST FRAN.
This is the place.

LUC. [*Pointing at* SAV.]
And this the man! [*Aside.*] And I—
By the hot blood that courses i' my veins
I swear it ineluctably—the woman!

SAV.
Who is this wanton?

[LUC. *throws back her hood, revealing her face.*
SAV. *starts back, gazing at her.*]

ST FRAN.
Hush, Sir! 'Tis my little sister
The poisoner, right well-belov'd by all
Whom she as yet hath spared. Hither she came
Mounted upon another little sister of mine—
A mare, caparison'd in goodly wise.
She—I refer now to Lucrezia—
Desireth to have word of thee anent
Some matter that befrets her.

SAV. [*To* LUC.]
Hence! Begone!

Savonarola will not tempted be
By face of woman e'en tho' be, tho' 'tis,
Surpassing fair. All hope abandon therefore.
I charge thee: Vade retro, Satanas!

LEONARDO.
Sirrah, thou speakst in haste, as is the way
Of monkish men. The beauty of Lucrezia
Commends, not discommends, her to the eyes
Of keener thinkers than I take thee for.
I am an artist and an engineer,
Giv'n o'er to subtile dreams of what shall be
On this our planet. I foresee a day
When men shall skim the earth i' certain chairs
Not drawn by horses but sped on by oil
Or other matter, and shall thread the sky
Birdlike.

LUC.
          It may be as thou sayest, friend,
Or may be not. [*To* SAV.] As touching this our errand,
I crave of thee, Sir Monk, an audience
Instanter.

FRI.
          Lo! Here Alighieri comes.
I had methought me he was still at Parma.

                    [*Enter* DANTE.]

ST FRAN. [TO DAN.]
How fares my little sister Beatrice?

DAN.
She died, alack, last sennight.

ST FRAN.
                              Did she so?
If the condolences of men avail
Thee aught, take mine.

DAN.
They are of no avail.

SAV. [*To* LUC.]
I do refuse thee audience.

LUC.
Then why
Didst thou not say so promptly when I ask'd it?

SAV.
Full well thou knowst that I was interrupted
By Alighieri's entry.

> [*Noise without. Enter Guelfs and Ghibellines fighting.*]

What is this?

LUC.
I did not think that in this cloister'd spot
There would be so much doing. I had look'd
To find Savonarola all alone
And tempt him in his uneventful cell.
Instead o' which—Spurn'd am I? I am I.
There was a time, Sir, look to 't! O damnation!
What is 't? Anon then! These my toys, my gauds,
That in the cradle—aye, 't my mother's breast—
I puled and lisped at,—'Tis impossible,
Tho' faith, 'tis not so, forasmuch as 'tis.
And I a daughter of the Borgias!—
Or so they told me. Liars! Flatterers!
Currying lick-spoons! Where's the Hell of 't then?
'Tis time that I were going. Farewell, Monk,
But I'll avenge me ere the sun has sunk.

> [*Exeunt* LUC., ST FRAN., *and* LEONARDO, *followed by* DAN. SAV., *having watched* LUC. *out of sight, sinks to his knees, sobbing.* FRI. *and* SACR. *watch him in amazement. Guelfs and Ghibellines continue fighting as the Curtain falls.*]

ACT II

TIME: *Afternoon of same day.*

SCENE: *Lucrezia's Laboratory. Retorts, test-tubes, etc. On small Renaissance table, up* C., *is a great poison-bowl, the contents of which are being stirred by the* FIRST APPRENTICE. *The* SECOND APPRENTICE *stands by, watching him.*

SECOND APP.
For whom is the brew destin'd?

FIRST APP.

I know not.
Lady Lucrezia did but lay on me
Injunctions as regards the making of 't,
The which I have obey'd. It is compounded
Of a malignant and a deadly weed
Found not save in the Gulf of Spezia,
And one small phial of 't, I am advis'd,
Were more than 'nough to slay a regiment
Of Messer Malatesta's condottieri
In all their armour.

SECOND APP.

I can well believe it.
Mark how the purple bubbles froth upon
The evil surface of its nether slime!

[*Enter* LUC.]

LUC. [*To* FIRST APP.]
Is 't done, Sir Sluggard?

FIRST APP.

Madam, to a turn.

LUC.
Had it not been so, I with mine own hand
Would have outpour'd it down thy gullet, knave.

See, here's a ring of cunningly-wrought gold
That I, on a dark night, did purchase from
A goldsmith on the Ponte Vecchio.
Small was his shop, and hoar of visage he.
I did bemark that from the ceiling's beams
Spiders had spun their webs for many a year,
The which hung erst like swathes of gossamer
Seen in the shadows of a fairy glade,
But now most woefully were weighted o'er
With gather'd dust. Look well now at the ring!
Touch'd here, behold, it opes a cavity
Capacious of three drops of yon fell stuff.
Dost heed? Whoso then puts it on his finger
Dies, and his soul is from his body rapt
To Hell or Heaven as the case may be.
Take thou this toy and pour the three drops in.

[*Hands ring to* FIRST APP. *and comes down* C.]

So, Sav'narola, thou shalt learn that I
Utter no threats but I do make them good.
Ere this day's sun hath wester'd from the view
Thou art to preach from out the Loggia
Dei Lanzi to the cits in the Piazza.
I, thy Lucrezia, will be upon the steps
To offer thee with phrases seeming-fair
That which shall seal thine eloquence for ever.
O mighty lips that held the world in spell
But would not meet these little lips of mine
In the sweet way that lovers use—O thin,
Cold, tight-drawn, bloodless lips, which natheless I
Deem of all lips the most magnifical
In this our city——

[*Enter the Borgias'* FOOL.]

Well, Fool, what's thy latest?

FOOL
Aristotle's or Zeno's, Lady—'tis neither latest nor last.

For, marry, if the cobbler stuck to his last, then were his latest his last *in rebus ambulantibus*. Argal, I stick at nothing but cobble-stones, which, by the same token, are stuck to the road by men's fingers.

Luc.
How many crows may nest in a grocer's jerkin?

Fool
A full dozen at cock-crow, and something less under the dog-star, by reason of the dew, which lies heavy on men taken by the scurvy.

Luc. [*To* First App.]
Methinks the Fool is a fool.

Fool
And therefore, by auricular deduction, am I own twin to the Lady Lucrezia!

[*Sings.*]

When pears hang green on the garden wall
    With a nid, and a nod, and a niddy-niddy-o
Then prank you, lads and lasses all
    With a yea and a nay and a niddy-o.

But when the thrush flies out o' the frost
    With a nid, [*etc.*]
'Tis time for loons to count the cost,
    With a yea [*etc.*]

[*Enter the* Porter.]

Porter
O my dear Mistress, there is one below
Demanding to have instant word of thee.
I told him that your Ladyship was not
At home. Vain perjury! He would not take
Nay for an answer.

LUC.
                    Ah? What manner of man
Is he?

PORTER
    A personage the like of whom
Is wholly unfamiliar to my gaze
Cowl'd is he, but I saw his great eyes glare
From their deep sockets in such wise as leopards
Glare from their caverns, crouching ere they spring
On their reluctant prey.

LUC.
                    And what name gave he?

PORTER [*After a pause.*]
Something-arola.

LUC.
            Savon-? [PORTER nods.] Show him up.

                            [*Exit* PORTER.]
FOOL
If he be right astronomically, Mistress, then is he the
greater dunce in respect of true learning, the which goes
by the globe. Argal, 'twere better he widened his wind-
pipe.

                    [*Sings.*]

            Fly home, sweet self,
            Nothing's for weeping,
            Hemp was not made
            For lovers' keeping,
                Lovers' keeping,
        Cheerly, cheerly, fly away.

            Hew no more wood
            While ash is glowing,
            The longest grass
            Is lovers' mowing,
                Lovers' mowing,
        Cheerly, [*etc.*]

[*Re-enter* PORTER, *followed by* SAV. *Exeunt* PORTER,
FOOL, *and* FIRST *and* SECOND APPS.]

SAV.

I am no more a monk, I am a man
O' the world.

> [*Throws off cowl and frock, and stands forth in the
> costume of a Renaissance nobleman.* LUCREZIA *looks
> him up and down.*]

LUC.

> Thou cutst a sorry figure.

SAV.

>> That
Is neither here nor there. I love you, Madam.

LUC.

And this, methinks, is neither there nor here,
For that my love of thee hath vanishèd,
Seeing thee thus beprankt. Go pad thy calves!
Thus mightst thou, just conceivably, with luck
Capture the fancy of some serving-wench.

SAV.

And this is all thou hast to say to me?

LUC.

It is.

SAV.

> I am dismiss'd?

LUC.

> Thou are.

SAV.

>> 'Tis well.

> [*Resumes frock and cowl.*]

Savonarola is himself once more.

Luc.
And all my love for him returns to me
A thousandfold!

Sav.
                    Too late! My pride of manhood
Is wounded irremediably. I'll
To the Piazza, where my flock awaits me.
Thus do we see that men make great mistakes
But may amend them when the conscience wakes.

                                        [*Exit.*]

Luc.
I'm half avengèd now, but only half:
'Tis with the ring I'll have the final laugh!
Tho' love be sweet, revenge is sweeter far.
To the Piazza! Ha, ha, ha, ha, har!

> [*Seizes ring, and exit. Through open door are heard,
> as the Curtain falls, sounds of a terrific hubbub in the
> Piazza.*]

ACT III

Scene: *The Piazza.*

Time: *A few minutes anterior to close of preceding Act.*

*The Piazza is filled from end to end with a vast seething
crowd that is drawn entirely from the lower orders. There
is a sprinkling of wild-eyed and dishevelled women in it.
The men are lantern-jawed, with several days' growth of
beard. Most of them carry rude weapons—staves, bill-
hooks, crow-bars, and the like—and are in as excited a
condition as the women. Some are bare-headed, others
affect a kind of Phrygian cap. Cobblers predominate.*

Enter Lorenzo de Medici *and* Cosimo de Medici.
*They wear cloaks of scarlet brocade, and, to avoid notice,
hold masks to their faces.*

Cos.

What purpose doth the foul and greasy plebs
Ensue to-day here?

Lor.

                    I nor know nor care.

Cos.

How thrall'd thou art to the philosophy
Of Epicurus! Naught that's human I
Deem alien from myself. [*To a* Cobbler.] Make answer,
      fellow!
What empty hope hath drawn thee by a thread
Forth from the *ob*scene hovel where thou starvest?

Cob.

No empty hope, your Honour, but the full
Assurance that to-day, as yesterday,
Savonarola will let loose his thunder
Against the vices of the idle rich
And from the brimming cornucopia
Of his immense vocabulary pour
Scorn on the lamentable heresies
Of the New Learning and on all the art
Later than Giotto.

Cos.

                    Mark how absolute
The knave is!

Lor.

                    Then are parrots rational
When they regurgitate the thing they hear!
This fool is but an unit of the crowd,
And crowds are senseless as the vasty deep
That sinks or surges as the moon dictates.
I know these crowds, and know that any man
That hath a glib tongue and a rolling eye
Can as he willeth with them.

[*Removes his mask and mounts steps of Loggia.*]

Citizens!

[*Prolonged yells and groans from the crowd.*]

Yes, I am he, I am that same Lorenzo
Whom you have nicknamed the Magnificent.

[*Further terrific yells, shakings of fists, brandishings
of bill-hooks, insistent cries of 'Death to Lorenzo!'
'Down with the Magnificent!' Cobblers on fringe of
crowd, down* C., *exhibit especially all the symptoms
of epilepsy, whooping-cough, and other ailments.*]

You love not me.

[*The crowd makes an ugly rush.* LOR. *appears likely
to be dragged down and torn limb from limb, but
raises one hand in nick of time, and continues:*]

Yet I deserve your love.

[*The yells are now variegated with dubious murmurs.
A cobbler down* C. *thrusts his face feverishly in the
face of another and repeats, in a hoarse interrogative
whisper, 'Deserves our love?'*]

Not for the sundry boons I have bestow'd
And benefactions I have lavishèd
Upon Firenze, City of the Flowers,
But for the love that in this rugged breast
I bear you.

[*The yells have now died away, and there is a sharp
fall in dubious murmurs. The cobbler down* C. *says,
in an ear-piercing whisper, 'The love he bears us',
drops his lower jaw, nods his head repeatedly, and
awaits in an intolerable state of suspense the orator's
next words.*]

I am not a blameless man,

[*Some dubious murmurs.*]

Yet for that I have lov'd you passing much,
Shall some things be forgiven me.

                              [*Noise of cordial assent.*]

                              There dwells
In this our city, known unto you all,
A man more virtuous than I am, and
A thousand times more intellectual;
Yet envy not I him, for—shall I name him?—
He loves not you. His name? I will not cut
Your hearts by speaking it. Here let it stay
On tip o' tongue.

                              [*Insistent clamour.*]

                    Then steel you to the shock!—
Savonarola.

        [*For a moment or so the crowd reels silently under
        the shock. Cobbler down* c. *is the first to recover
        himself and cry 'Death to Savonarola!' The cry in-
        stantly becomes general.* LOR. *holds up his hand and
        gradually imposes silence.*]

                    His twin bug-bears are
Yourselves and that New Learning which I hold
Less dear than only you.

        [*Profound sensation. Everybody whispers 'Than only
        you' to everybody else. A woman near steps of Loggia
        attempts to kiss hem of* LOR.'*s garment.*]

                              Would you but con
With me the old philosophers of Hellas,
Her fervent bards and calm historians,
You would arise and say 'We will not hear
Another word against them!'

        [*The crowd already says this, repeatedly, with great
        emphasis.*]

Take the Dialogues
Of Plato, for example. You will find
A spirit far more truly Christian
In them than in the ravings of the sour-soul'd
Savonarola.

[*Prolonged cries of 'Death to the Sour-Souled Savonarola!' Several cobblers detach themselves from the
crowd and rush away to read the Platonic Dialogues.
Enter* SAVONAROLA. *The crowd, as he makes his way
through it, gives up all further control of its feelings,
and makes a noise for which even the best zoologists
might not find a good comparison. The staves and
bill-hooks wave like twigs in a storm. One would say
that* SAV. *must have died a thousand deaths already.
He is, however, unharmed and unruffled as he reaches
the upper step of the Loggia.* LOR. *meanwhile has
rejoined* COS. *in the Piazza.*]

SAV.

Pax vobiscum, brothers!

[*This does but exacerbate the crowd's frenzy.*]

VOICE OF A COBBLER.
Hear his false lips cry Peace when there is no
Peace!

SAV.

Are you not ashamed, O Florentines,

[*Renewed yells, but also some symptoms of manly
shame.*]

That hearken'd to Lorenzo and now reel
Inebriate with the exuberance
Of his verbosity?

[*The crowd makes an obvious effort to pull itself
together.*]

A man can fool
Some of the people all the time, and can
Fool all the people sometimes, but he cannot
Fool *all* the people *all* the time.

> [*Loud cheers. Several cobblers clap one another on
> the back. Cries of 'Death to Lorenzo!' The meeting
> is now well in hand.*]

To-day
I must adopt a somewhat novel course
In dealing with the awful wickedness
At present noticeable in this city.
I do so with reluctance. Hitherto
I have avoided personalities.
But now my sense of duty forces me
To a departure from my custom of
Naming no names. One name I must and shall
Name.

> [*All eyes are turned on* LOR., *who smiles uncomfort-
> ably.*]

No, I do not mean Lorenzo. He
Is 'neath contempt.

> [*Loud and prolonged laughter, accompanied with
> hideous grimaces at* LOR. *Exeunt* LOR. *and* COS.]

I name a woman's name,

> [*The women in the crowd eye one another suspi-
> ciously.*]

A name known to you all—four-syllablèd,
Beginning with an L.

> [*Tense pause. Enter* LUC., *carrying the ring, and
> stands, unobserved by any one, on outskirt of crowd.*
> SAV. *utters the name:*]

Lucrezia!

Luc. [*With equal intensity.*]
Savonarola!

[Sav. *starts violently and stares in direction of her voice.*]

Yes, I come, I come!

[*Forces her way to steps of Loggia. The crowd is much bewildered, and the cries of 'Death to Lucrezia Borgia!' are few and sporadic.*]

Why didst thou call me?

[Sav. *looks somewhat embarrassed.*]

What is thy distress?
I see it all! The sanguinary mob
Clusters to rend thee! As the antler'd stag,
With fine eyes glazèd from the too-long chase,
Turns to defy the foam-fleck'd pack, and thinks,
In his last moment, of some graceful hind
Seen once afar upon a mountain-top,
E'en so, Savonarola, didst thou think,
In thy most dire extremity, of me.
And here I am! Courage! The horrid hounds
Droop tail at sight of me and fawn away
Innocuous.

[*The crowd does indeed seem to have fallen completely under the sway of* Luc.'s *magnetism, and is evidently convinced that it had been about to make an end of the monk.*]

Take thou, and wear henceforth,
As a sure talisman 'gainst future perils,
This little, little ring.

[Sav. *makes awkward gesture of refusal. Angry murmurs from the crowd. Cries of 'Take thou the ring!' 'Churl!' 'Put it on!' etc.*
Enter the Borgias' Fool *and stands unnoticed on fringe of crowd.*]

I hoped you'ld like it—
Neat but not gaudy. Is my taste at fault?
I'd so look'd forward to—[*Sob.*] No, I'm not crying. But
just a little hurt.

> [*Hardly a dry eye in the crowd. Also swayings and
> snarlings indicative that* SAV.*'s life is again not worth
> a moment's purchase.* SAV. *makes awkward gesture of
> acceptance, but just as he is about to put ring on
> finger, the* FOOL *touches his lute and sings:—*]

> Wear not the ring
> It hath an unkind sting,
>   Ding, dong, ding.
> Bide a minute,
> There's poison in it,
>   Poison in it,
>   Ding-a-dong, dong, ding.

LUC.

                  The fellow lies.

> [*The crowd is torn with conflicting opinions. Mingled
> cries of 'Wear not the ring!' 'The fellow lies!' 'Bide
> a minute!' 'Death to the Fool!' 'Silence for the Fool!'
> 'Ding-a-dong, dong, ding!' etc.*]

FOOL

                  [*Sings.*]

> Wear not the ring,
> For Death's a robber-king,
>   Ding, [*etc.*]
> There's no trinket
> Is what you think it,
>   What you think it,
>   Ding-a-dong, [*etc.*]

> [SAV. *throws ring in* LUC.*'s face. Enter* POPE JULIUS
> II, *with Papal army.*]

POPE
Arrest that man and woman!

> [*Re-enter Guelfs and Ghibellines fighting.* SAV. *and*
> LUC. *are arrested by Papal officers. Enter* MICHAEL
> ANGELO. ANDREA DEL SARTO *appears for a moment
> at a window.* PIPPA *passes. Brothers of the Miseri-
> cordia go by, singing a Requiem for Francesca da
> Rimini. Enter* BOCCACCIO, BENVENUTO CELLINI, *and
> many others, making remarks highly characteristic of
> themselves but scarcely audible through the terrific
> thunderstorm which now bursts over Florence and is
> at its loudest and darkest crisis as the Curtain falls.*]

ACT IV

TIME: *Three hours later.*
SCENE: *A Dungeon on the ground-floor of the Palazzo
Civico.*

*The stage is bisected from top to bottom by a wall, on
one side of which is seen the interior of* LUCREZIA's *cell,
on the other that of* SAVONAROLA's.

*Neither he nor she knows that the other is in the next
cell. The audience, however, knows this.*

*Each cell (because of the width and height of the pro-
scenium) is of more than the average, Florentine size, but
is bare even to the point of severity, its sole amenities being some straw, a hunk of bread, and a stone pitcher. The
door of each is facing the audience. Dim-ish light.*

LUCREZIA *wears long and clanking chains on her wrists,
as does also* SAVONAROLA. *Imprisonment has left its mark
on both of them.* SAVONAROLA's *hair has turned white.
His whole aspect is that of a very old, old man.* LUCREZIA
looks no older than before, but has gone mad.

SAV.
Alas, how long ago this morning seems
This evening! A thousand thousand æons

Are scarce the measure of the gulf betwixt
My then and now. Methinks I must have been
Here since the dim creation of the world
And never in that interval have seen
The tremulous hawthorn burgeon in the brake,
Nor heard the hum o' bees, nor woven chains
Of buttercups on Mount Fiesole
What time the sap lept in the cypresses,
Imbuing with the friskfulness of Spring
Those melancholy trees. I do forget
The aspect of the sun. Yet I was born
A freeman, and the Saints of Heaven smiled
Down on my crib. What would my sire have said,
And what my dam, had anybody told them
The time would come when I should occupy
A felon's cell? O the disgrace of it!—
The scandal, the incredible come-down!
It masters me. I see i' my mind's eye
The public prints—'Sharp Sentence on a Monk.'
What then? I though I was of sterner stuff
Than is affrighted by what people think.
Yet thought I so because 'twas thought of me,
And so 'twas thought of me because I had
A hawk-like profile and a baleful eye.
Lo! my soul's chin recedes, soft to the touch
As half-churn'd butter. Seeming hawk is dove,
And dove's a gaol-bird now. Fie, out upon 't!

Luc.
How comes it? I am Empress Dowager
Of China—yet was never crown'd. This must
Be seen to.

> [*Quietly gathers some straw and weaves a crown,
> which she puts on.*]

Sav.
        O, what a degringolade!
The great career I had mapp'd out for me—

Nipp'd i' the bud. What life, when I come out,
Awaits me? Why, the very Novices
And callow Postulants will draw aside
As I pass by, and say 'That man hath done
Time!' And yet shall I wince? The worst of Time
Is not in having done it, but in doing 't.

Luc.
Ha, ha, ha, ha! Eleven billion pig-tails
Do tremble at my nod imperial,—
The which is as it should be.

Sav.
                                        I have heard
That gaolers oft are willing to carouse
With them they watch o'er, and do sink at last
Into a drunken sleep, and then's the time
To snatch the keys and make a bid for freedom.
Gaoler! Ho, Gaoler!

          [*Sounds of lock being turned and bolts withdrawn.
          Enter the Borgias' FOOL, in plain clothes, carrying
          bunch of keys.*]

                              I have seen thy face
Before.

Fool
          I saved thy life this afternoon, Sir.

Sav.
Thou art the Borgias' fool?

Fool
                              Say rather, was.
Unfortunately I have been discharg'd
For my betrayal of Lucrezia,
So that I have to speak like other men—
Decasyllabically, and with sense.
An hour ago the gaoler of this dungeon
Died of an apoplexy. Hearing which,
I ask'd for and obtain'd his billet.

SAV.

        Fetch
A stoup o' liquor for thyself and me.

          [*Exit* GAOLER.]

Freedom! there's nothing that thy votaries
Grudge in the cause of thee. That decent man
Is doom'd by me to lose his place again
To-morrow morning when he wakes from out
His hoggish slumber. Yet I care not.

    [*Re-enter* GAOLER *with a leathern bottle and two
    glasses.*]

          Ho!
This is the stuff to warm our vitals, this
The panacea for all mortal ills
And sure elixir of eternal youth.
Drink, bonniman!

    [GAOLER *drains a glass and shows signs of instant
    intoxication.* SAV. *claps him on shoulder and re-
    plenishes glass.* GAOLER *drinks again, lies down on
    floor, and snores.* SAV. *snatches the bunch of keys,
    laughs long but silently, and creeps out on tip-toe,
    leaving door ajar.*

     LUC. *meanwhile has lain down on the straw in her
    cell, and fallen asleep.*

     Noise of bolts being shot back, jangling of keys,
    grating of lock, and the door of* LUC.'s *cell flies open.*
    SAV. *takes two steps across the threshold, his arms
    outstretched and his upturned face transfigured with
    a great joy.*]

       How sweet the open air
Leaps to my nostrils! O the good brown earth
That yields once more to my elastic tread
And laves these feet with its remember'd dew!

    [*Takes a few more steps, still looking upwards.*]

Free!—I am free! O naked arc of heaven,
Enspangled with innumerable—no,
Stars are not there. Yet neither are there clouds!
The thing looks like a ceiling! [*Gazes downward.*]
    And this thing
Looks like a floor. [*Gazes around.*] And that white bundle
    yonder
Looks curiously like Lucrezia.

    [LUC. *awakes at sound of her name, and sits up sane.*]

There must be some mistake.

LUC. [*Rises to her feet.*]

                There is indeed!
A pretty sort of prison I have come to,
In which a self-respecting lady's cell
Is treated as a lounge!

SAV.
              I had no notion
You were in here. I thought I was out there.
I will explain—but first I'll make amends.
Here are the keys by which your durance ends.
The gate is somewhere in this corridor,
And so good-bye to this interior!

    [*Exeunt* SAV. *and* LUC. *Noise, a moment later, of a
    key grating in a lock, then of gate creaking on its
    hinges; triumphant laughs of fugitives; loud slam-
    ming of gate behind them.*
        In SAV.'s *cell the* GAOLER *starts in his sleep, turns
    his face to the wall, and snores more than ever
    deeply. Through open door comes a cloaked figure.*]

CLOAKED FIGURE
Sleep on, Savonarola, and awake
Not in this dungeon but in ruby Hell!

    [*Stabs* GAOLER, *whose snores cease abruptly. Enter*
    POPE JULIUS II, *with Papal retinue carrying torches.*
    MURDERER *steps quickly back into shadow.*]

POPE [*To body of* GAOLER.]
Savonarola, I am come to taunt
Thee in thy misery and dire abjection.
Rise, Sir, and hear me out.

MURD. [*Steps forward.*]

        Great Julius,
Waste not thy breath. Savonarola's dead.
I murder'd him.

POPE

     Thou hadst no right to do so.
Who art thou, pray?

MURD.

    Cesare Borgia,
Lucrezia's brother, and I claim a brother's
Right to assassinate whatever man
Shall wantonly and in cold blood reject
Her timid offer of a poison'd ring.

POPE
Of this anon.

       [*Stands over body of* GAOLER.]

   Our present business
Is general woe. No nobler corse hath ever
Impress'd the ground. O, let the trumpets speak it!

        [*Flourish of trumpets.*]

This was the noblest of the Florentines.
His character was flawless, and the world
Held not his parallel. O, bear him hence
With all such honours as our State can offer.
He shall interrèd be with noise of cannon,
As doth befit so militant a nature.
Prepare these obsequies.

     [*Papal officers lift body of* GAOLER.]

A Papal Officer
                        But this is not
Savonarola. It is some one else.

Cesare
Lo! 'tis none other than the Fool that I
Hoof'd from my household but two hours agone.
I deem'd him no good riddance, for he had
The knack of setting tables on a roar.
What shadows we pursue! Good night, sweet Fool,
And flights of angels sing thee to thy rest!

Pope
Interrèd shall he be with signal pomp.
No honour is too great that we can pay him.
He leaves the world a vacuum. Meanwhile,
Go we in chase of the accursèd villain
That hath made escapado from this cell.
To horse! Away! We'll scour the country round
For Sav'narola till we hold him bound.
Then shall you see a cinder, not a man,
Beneath the lightnings of the Vatican!

> [*Flourish, alarums and excursions, flashes of Vatican
> lightning, roll of drums, etc. Through open door of
> cell is led in a large milk-white horse, which the*
> Pope *mounts as the Curtain falls.*]

Remember, please, before you formulate your impressions, that saying of Brown's: 'The thing *must* be judged as a whole.' I like to think that whatever may seem amiss to us in these four Acts of his would have been righted by collation with that Fifth which he did not live to achieve.

I like, too, to measure with my eyes the yawning gulf between stage and study. Very different from the message of cold print to our imagination are the messages of flesh and blood across footlights to our eyes and ears. In the warmth and brightness of a crowded theatre 'Savonarola' might, for aught one knows, seem perfect. 'Then why', I hear my gentle readers asking, 'did you thrust the play on *us*, and, not on a theatrical manager?'

That question has a false assumption in it. In the course of the past eight years I have thrust 'Savonarola' on any number of theatrical managers. They have all of them been (to use the technical phrase) 'very kind'. All have seen great merits in the work; and if I added together all the various merits thus seen I should have no doubt that 'Savonarola' was the best play never produced. The point on which all the managers are unanimous is that they have no use for a play without an ending. This is why I have fallen back, at last, on gentle readers, whom now I hear asking why I did not, as Brown's literary executor, try to finish the play myself. Can they never ask a question without a false assumption in it? I did try, hard, to finish 'Savonarola'.

Artistically, of course, the making of such an attempt was indefensible. Humanly, not so. It is clear throughout the play—especially perhaps in Acts III and IV—that if Brown had not steadfastly in his mind the hope of production on the stage, he had nothing in his mind at all. Horrified though he would have been by the idea of letting me kill his Monk, he would rather have done even this than doom his play to everlasting unactedness. I took, therefore, my courage in both hands, and made out a scenario. . . .

Dawn on summit of Mount Fiesole. Outspread view of Florence (Duomo, Giotto's Tower, etc.) as seen from that eminence.—NICCOLO MACHIAVELLI, *asleep on grass, wakes as sun rises. Deplores his exile from Florence,* LORENZO's *unappeasable hostility, etc. Wonders if he could not somehow secure the* POPE's *favour. Very cynical. Breaks off:* But who are these that scale the mountainside? | Savonarola and Lucrezia | Borgia!—*Enter through a trap-door, back* C. [*trap-door veiled from audience by a grassy ridge*], SAV. *and* LUC. *Both gasping and footsore from their climb.* [*Still with chains on their wrists? or not?*]—MACH. *steps unobserved behind a cypress and listens.*—SAV. *has a speech to the rising sun*—Th' effulgent hope that westers from the east | Daily. *Says that his hope, on the contrary, lies in escape.* To that which easters not from out the west, | That fix'd abode of freedom which men call | America! *Very bitter against* POPE.—LUC. *says that she, for her part, means* To start afresh in that uncharted land. | Which austers not from out the antipod, | Australia! *Exit* MACH., *unobserved, down trap-door behind ridge, to betray* LUC. *and* SAV.—*Several longish speeches by* SAV. *and* LUC. *Time is thus given for* MACH. *to get into touch with* POPE, *and time for* POPE *and retinue to reach the slope of Fiesole.* SAV., *glancing down across ridge, sees these sleuth-hounds, points them out to* LUC. *and cries* Bewray'd! LUC. By whom? SAV. I know not, but suspect | The hand of that sleek serpent Niccolo | Machiavelli.—SAV. *and* LUC. *rush down* C. *but find their way barred by the footlights.*— LUC. We will not be ta'en | Alive. And here availeth us my lore | In what pertains to poison. Yonder herb | [*points to a herb growing down* R.] Is deadly nightshade. Quick, Monk! Pluck we it!—SAV. *and* LUC. *die just as* POPE *appears over ridge, followed by retinue in full cry.*— POPE'S *annoyance at being foiled is quickly swept away on the great wave of Shakespearean chivalry and charity that again rises in him. He gives* SAV. *a funeral oration similar to the one meant for him in Act IV, but even more laudatory and more stricken. Of* LUC., *too, he enumerates the virtues, and hints that the whole terrestrial globe shall be hollowed to receive her bones. Ends by saying:* In deference to this our double sorrow | Sun shall not shine to-day nor shine to-morrow.—*Sun drops quickly back behind eastern horizon, leaving a great darkness, on which the Curtain slowly falls.*

All this might be worse, yes. The skeleton passes muster. But in the attempt to incarnate and ensanguine it I failed wretchedly. I saw that Brown was, in comparison with me, a master. Thinking I might possibly fare better in his method of work than in my own, I threw the skeleton into a cupboard, sat down, and waited to see what Savonarola and those others would do.

They did absolutely nothing. I sat watching them, pen in hand, ready to record their slightest movement. Not a little finger did they raise. Yet I knew they must be alive. Brown had always told me they were quite independent of him. Absurd to suppose that by the accident of his own death they had ceased to breathe. . . . Now and then, overcome with weariness, I dozed at my desk, and whenever I woke I felt that these rigid creatures had been doing all sorts of wonderful things while my eyes were shut. I felt that they disliked me. I came to dislike them in return, and forbade them my room.

Some of you, my readers, might have better luck with them than I. Invite them, propitiate them, watch them! The writer of the best Fifth Act sent to me shall have his work tacked on to Brown's; and I suppose I could get him a free pass for the second night.

FELIX ARGALLO
AND WALTER LEDGETT

I MARK YESTERDAY WITH a white stone. I made £900 yesterday.

Of this exploit I am all the gladder to write because it was not a mere vulgar fluke of the race-course or the stock-market, such as might befall me were I rich. It was the decent result of a wise step that I took quietly fifteen years ago. And that step would never have been taken had I not previously, in sheer kindness of heart, done a deed for which, when I shall have told you of it, you will praise

me. And yet another reason for me to unfold my tale is
that I shall thereby link my name with two names that are
very illustrious—those of Felix Argallo and Walter
Ledgett.

It may be that in these days, among the young,
Argallo's name is the main thing about him. His books
are but little read, I daresay, save by us elders. Argallo
was primarily a man of feeling: his whole philosophy was
founded on his emotions; and I am told that emotions are
now not held in high esteem by the young. To take things
as they come, and to examine them rather carefully, and to
dismiss them rather lightly, appears to be the present
fashion. Such things as pity and love and joy and indignation are incorrect. Joy was a thing alien to Argallo's
nature, certainly; but of what avail would this point in
his favour be as against his genius for pity? Pity, profound
and austerely tender pity, was the keynote of all his writings. He could not, as has often been pointed out, write
of anything that did not sadden him. This would have
been a serious limitation to his genius, but for the fact
that so few things in this world did *not* sadden him.
Sometimes it was not quite easy to understand what he
was pitying—what maiden in distress the old knight-errant
was eager to rescue, and just what her distress was. His
style was difficult. But it was not the less magnificent.
Those long-drawn cadences of his, those never-faltering
sonorousnesses, which were the voice of his soul, are
surely among the highest achievements in English prose;
and it is doubtful whether any man of purely English
blood could have given them to us; beside them Ruskin's
style seems tame, halting. But eloquence, with what it
springs from, is out of date. It may come in again? Well,
then Argallo will come in again, amidst the plaudits of
the young.

His first entry had made no stir at all. Few people had
been aware of it. Many years passed before his presence
was noticed by others than those few. In 1894, when I

came down from Oxford, I had never heard his name;
and it was only because his name looked rather promising,
somehow, that I one day paid threepence to the keeper of
a second-hand bookshop in Praed Street and bore away
with me a copy of *The Wall of Aloes*. The book was
twelve years old, its cover was very dingy, its pages were
mostly uncut; and as I cast my eye over some of the pages
that were open to inspection I felt that the author's name
had raised false hopes. But, unlike the critics of that
period and of the foregoing period, I persevered; and soon
I was enthralled. I do not say that a new star had swum
into my ken. That would strike too cheery a note. Rather
had I roamed into a dim twilight where great and noble
things were faintly discernible, looming suddenly out
upon me, and giving place to others before I had gauged
their import. Next day, when I had finished the book, I
was already a keen enough Argalloist to read it all over
again. With clearer understanding came a higher enthusiasm, on the wings of which I sped around to many
bookshops in quest of other works by the unknown god.
I would not believe that there were no others; but my
incredulity was not confirmed by any of my friends, and
I might have begun to waver had I not—suddenly,
blessedly—happened upon *A Bare Bodkin*.

This work was at that time aged only five years, and
thus gave me a sense of comparative nearness to its
creator; but it gave me also a sense of remoteness from
him: I doubted whether he were still alive. The idea of
suicide had often commended itself to the weak and
flaccid—to just the kind of people who would not carry
it out. But Argallo, as I had discerned through *The
Wall of Aloes*, had at some time been a man of action, a
fighter. Had he since been fighting his own theories? Or
had he strengthened them with his own death? I tried to
believe that he would in his austerity withhold from himself the pity that he lavished on his fellow-beings, and
would go stoically on to the natural end. But I was as

surprised as I was glad to hear, a month or so after my purchase of *A Bare Bodkin*, that he was still with us.

'With us' is perhaps not quite the phrase to use about a man living at Penge; and Penge was the scene of the great survival. Professor James Fitzmaurice Kelly, whom I met now for the first time, was my informant. I gathered that he (great gun that he was in Anglo-Hispanic scholarship) had helped Argallo by getting him commissions to translate Spanish works. I gathered also that Argallo had been born and bred in England, son of an Englishwoman and of a Spanish refugee who had fought in the first Carlist War. He himself, filially Carlist in his early manhood, had gone out to Spain and fought, with much gallantry and many wounds, throughout the insurrections of 1872–1876, afterwards returning to England and trying, with scant success, to live by his pen. He had at some time married an Englishwoman, but was now a widower, and rather a recluse. The Professor highly praised Argallo as translator, and seemed glad that I liked—glad that any one should like—Argallo's own books. Of these, he said, there must be quite half-a-dozen. He had them and would lend me them. He lent me them, and soon my fervour was such that he asked me to meet Argallo himself at luncheon. 'You must be prepared for a queer sad old fellow,' he said; but I needed no such warning.

Face to face with Argallo, I wondered only that he fitted so exactly my preconception of him. The long, gaunt, concave figure; the great melancholy dark eyes deep-set beneath a brow so wide that it seemed disproportionate even on so tall a man; the great aquiline nose; the small lips compressed into a short tight line by the soul's need to govern its sensibility; the sallowness, the shawnness, the close-cropped iron-grey hair; the shabbiness, but scrupulous neatness, of the clothes; the dignity, coupled with the painful shyness of the demeanour—all these things and all else about Mr Argallo were as I had expected and had wished. He had not been told that a third person was to be present; otherwise, said the

Professor, he might not have come. I effaced myself as
much as possible, so that the stormer of Castilian barri-
cades should not be frightened. I hoped he would presently
like me. That he already pitied me as much as he feared
me was a matter of course; but I wanted to be liked too.
And so well did I strive towards that goal that Mr Argallo
actually said, when he took leave of us, that if ever I
found myself in his neighbourhood he would be very glad
to see me.

Most of my elder readers, doubtless, visited that little
house in Penge as soon as it was acquired for the nation.
Ermyntrude Road, they will agree, is a deadly thorough-
fare. It was just as deadly in the 'nineties. Nor was
Argallo's home brighter than it is to-day. It was the
saddest of settings for the saddest of hidalgos. And the
measure of my fervour is that I did, in the course of years,
go to it frequently, and loved going.

I never asked leave to bring anybody with me. Others
there soon were who would have liked to come, for my
fervour had soon infected many of my friends—all of
them, indeed, who had spiritual insight and a scent for
fine literature. But Moses, that egoist, had gone alone up
Mount Sinai, and always alone went I down to Penge,
there to breathe, between the hours of four and six—
four, the hour when Argallo ceased work, and six, the
hour when he ate something—an atmosphere heavily-laden
with Castilian courtesy and gloom and genius. I never
told him that I constantly referred to him and to his
works in articles for the weekly press; nor did I let him
know that some of my friends were doing so. His pride
would have been wounded to the quick by any inkling
of any such aid. He earned enough by his translations to
keep body and soul together; and his desire that his
present and future work should be published in book-
form was balanced by that power for pity which was so
great as to exclude not even publishers from its scope.
When the great change in his life came I never hinted
to him that I and my friends and *their* friends—the ever-

growing band of us perceivers—were in any sort respon-
sible for it.

And indeed this change, which occurred in the Spring
of 1905, immediately after the publication of *Last Shadows*, was so abrupt and complete a peripety that we
ourselves were too dazed to take full credit for it. We poor
sappers and miners were blinded, were deafened, by the
vast explosion. It seemed less like a work of our own than
like some awful phenomenon of brute Nature. We had
never supposed that Argallo was the one and only great
writer the world had yet possessed. But the Press, for the
most part, held that opinion.

Walter Ledgett, I remember, was in frank agreement
with the Press. It would have been strange if so generous,
so swiftly impressionable a creature had felt any doubts in
the matter. In the earlier years of my acquaintance with
him, he too had been a reviewer of books, and had seldom
written a review without heartfelt conviction that the
occasion was unique. Deeply as he revered the established
names in literature, he was wildly susceptible to almost
anybody's 'latest'. He was a true book-lover. I had not,
however, at any time, breathed to him the name of Argallo.
I had felt that he would not be of service to the cause.
Only about his own books did his judgment seem to me
sound. 'My stuff' he called them; and his modesty, like
everything else about him (except, as I thought, his talent),
was perfectly genuine. He was the most unpretentious of
dear little men. At the Savage Club and the Authors', at
the Playgoers and the Yorick, there was no man more
popular than 'Walt'; and he seemed to be always at all
four of them, bustling around, buttonholing, radiating
innocence from his fresh round face. He was the brightest
of untiring little busybodies—always joyously organising a
dinner in honour of somebody, or a subscription for somebody's widow, or an illuminated address to some great
man. In the year of Argallo's apocalypse he was nearing the
age of forty, and was making a great deal of money by his

work; but his eye was as guileless, and his hair as curly, and his bearing as undistinguished as ever. He had dramatised his last year's novel, *Sweet Lady Caprice*; and this was being played with great success at the Strand Theatre. His cape-and-sword drama, *A Berserker in the Bastille*, had been produced elsewhere a year or so before, with equal success, and in the subsequent form of a novel was widely read by adults of the infantile persuasion. These plays of his, with two or three others that had held the boards, created a demand for even the things he did as a labour of love—the dear offspring of his veneration for mighty names and of his annual walking tour in the month of August. *Wordsworth's Windermere, In Stevenson's Cevennes, A Tramp Through Hardy-Land, Where Shelley Roamed*—and all the rest of them—became very marketable indeed. But their author was quite unspoilt. Nor indeed did his clubmates try to spoil him. He was, as ever, the victim of many hoaxes. Anybody with a solemn face could tell him the most preposterous things and be believed. Frank chaff, on the other hand, was understood by him quite well and taken with delight. Whenever he was in the chair at a house-dinner, some one would be sure to shout along the table, 'Hullo, Walt! What are *you* doing there?' and 'My dear chap, ask me another!' he would beamingly shout back.

It is true that in the photographs that were taken of him for the illustrated papers there was a touch of solemnity, of cerebration. Either the brow would be propped up by the right hand and partly covered by it, or the left hand would be clutching and wholly covering the chin. One day when I was lunching at the Savage, as guest of my friend Mostyn Pigott, Ledgett joined us at table; and my host insisted to him that those pensive attitudes towards the camera were obvious precautions—'At Elliott and Fry's, Walt, you feel that your forehead is unimpressive: you daren't show it. At Russell's you remember your weak chin: you hastily hide it. Quite right too! But not thorough enough! Next time you go to Baker Street, you must have one hand across your chin *and* the other across your forehead. And by Jove, I'll go with you, out of friend-ship, and stand behind you, holding my hands across the middle part of your face, old boy!' Ledgett almost rolled off his chair, in spasms of delight at Mostyn's affectionate onslaught. He simply could not take offence at anything a friend said.

This disability was the more loveable because he was not insensitive. So early as 1899 I had discovered that outside the realms of good-fellowship he was quite thin-skinned. Stevenson's Letters had recently been published, and I had just begun to read them. I met Ledgett in the Strand and asked if he had read them yet. 'Yes—oh, yes—capital, aren't they?' This was faint praise from Ledgett. More-over, he blushed as he spoke it, and parted from me rather abruptly. I remembered these things when I came to a passage in one of the later Samoan letters to R. A. M. ('Bob') Stevenson:—'Dost knaw aught of a lad named Leget or Legget? He writ me (but mon, I hae na keppit his horrid screed) wanting to write a wee bookie anent me. He claimed to have met you. If you know him, do, like a good fellow, write to him—and tell him not to.' Poor little Ledgett! What a shame!

In the following Spring appeared the Life and Letters of Coventry Patmore, and I was very sorry to find there, at the close of an interesting letter to Mr Wilfrid Meynell, 'Please say a sharp word to this Mr L——. A man making his soul under the shadow of the Awful Gate doesn't want to be pestered to be the guest of a dining-club.' I made no reference to Patmore's epistolary charm when next I came across Ledgett, and was the more careful not to do so because I had heard that some friends of his at the Authors' Club had jovially greeted him as Mr L—— and been stricken with remorse at sight of sudden moisture in his eyes. Not even by his cronies, from whom he could stand any amount of direct banter, could he bear to be rallied on an unkind snub.

When, a few years later, Bram Stoker's Life of Henry

Irving was published, I was again very sorry. The biographer quoted, as 'an example both of the Chief's good judgment and of his diplomacy', the following note:—
'Dear Stoker,—Have read W—— L——'s drama. Decidedly *not*, eh? Let the man down lightly. Greetings, H.I.'

This was less bad. There was a touch of kindness about it. But it was bad enough. And, though I am not of a nervous or suspicious habit, I began now to believe there was a conspiracy among the Fates that all Ledgett's failures to please great men should ultimately be brought to light. I wished great men would not die. I wished that if die they must their letters should be destroyed. And when, in the Spring of 1912, the Letters of George Meredith were given to us, it was with a deep groan that I beheld these words at the end of a letter written in 1889 to Leslie Stephen:—
'Yesterday an eager homunculus named L—— struck foot across this threshold, sputtering encomiastic cackle. He wanted me to be guest of honour at some festal junket in town. Such are the signs that England has heard of one's existence. I salaam'd him off, but he was not an easy goer.'

This was too much. I rose from my chair. Something must be done. I threw open the window and leaned out into the night. This constant persecution of Ledgett by the mighty dead must be put a stop to. But how? I regretted that I was not a man of resource. And in so doing (not that I would boast) I rather underrated myself. For there came to me suddenly an idea for a course of action. Nothing perhaps could be done to deter the malignant Fates. But the evil they were bent on could be somewhat counteracted. Having paced my room awhile, I sat down to my writing-table.

And early in the afternoon of the next day I took a cab to Wimbledon. Felix Argallo had now lived there for six years, in an old house with a high-walled garden. Penge had become impossible soon after the apocalypse. Within a month of its publication in the Spring, *Last Shadows*—and with it all the previous works—had come out in

America too, of course. America in such crises is less self-
controlled than England. There were strange doings. The
principal literary critic in Pittsburg lost his reason and had
to be placed under restraint; and the number of suicides
here and there was so large that in some of the States the
sale of *A Bare Bodkin* was banned by the authorities.
And during the Summer months in Ermyntrude Road the
crowds of American tourists standing outside Argallo's
exposed refuge were too great for his endurance. He had to
live with the blinds down; he could take exercise only after
dark; his health suffered. He didn't ever say he had heard
that I was the origin of all the new woes which had come
on him. But I think some ill-natured person must have
hinted as much to him; for his manner to me, in that
darkened sitting-room, was cold. Darkness and confine-
ment in a glare of bi-hemispheric publicity—with the be-
ginnings of hideously vast wealth thrown in—were too
much for Argallo's inveterate stoicism. He began to pity
himself.

Nor did the irruption of George Batford into his life
seem to comfort him. This youth, a nephew of the late
Mrs Argallo, had been a clerk in some provincial firm of
business, but had very unselfishly thrown up his post in
order to 'look after the old gentleman'. He was a brisk,
sensible young fellow; and he 'handled' Argallo's 'rights'
with great gusto, and in a manner that wrung admiration
from the various publishers involved. It was he, too, that
hit on the house at Wimbledon and effected the purchase
of it and now 'ran' it very smoothly and well. It was he
that sent interviewers and photographers empty away.
'Privacy is the biggest Ad', he once said to me, with a wink.
He may have indiscreetly made this remark to his uncle
also. For Argallo seemed to be oppressed even by the
dignity of seclusion. His health had been restored by his
daily walks around the garden. But his spirit had been
well-nigh broken by success. When he was not walking
in the garden, he was translating. The nephew obtained

fabulous offers even for these translations. The uncle
shook his head.

However, as I drove down to Wimbledon through the
Spring sunshine, I had little doubt that I could persuade
Argallo to grant me the MSS that I needed. I needed
neither translations nor original work; merely some to-be-
dictated matter, for a purpose which I thought would commend itself to him. True, his self-pity had become a formidable rival to his sorrow for mankind; but surely the
special case that I was going to lay before him would not
leave him unmoved, unhelpful? Nor was I disappointed.
As we paced the garden together (unbothered by prosaic
George, who was up in town on business) he was moved,
he was won; and presently, without a word, he led me
indoors to his study. There, with his grave old courtesy,
he placed a chair for me near to his writing-table. I laid
before him some sheets of notepaper—several kinds of
cheap note-paper—which I had bought that morning. I sat
down and sorted out in my hands the MSS that I had
written overnight. I cleared my throat. He dipped his pen
in the ink and wrote, at my dictation, as follows:

> 43, Ermyntrude Road, Penge, S.E.
> Monday, February 27th, 1898.

Dear Mr Beerbohm,—I must unburden my heart in
thanks to you for bringing me acquainted with Walter
Ledgett. He spent the day here yesterday, and it was a
day that will be in my memory while life lasts. What a
man! I have known in my time many men of divers
races. But I swear on my conscience I have never known
one who—how shall I say it?—*gives* more than your
friend Ledgett. Others may have his abundance. But
they do not scatter it, as he does. He arrived in a hansom
in the morning, I offered him what poor hospitality I
could, he did not leave me before dusk. During the
afternoon, W. E. Henley—himself a fine talker, as you
know—came in to see me.

Argallo paused in his penmanship and looked at me. 'W. E. Henley, the poet and critic?'

'Of course.'

'But I never knew him.'

'No? But what matter, Mr Argallo? You never knew Ledgett either.'

'True.'

And all the time Ledgett talked, talked, while we listened, Henley and I, much as the fishes listened to Arion's singing. You know my feelings about Ledgett's work. Well, the impression that I had the other evening, when I met him under your auspices, was right. The man is greater than his work. *Credo quia incredibile.*

When Henley and I were alone, I said: 'How horrible that of all that he poured out to us nothing will remain!' And presently we had a sort of paper-game—Henley and I separately writing out all the best single phrases we could remember of his talk. Thank God, there is no jealousy in my nature. Ledgett makes a worm of me, but if I writhe it is only for joy. He promised he would come and see me again some day. I wonder if he will? How hideous an irony that such a man should be born into such a world as ours!

Thank you again.

Yours faithfully,
Felix Argallo.

P.S. L. spoke most kindly of you and of your work, which he thinks *extremely promising*—his own words, and he spoke them with great emphasis.

'End of first letter,' I said. 'Another sheet of paper now. That yellowish-greyish kind, perhaps' . . .

Clarke's Temperance Hotel,
    Walford Street,
        Tottenham Court Road.
        October 23rd, 1903.   Midnight.

Dear Max Beerbohm,—I came up to town this morning, for though I am, as you know, no playgoer and detest the English theatre, I never miss a Ledgett first night. What a play! Has he ever done anything so fine as that third act? I took my stand outside the Pit entrance early in the afternoon, so as to be sure to have a place in the front row. It was a long wait, but really, such was my excitement, it passed almost in a flash. I think the gradual unfolding of the woman's character, as wrought on by the situation in the third act, is the finest *technical* feat Ledgett has yet achieved. Could you lunch with me here to-morrow? Table-d'hôte is at one o'clock. I want to talk of the play to some one who I know shares my feeling for Ledgett's work.

Yours sincerely,
Felix Argallo.

P.S. There was a man sitting next to me who did not applaud at the end of the first act, and I said something to him which I instantly regretted. Afterwards we became quite good friends. I could not help telling him that I knew Ledgett personally—that he had once come to my house. What weak vain creatures God's creatures are!

'End of letter. Thank you, Mr Argallo. Take another sheet, please. This one is from Penge again. You're sure I'm not tiring you?—no?'

43, Ermyntrude Road, Penge.
May 4th, 1904.

In strictest confidence.

My dear Max Beerbohm,—I came up to London yesterday to see my 'literary agent'. He had to give me the usual discouragement, poor man. But it is not about him that I am writing to you.

Leaving the Strand, I turned aimlessly westward and passed through Piccadilly (more than ever oppressed by the sadness of its gaiety). I then wandered into the Park. About halfway up the Drive (is that what it is called?) I, feeling tired, sat down on one of those green

chairs, facing eastward. Presently a 'brougham' drew up
at the break in the railings just opposite to me, and out of
it stepped a tall young woman of extreme beauty. She
gave some order to the coachman, who touched his hat,
said 'Yes, your Excellency', and drove away. What struck
me even more than the beauty of her face was the expression of it—an extraordinary mingling, as it seemed
to me, of hope and despair. She passed very quickly
across the pathway to the grass beyond, nor had she
gone far when I found myself following her, urged forward by the belief that I might somehow be of service
to her. She made straight for a distant tree—an elm—
under which were two chairs. I seated myself under
another tree—a plane—some twenty yards away. She sat
quite unconscious of any observer, straining her eyes
in the direction whence she had come—always with
that strange duality of expression. I was filled with all
the deeper compassion for her because, though evidently
a married woman, she was hardly more than a girl in
her teens, and also because, for all her high elegance
and her air as of one accustomed to command, there was
yet about her something that I can only describe
as *servile*. Suddenly after 20 minutes or so of tense and
rigid waiting, she sprang to her feet. A man was
approaching from the distance. He came sauntering
along, twirling his stick round and round in the air, with
his hat tilted back from his forehead. My first impression of his face, as he drew near, was not pleasant. It
seemed to me a cold and a hard face. A moment later,
repressing a cry, I recognised the face of Walter Ledgett.

Argallo looked up from his task. 'Surely,' he said, 'this
can only injure your friend.'
'Oh, not at all—quite the contrary. And of course the
name *Walter Ledgett* won't appear on the printed page.
When the time comes for your Letters to appear, I shall
ask the editor of them to omit *Walter Ledgett* from this
particular letter and to substitute two strokes.'

'Then how is anybody to know whom you mean?'

'Whom *you* mean, Mr Argallo. They'll know whom you mean, or rather meant, by collating this letter with your other letters to me. You never seemed able to write to me about *anybody* but Ledgett. . . . Shall we go on now?'

'Certainly, yes. Pardon me.' Argallo took up his pen.

I rose to my feet, stepped quickly behind my plane tree—but not, I fear, before the newcomer had seen and recognised me. I then walked rapidly away, not once looking back. I felt, as you may imagine, a great heaviness at my heart. I had pitied the woman, but to her, now, I gave hardly a thought——

'I don't at all like that,' muttered my amanuensis.

'Why not? It shows the intensity of your feeling for Ledgett. Besides, the woman never existed—she's a figment, don't you see? Ledgett's a man of flesh and blood.'

'H'm. You're very glib. Well?'

—gave hardly a thought, except in so far as she might yet be a source of trouble to our friend. That wonderful white face was as full of strength as of beauty. It was the face of one who, cast off, might by some kind of persecution hinder our friend in his creative work. You yourself see much of Ledgett, and are in his confidence. Perhaps you know of this affair?—though, from hints you have let drop, I suppose it is only one of many. I should be glad if you could reassure me that there is nothing to fear for him and for his art.

Ever sincerely yours,
Felix Argallo.

'I sign my name to that with great reluctance,' growled the signatory.

'Well, then, let's have a postscript.'

P.S. I am less callous than I seem. That young face of anguish will haunt me always.

'Only one more, Mr Argallo. This one may as well have a recent date—to show that you never faltered in the faith.'

Wimbledon.
December, 1911.

My dear Max,—

Argallo looked at me with sombre irony. 'Would that not be taking rather a liberty?'

'It is a liberty only on *my* part, Mr Argallo. I take it because it would help me. *I* can't be always thinking *only* of Ledgett.'

'Very well.'

My dear Max,—You must forgive me for not having thanked you sooner for your very pleasant letter. It came when I was stretched on a bed of sickness, suffering from a severe internal chill. I do not, however, regret that period of enforced rest, for it gave me the opportunity of reading once again, from first to last, *all* of Ledgett's books—besides the whole of that great album (which I once showed you) containing all that I have been able to collect of his not-republished work for the daily and weekly press. I found in this exercise a sovereign anodyne for pain. You know of old my feeling about Ledgett's work. Time has but intensified that passion, just as Time has deepened the genius of that man. Ledgett's later work is (not merely seems) his best. And yet, no! For who shall say the great wide-bosomed river is better than the little mountain-spring?

'Stop!' cried Argallo, and he read aloud the last sentence. 'Two lines of sheer blank verse! I don't like that at all.'

'Neither do I, Mr Argallo. But there it is. I hope you don't think I did it through lack of ear? I did it to show how carried out of yourself you were at the moment of writing. Nature took the pen and wrote *for* you; and she's not, as we know, a very good writer. However, it's a small point: I'm quite ready to waive it. Put in *that* after *say*, and strike out *little* ... So! Now let's finish up the letter. ... No break in paragraph. You were too excited not to write straight on.'

> And now I have a question to ask. Could you tell me whether there is any possibility of obtaining a scrap of Ledgett's MS? I have always refrained from writing to him—or rather (for I have written to him again and again) I have never posted any letter to him. To push and to pester is alien from my nature. Else, doubtless, I might be the possessor of many letters from L. I do in fact possess three, and they have always been among my most cherished possessions; but they are typewritten, circular letters— impersonal letters sent out, I conceive, to a great number of people. They are strong and cogent work, and not without that something of magic which is in everything that L. touches. (One of them, especially, about a luncheon to be offered at the Holborn Restaurant to the widow of an eminent Swedish novelist, is a masterpiece in its kind.) But they are *not enough*. 'I want, I want'—you remember that cry of Blake's?—a holograph letter written to some one person, and should deem it a bargain at whatever price the vendor might name.
>
> Forgive me, dear Max, for troubling you.
>
> Yours affectionately,
F. A.

'Or rather,' I added with a smile, 'forgive *me* for troubling *you*, Mr Argallo. And accept my profoundest thanks.'

He rose from his table, and 'Believe me,' he said, 'the power to serve that poor man—if these letters *will* serve him, as you think—is the one good thing my—my wretched notoriety has brought me.'

'Ah, don't say that!—However,' I suggested, while I tore up the pages I had brought with me, 'since such work pleases you, you might write to me, from time to time, of your own accord, about Ledgett.'

He repeated the words 'from time to time', and stood gazing down into the fire. There was silence while I took and folded and thrust into my pocket-book the letters already written. Suddenly, in a low voice, he broke this silence: 'There might then be many letters.' Still gazing into the fire, 'There might', he said in a yet lower voice, 'be a long time for your friend to wait. My bodily health is sound.' I was about to speak when suddenly he looked at me, in the strangest way. There had come into his eyes a light that I had never seen in them. There had come a look of veritable youth to his furrowed face. I could utter no word as he stood there strangely erect, soldierly—young. And it was in silence that I took leave of him.

'Tragic', a very apt word to describe Argallo's life, was the word that all the newspapers next morning used about his death. I, remembering what I had seen, knew better. However, the newspapers meant well. Their tributes to Argallo's genius in literature were whole-hearted; and on the ethical side they argued that, though the Almighty had set his canon against self-slaughter, their readers must remember that Argallo, wrongly no doubt, but honestly and with deep conviction, had held views of his own in the matter. One of the younger and more strenuous journals said that if the usual verdict were brought in by the Coroner's jury there would go up throughout the land such a howl of execration as would sweep away into limbo that whole fabric of 'Crowner's Quest Law' which had been a by-word and a mock ever since the days of the First Gravedigger in 'Hamlet', and that such a verdict would moreover cause deep offence in Spain at a moment when it was vitally necessary for the peace of Europe that Spain and England should draw closer and yet closer together. I, of course, had to attend the inquest and give evidence; and I too (though rather for truth's and memory's sake than for Europe's) tried to avert the usual verdict. Asked whether Mr Argallo had seemed to have anything on his mind, I said that he was a man who had always had much on his mind, and that my last impression of him was that he was exceptionally free from care or distress. The usual verdict was brought in, however. And I consoled myself with the reflection that it might make more acceptable to the Dean of Westminster the hasty but weighty petition that had been made to him. He, however, ran true to form. Argallo was buried, as Argallo would have wished, without official pomp.

He had made no will. But George Batford was of course the next of kin, and he told me that he would continue to devote his whole life to his uncle's service. This resolve, I inwardly foresaw, would entail vast exertions in the immediate future. Even the natural death of an eminent writer greatly intensifies, for a little while, the general desire to read him. The need for relays of new editions of Argallo's books would be specially urgent. Batford mentioned to me that all the translations would be issued 'shortly', and that there would also be a folio edition of them, entitled 'The Wimbledon Edition'. 'And of course there's the "Life and Letters" to be done. I shall do that myself,' he said with a thrifty look. 'I'm not a practised hand, I know. But I wouldn't let the dear old gentleman's Life be written by any cold-blooded stranger. By the way, I suppose you've some letters from him?' I said that I had a few.

Within a month the newspapers had duly received and published a letter from the biographer saying that he would esteem it a favour if possessors of letters written by Felix Argallo would etc, etc. I would not of course lend the letters in my possession until I had done some necessary spade-work on the mind of Ledgett. One is apt to postpone ticklish interviews, and, beautifully ingenuous though Ledgett was, and armed though *I* was with a Græco-medical word on which I placed great reliance, I had felt that my task might not be quite easy. But

I hastened forth now to accomplish it. Woe to my old illusion that he was always at all his four clubs simultaneously!—he was not at the Savage. But I found him at the Authors'; and (good omen) he believed me that I had come just for the pleasure of his company. After we had sat talking for a while and were halfway through our whisky-and-soda, 'Sad, wasn't it,' I said, 'about Felix Argallo?'

'Dreadful! The greatest loss of our time. I'd give anything to bring that man back to life.'

'Ah. You feel that you rather neglected him?'

'No, not that. Hang it all, I've read every line—or almost every line—he ever wrote. But you mean I might have tried to organise some sort of——'

'No. Only I think perhaps you might have called on him again from time to time. He was a lonely man. And that one visit that you did pay him, all those years ago, at Penge,'—

'I? What years ago? What visit?'

'Oh, well, your life has been a very full one, of course. And in those days Argallo was an almost unknown writer. Still, I wonder that you have forgotten. *He* didn't forget. Nor did W. E. Henley, I'll wager. Don't you remember that Henley was there that day?'

'He couldn't have been. I mean *I* couldn't have been. I never once met him. I did once, when he was living at Muswell Hill, go to see him about something. But he was out.'

'Perhaps when Argallo introduced you to him that day at Penge, you didn't catch his name?'

'But I tell you,' said Ledgett, flushed and almost angry, 'I never set eyes on Argallo.'

'Curious. Very curious. You don't remember dining with me, to meet him, at the little Solferino restaurant? I myself forget the exact date. But it must have been early in February, '98. You and he and I, nobody else. We were at that corner table—don't you remember?—to the left. You did most of the talking. You were in great form that night. But I gather you were in still greater when you went down to Penge.'

'But—look here! You must have got some sort of—hallucination.'

'Strange that Argallo should have shared it with me, Ledgett.' I had drawn out my pocket-book, and I now selected from its contents the first of Argallo's letters. 'This', I said, handing it over, 'may help you to recall things.'

His mind worked in obviously feverish confusion as he pored over the script. 'Look here!' he said to me at last. 'Somebody must have impersonated me!'

'You mean that *you* would never have said you thought my work extremely promising?'

'No—I think it is. I mean, I like it immensely, but——'

'If anybody did impersonate you, Ledgett—and frankly I don't see why anybody should—his face must have resembled yours exactly. Argallo had various photographs of you—reproductions of them, at least. He cut them out of newspapers, he kept them in an album, with the articles that you wrote. He knew your whole face—forehead and chin and everything—by heart. He often showed me the album. He mentions it in one of the other letters about you.'

'He wrote other letters about me? I mean about——'

'The second one is more about your work than about you.' I passed it on to him.

'I never,' he said after a while, huskily, 'I never could have believed—that such a man—that my stuff——'

'Well, those were his feelings, anyhow. Let's see: the third letter is of a more personal kind. But he speaks of your work on the last page, I think, yes.'

Presently, as he read, the veins stood out upon his temples. He was so bewildered that I felt quite guilty. But there could be no going back. I had to carry the good work—Argallo's and mine—through.

'Well?' I said, meeting his gaze sardonically. 'The mystic impersonator again? Or what?'

'Surely,' he gasped, 'you didn't believe, when you got this letter, that *I* was the——'

'My dear fellow, it was none of my business. I dismissed the matter from my mind.'

'But you don't seriously believe it *was* me?'

I laughingly lit a cigarette. Ledgett pressed his question.

'I know nothing about it, my dear fellow. I simply think you may have forgotten.'

'How could I forget a thing of that kind?'

'Well, it rather depends on how many things of that kind have happened to you. I take it that you aren't a misogynist. You could hardly have evolved *all* the delightful heroines of your novels without a fairly—or call it a terribly—wide experience. Cast your mind back. May the 4th, 1904. What were you doing on the afternoon of that day?'

'How on earth should I know?'

'You weren't keeping a diary in that year?'

'No. I've never kept a diary.'

'That in itself looks fishy. But come, man!—jog your wretched memory and then be quite frank with me! An afternoon in May—an elm tree—two green chairs under it. Do these things suggest *nothing* to you?'

'Oh, I don't say I've never had an appointment with a girl in a park. But never with—with *that* kind of girl.'

'You wouldn't have *kept* an appointment with that kind?'

'I don't say that.'

'Ah, Ledgett, Ledgett!'

'What I do say is that I should remember about it.'

'As clearly, perhaps, as you remember that evening at the Solferino, and that long day at Penge?'

He looked at me with dazed eyes.

'Don't worry,' I said. 'Your mind is all right—in all other ways, I'm quite sure. You've only got monoutinos-amnesia.'

'What's that?'

'Oh, a very common thing. I've heard of heaps of cases

of it. The word means "forgetfulness of some one thing".
Just as some people are always remembering some one
thing, others permanently forget some one thing. Doctors
say it's due to some infinitesimal lesion in the brain.'

'Then I'd better go straight to some good doctor.'

'Don't do that. Sheer waste of time. Such lesions can't
be cured—any more than they can be accounted for. And
they have no effect on the rest of the brain. They're
secerned.'

'Secerned?'

'Yes, to all intents and purposes they are. But of course,'
I was careful to add, 'they have what's called enviroactivity.'

'What's that?'

'It means that the patient—I mean the man—not only
forgets some one thing, but also forgets everything connected with it. You, for example, remember nothing
connected with Argallo.'

'Surely,' said Ledgett, with a dangerous gleam of intelligence, 'his books are connected with him? Yet I
remember *them* well enough.'

'You do. Yes. That's so. ... But his books aren't connected with his actual physical presence; and it's that
presence which is the some one thing in your case. Anything that you saw when you were *in* that presence is
blotted out. You remember having been in the Solferino
at various times; but the Solferino with Argallo in it eludes
you—and so do I, your attentive host there. The little
house at Penge, too, the listening Henley, that old elm
tree in the Park, that poor lady—all gone irrevocably,
Ledgett, all snatched away forever by enviroactivity.'

'But,' my friend had a second gleam, 'if I really did go
and meet that lady, I must have met her before somewhere. Why should I forget that?'

'*Have* you forgotten it, Ledgett? Honour bright? Well,
I'll believe you. Enviroactivity often effaces previous
events. And subsequent ones too. I daresay you don't

remember whether or not she did persecute you. Strange, isn't it? Stranger than anything in all your novels.'

'Yes, it's stranger than anything I could have imagined.'

'And somehow ridiculous, too. I wouldn't tell anybody about it, if I were you. You see, when these letters of Argallo's are published they'll make rather an impression on people. And if you went around saying you didn't remember him, people would wonder. You wouldn't want to say, "The fact is, I'm a monoutinosamnesiac." And without that explanation people might think you rather heartless. By the way, talking of supposed heartlessness, would you rather I didn't send in that third letter?'

Ledgett, who had one elbow on the arm of his chair, raised one hand to his forehead. I had never seen him do that. 'It is a very fine letter in itself,' he said, with deliberation. 'Finely felt and finely expressed. To keep it back would hardly be loyal, Beerbohm, to our friend's memory.' I asked whether he would prefer that two strokes should be substituted for his name. He said firmly that it would not be right to tamper with anything. He removed his hand from his forehead and held it out for the fourth letter. 'Anything personal in this one?' he asked.

'No, I'm afraid there isn't. But it's a very nice letter. It's finely felt and finely expressed. And I believe it's the last letter he wrote to anybody.'

'It's the greatest tribute', Ledgett presently said, 'ever paid to my work.' And he nursed his chin.

Nor, when I rose to go, did he rise and see me off the premises. He shook hands with me from his chair.

However, I posted the letters, to George Batford, that evening.

Next day, full of a happy inspiration, I went to a second-hand bookseller in the Charing Cross Road. The craze for first editions of modern authors had already, in a small way, begun; and I had an inkling that it would grow—though I no more foresaw the vast dimensions it would attain than I foresaw the War that for a time

stopped its growth. While I gave my order to the bookseller, I expected to reap ultimately a fair profit, but
nothing grandiose.

Meanwhile, the principal publishers strove fiercely with
one another for acquisition of the Life and Letters; and
the 'advance' paid to George Batford by the victor was
commensurate with the fury of the fray. The two handsome volumes were out early in November. The victor
advertised them as one of the greatest of English
biographies, and also as an ideal gift-book for the Christmas Season. To me it seemed that George's nepotic piety
did not atone for certain drawbacks. I found in his work
a lack of discernment, style, and lucid order. Of course
he had been heavily handicapped. Very little was known
of Argallo's early exploits in Spain; very little had happened to him in Penge, before the boom; practically nothing had happened to him in Wimbledon, before the end.
But George's innumerable long quotations from Tuck-
man's 'History of the Carlist Wars', and from the Rev. J.
F. Copley's book about the antiquities of Penge, and
from several books about the topography of Wimbledon,
were not in themselves interesting, had not been well-
chosen; and his history of the boom, with some eighty
reviews of *Last Shadows* quoted verbatim from the English and American press, was a dreadful muddle. Nor was
he better in touching the personal note. The last chapter
—from its opening words—'I will now attempt a pen-
picture of my Uncle when I first saw him. He was very
tall in height with a dark Spanish complexion which
showed his Spanish blood on the father's side, and spoke
in a low sort of voice,' to its closing words, 'But his
memory lives in the remembrance of all the English-
speaking public both of the British Empire and America'
—was a singularly infelicitous piece of writing. Argallo's
own letters were the one strong point in the book. True,
he had written few in his later age; and of his early letters
few had been preserved. But there was a general agreement among the critics that he was certainly in the fore-

most rank of English letter-writers. This opinion I shared. I found Argallo's letters very splendid. I was therefore surprised that by several critics the four letters addressed to myself were singled out as among the most characteristic and the best.

And there was another thing that rather took me aback. I had supposed that the revelation of Argallo's feeling about Ledgett's work would violently flutter the dovecots. There was not the stirring of a wing. There was but a bland cooing. 'It is pleasant to find that he was among the first to appreciate the genius of Mr Walter Ledgett.' —'He gives us the penetrating criticism that can be had only from a master-craftsman. What he wrote about Browning in his youth is hardly less fine than his later appreciations of Joseph Conrad, of D'Annunzio, and of Walter Ledgett.'—'The dark beads of his later years are strung on the golden thread of his generous passion for Ledgett's work.' Absurd as it may seem, even I, knowing what I knew, was beguiled by the melodious chorus, and did not wonder that Ledgett's manner, whenever I came across him, was so off-hand as to be not even patronising. From many people Argallo's 'Max' received an unwonted deference. But how should Argallo's idol be one of these?

I was told that to such people as the Bishop who put him up for The Athenæum, and the Field-Marshal who seconded him, his manner was fairly cordial. But when, in the following Spring, he was elected under Rule 2, he did not forgather much with the literary members. From his other clubs he had resigned soon after my chat with him at the Authors'. His old friends, behaving to him in the old way, had given him deep offence, and at the Savage especially he had made some unpleasant scenes. Even at The Athenæum, I heard, his temper was by no means equable. He was reported to have been unjustifiably caustic to an eminent old scientist who had said that it must be a great satisfaction to him to have been esteemed so highly by such a man as Felix Argallo. Stupendous though the sales of his books now were, and

undisputed though his genius was by even the most acrid
young persons, he did not appear to be a contented man.
Oxford, always rather slow in the uptake, did not offer
him a Doctorate of Letters that Summer. He very wrongly
took this as a personal slight. Argallo's letter to Lord
Curzon (May, 1907), begging to decline that high honour,
was a noble and touching document, a classic letter. But
I would barter its existence to have seen Ledgett turn on
his heel, as he did, one day in the Autumn of 1913, when
Lord Curzon came towards him, with outstretched hand,
in the library of The Athenæum. In 1914, you will remember, Oxford did the correct thing; but all who
attended the Encaenia agreed that Valterius Ledgett
looked very sulky, very stern and unbending, in his scarlet
gown.

I have always loved Oxford. I welcomed, as a sign of her
undiminished power, the fact that Ledgett's Doctorate
sent up by ten points the market-price of 'Ledgett Firsts'.
I wondered whether this were the moment to 'unload'.
I was greatly tempted. Even one of Ledgett's books,
despite the spell his fame had cast on me, was more than
I really wanted. It was awful to have to go on harbouring
two 'clean copies' of the first edition of everything he had
proliferated. My sleuth-hound of the Charing Cross Road
had carried out my order with appalling thoroughness. I
had two clean copies of every brochure that Ledgett had
written in his youth for the lesser railway-companies, for
keepers of seaside hotels, for keepers of hotels inland, for
heaven knows whom. I had two clean copies of every
song for which he had written words. And *what* words!
Surely I should unload now? 'Not yet,' whispered my
wiser self. 'The market price for Firsts is nothing to what
it will yet be. And every year of Ledgett's life will send up
Ledgett's value.' Two months later came the War; and
one forgot everything else.

Even Ledgett was forgotten. Practically no notice was
taken of the sonnet in which he expressed his envy of

Youth, and his regret that he personally could not go out
'And fight the accursed Kaiser face to face'. The continuance of the War weighed heavily on him. He did not
go so far as to try to stop it, but, as he said to me one day
when I met him in Pall Mall, he felt that 'this total abey-
ance of the things of the mind' was in itself a great danger
to the country. The air-raids, I think, he took as a personal
insult. Anyway, before the end of 1915, he retired to
Wordsworth's Windermere. And one likes to think of
him there among the unbombed Lakes, reading his own
books incessantly. When the War was over, the things of
the mind were remembered. John Bull sat down to feast
on them with the appetite of a starved man. Ledgett's
name shone now the more lustrously for its long occlusion.
Ledgett Firsts rose 15 points above pre-war value. Should
I unload now? But again my wiser self restrained me.

Not long after the Armistice, I went to Italy, where
I had mostly lived for a while before the War; and in
Italy I now settled. A few days before my departure I had
a glimpse—my last—of Ledgett. He was walking towards
The Athenæum—walking very slowly, leaning heavily on
a stick, for he had become, in spite of the food-restrictions
of the past years, enormously fat. Too intense contemplation of his own genius had begun to undermine his health,
I was sure. His face was flabby, and his eyes were lack-
lustre. I did not foresee that his naturally strong con-
stitution would preserve him for eight more years.

Happening to have come over from Italy a fortnight
ago, I attended, of course, the service in the Abbey last
Tuesday. I was glad to be able to pay this last tribute to
my friend's memory. I was glad also, on the following
day, to hear that Mr Nat Heinz, the famous 'Firsts Agent',
had recently come over from New York on one of his
periodical visits to London, and was staying at the Ritz.
I wrote at once a respectful note to this magnoperator,
telling him that if he would do me the honour to call on
me at the Charing Cross Hotel I could show him some

things that might interest him. I then drove to the storage warehouse that harboured the packing-case in which were my duplicated copies of Ledgett Firsts. This possession I transported to my hotel and, with a view to the magno-perator, dashingly engaged a private sitting-room. There, yesterday morning, with my baits outspread on two tables, three chairs and a sofa, I awaited the hour fixed by Mr Heinz for his visit. I was prepared for a man with a cool, depreciative manner. Such a manner is essential to such men's business. But the small dark eyes of Mr Heinz, as they alighted on treasure after treasure, gave forth un-controllable gleams.

Between the pages of some of the books were insertions of what is called 'relative matter'. There were letters that I had received from Ledgett at various dates, there were *menus* that had been handed round after convivial dinners and signed by diners of whom Ledgett was one, there were several sketches of Ledgett made by Phil May. I especially drew Mr Heinz's attention to the books in which I had inserted my four letters from Argallo. But I had set overmuch store on these. 'Ar-*what*?' said Mr Heinz. 'Oh, Argallo; yes; I reckle-ect. The author who took his own life. I handled Argallo wares extens'vely at one time. They've greatly dee-preciated.'

He made, however, no other cavils. And he presently drew, without a murmur, a cheque for the amount that I firmly named to him. With this in my pocket, I lunched heartily, but, before going forth from my hotel to pay it into my bank, I told the young lady at the bureau that I should not need my private sitting-room any more. The bank-clerk who received my cheque, and knew my affairs, saw through my assumption of languor instantly and gave me a very human smile of congratulation.

On my way back to Charing Cross, I met a friend and fellow-writer who is noted for his acumen in matters of business; and, to impress him, I poured forth the story of my transaction.

He gave a sharp whistle. 'My dear good fool, you've put nine hundred pounds into Nat Heinz's pocket!'

'Well, after all,' I reasoned with him, 'that's exactly the sum he put into *my* pocket. So we're quits. I never want to get the better of anybody. Enough that for once Europe has held her own!'

'But she hasn't!' my friend retorted. 'America has got the books!'

This, I confessed, was a point I hadn't thought of. But perhaps also it is a point which Mr Heinz's clients, when these pages shall have appeared, won't think very much of.

From

ZULEIKA DOBSON
[1911]

Extracts from

I

ZULEIKA'S ARRIVAL

THAT OLD BELL, PRESAGE of a train, had just sounded
through Oxford station; and the undergraduates who were
waiting there, gay figures in tweed or flannel, moved to
the margin of the platform and gazed idly up the line.
Young and careless, in the glow of the afternoon sunshine,
they struck a sharp note of incongruity with the worn
boards they stood on, with the fading signals and grey
eternal walls of that antique station, which, familiar to
them and insignificant, does yet whisper to the tourist the
last enchantments of the Middle Age.

At the door of the first-class waiting-room, aloof and
venerable, stood the Warden of Judas. An ebon pillar of
tradition seemed he, in his garb of old-fashioned cleric.
Aloft, between the wide brim of his silk hat and the white
extent of his shirt-front, appeared those eyes which hawks,
that nose which eagles, had often envied. He supported his
years on an ebon stick. He alone was worthy of the background.

Came a whistle from the distance. The breast of an
engine was descried, and a long train curving after it,
under a flight of smoke. It grew and grew. Louder and
louder, its noise foreran it. It became a furious, enormous
monster, and, with an instinct for safety, all men receded
from the platform's margin. (Yet came there with it, unknown to them, a danger far more terrible than itself.)
Into the station it came blustering, with cloud and
clangour. Ere it had yet stopped, the door of one carriage
flew open, and from it, in a white travelling-dress, in a
toque a-twinkle with fine diamonds, a lithe and radiant
creature slipped nimbly down to the plaform.

A cynosure indeed! A hundred eyes were fixed on her, and half as many hearts lost to her. The Warden of Judas himself had mounted on his nose a pair of black-rimmed glasses. Him espying, the nymph darted in his direction. The throng made way for her. She was at his side.

'Grandpapa!' she cried, and kissed the old man on either cheek. (Not a youth there but would have bartered fifty years of his future for that salute.)

'My dear Zuleika,' he said, 'welcome to Oxford! Have you no luggage?'

'Heaps!' she answered. 'And a maid who will find it.'

'Then,' said the Warden, 'let us drive straight to College.' He offered her his arm, and they proceeded slowly to the entrance. She chatted gaily, blushing not in the long avenue of eyes she passed through. All the youths, under her spell, were now quite oblivious of the relatives they had come to meet. Parents, sisters, cousins, ran unclaimed about the platform. Undutiful, all the youths were forming a serried suite to their enchantress. In silence they followed her. They saw her leap into the Warden's landau, they saw the Warden seat himself upon her left. Nor was it until the landau was lost to sight that they turned—how slowly, and with how bad a grace!—to look for their relatives.

Through those slums which connect Oxford with the world, the landau rolled on towards Judas. Not many youths occurred, for nearly all—it was the Monday of Eights Week—were down by the river, cheering the crews. There did, however, come spurring by, on a polo-pony, a very splendid youth. His straw hat was encircled with a riband of blue and white, and he raised it to the Warden.

'That', said the Warden, 'is the Duke of Dorset, a member of my College. He dines at my table to-night.'

Zuleika, turning to regard his Grace, saw that he had not reined in and was not even glancing back at her over his shoulder. She gave a little start of dismay, but scarcely had her lips pouted ere they curved to a smile—a smile with no malice in its corners.

As the landau rolled into 'the Corn', another youth—a

pedestrian, and very different—saluted the Warden. He wore a black jacket, rusty and amorphous. His trousers were too short, and he himself was too short: almost a dwarf. His face was as plain as his gait was undistinguished. He squinted behind spectacles.

'And who is that?' asked Zuleika.

A deep flush overspread the cheek of the Warden. 'That', he said, 'is also a member of Judas. His name, I believe, is Noaks.'

'Is he dining with us to-night?' asked Zuleika.

'Certainly not,' said the Warden. 'Most decidedly not.'

Noaks, unlike the Duke, had stopped for an ardent retrospect. He gazed till the landau was out of his short sight; then, sighing, resumed his solitary walk.

The landau was rolling into 'the Broad', over that ground which had once blackened under the faggots lit for Latimer and Ridley. It rolled past the portals of Balliol and of Trinity, past the Ashmolean. From those pedestals which intersperse the railing of the Sheldonian, the high grim busts of the Roman Emperors stared down at the fair stranger in the equipage. Zuleika returned their stare with but a casual glance. The inanimate had little charm for her.

A moment later, a certain old don emerged from Blackwell's, where he had been buying books. Looking across the road, he saw, to his amazement, great beads of perspiration glistening on the brows of those Emperors. He trembled, and hurried away. That evening, in Common Room, he told what he had seen; and no amount of polite scepticism would convince him that it was but the hallucination of one who had been reading too much Mommsen. He persisted that he had seen what he described. It was not until two days had elapsed that some credence was accorded him.

Yes, as the landau rolled by, sweat started from the brows of the Emperors. They, at least, foresaw the peril that was overhanging Oxford, and they gave such warning as they could. Let that be remembered to their credit. Let that incline us to think more gently of them. In their lives we know, they were infamous, some of them—'nihil non commiserunt stupri, saevitiae, impietatis'. But are they too little punished, after all? Here in Oxford, exposed eternally and inexorably to heat and frost, to the four winds that lash them and the rains that wear them away, they are expiating, in effigy, the abominations of their pride and cruelty and lust. Who were lechers, they are without bodies; who were tyrants, they are crowned never but with crowns of snow; who made themselves even with the gods, they are by American visitors frequently mistaken for the Twelve Apostles. It is but a little way down the road that the two Bishops perished for their faith, and even now we do never pass the spot without a tear for them. Yet how quickly they died in the flames! To these Emperors, for whom none weeps, time will give no surcease. Surely, it is sign of some grace in them that they rejoiced not, this bright afternoon, in the evil that was to befall the city of their penance.

V

THE DUKE'S PROPOSAL

LUNCHEON PASSED IN ALMOST unbroken silence. Both Zuleika and the Duke were ravenously hungry, as people always are after the stress of any great emotional crisis. Between them, they made very short work of a cold chicken, a salad, a gooseberry-tart and a Camembert. The Duke filled his glass again and again. The cold classicism of his face had been routed by the new romantic movement which had swept over his soul. He looked two or three months older than when first I showed him to my reader.

He drank his coffee at one draught, pushed back his chair, threw away the cigarette he had just lit. 'Listen!' he said.

Zuleika folded her hands on her lap.

'You do not love me. I accept as final your hint that you never will love me. I need not say—could not, indeed, ever say—how deeply, deeply you have pained me. As lover, I am rejected. But that rejection', he continued, striking the table, 'is no stopper to my suit. It does but drive me to the use of arguments. My pride shrinks from them. Love, however, is greater than pride; and I, John, Albert, Edward, Claude, Orde, Angus, Tankerton,* Tanville-Tankerton,† fourteenth Duke of Dorset, Marquis of Dorset, Earl of Grove, Earl of Chastermaine, Viscount Brewsby, Baron Grove, Baron Petstrap, and Baron Wolock, in the Peerage of England, offer you my hand. Do not interrupt me. Do not toss your head. Consider well what I am saying. Weigh the advantages you would gain by acceptance of my hand. Indeed, they are manifold and tremendous. They are also obvious: do not shut your eyes to them. You, Miss Dobson, what are you? A conjurer, and a vagrant; without means, save such as you can earn by the sleight of your hand; without position; without a home; all unguarded but by your own self-respect. That you follow an honourable calling, I do not for one moment deny. I do, however, ask you to consider how great are its perils and hardships, its fatigues and inconveniences. From all these evils I offer you instant refuge. I offer you, Miss Dobson, a refuge more glorious and more augustly gilded than you, in your airiest flights of fancy, can ever have hoped for or imagined. I own about 340,000 acres. My town residence is in St James's Square. Tankerton, of which you may have seen photographs, is the chief of my country seats. It is a Tudor house, set on the ridge of a valley. The valley, its park, is halved by a stream so narrow that the deer leap across. The gardens are estraded upon the slope. Round the house runs a wide paven terrace. There are always two or three peacocks trailing their sheathed feathers along the balustrade, and stepping how stiffly! as though they had just been unharnessed from Juno's chariot. Two flights of shal-

---

* Pronounced as Tacton.　　　† Pronounced as Tavvle-Tacton

low steps lead down to the flowers and fountains. Oh, the gardens are wonderful. There is a Jacobean garden of white roses. Between the ends of two pleached alleys, under a dome of branches, is a little lake, with a Triton of black marble, and with water-lilies. Hither and thither under the archipelago of water-lilies, dart gold-fish—tongues of flame in the dark water. There is also a long strait alley of clipped yew. It ends in an alcove for a pagoda of painted porcelain which the Prince Regent—peace be to his ashes! —presented to my great-grandfather. There are many twisting paths, and sudden aspects, and devious, fantastic arbours. Are you fond of horses? In my stables of pine-wood and plated-silver seventy are installed. Not all of them together could vie in power with one of the meanest of my motor-cars.'

'Oh, I never go in motors,' said Zuleika. 'They make one look like nothing on earth, and like everybody else.'

'I myself', said the Duke, 'use them little for that very reason. Are you interested in farming? At Tankerton there is a model farm which would at any rate amuse you, with its heifers and hens and pigs that are like so many big new toys. There is a tiny dairy, which is called "Her Grace's". You could make, therein, real butter with your own hands, and round it into little pats, and press every pat with a different device. The boudoir that would be yours is a blue room. Four Watteaus hang in it. In the dining-hall hang portraits of my forefathers—*in petto*, your fore-fathers-in-law—by many masters. Are you fond of peasants? My tenantry are delightful creatures, and there is not one of them who remembers the bringing of the news of the Battle of Waterloo. When a new Duchess is brought to Tankerton, the oldest elm in the park must be felled. That is one of many strange old customs. As she is driven through the village, the children of the tenantry must strew the road with daisies. The bridal chamber must be lighted with as many candles as years have elapsed since the creation of the Dukedom. If you came into it, there would be'—and the youth, closing his eyes, made a rapid

calculation—'exactly three hundred and eighty-eight
candles. On the eve of the death of a Duke of Dorset two
black owls come and perch on the battlements. They remain there through the night, hooting. At dawn they fly
away, none knows whither. On the eve of the death of any
other Tanville-Tankerton comes (no matter what be the
time of year) a cuckoo. It stays for an hour, cooing, then
flies away, none knows whither. Whenever this portent
occurs, my steward telegraphs to me, that I, as head of the
family, be not unsteeled against the shock of a bereave-
ment, and that my authority be sooner given for the unseal-
ing and garnishing of the family vault. Not every forefather
of mine rests quiet beneath his escutcheoned marble.
There are they who revisit, in their wrath or their remorse,
the places wherein erst they suffered or wrought evil.
There is one who, every Halloween, flits into the dining-
hall, and hovers before the portrait which Hans Holbein
made of him, and flings his diaphanous grey form against
the canvas, hoping, maybe, to catch from it the fiery flesh-
tints and the solid limbs that were his, and so to be re-
incarnate. He flies against the painting, only to find himself t'other side of the wall it hangs on. There are five
ghosts permanently residing in the right wing of the house,
two in the left, and eleven in the park. But all are quite
noiseless and quite harmless. My servants, when they meet
them in the corridors or on the stairs, stand aside to let
them pass, thus paying them the respect due to guests of
mine; but not even the rawest housemaid ever screams or
flees at sight of them. I, their host, often waylay them and
try to communicate with them; but always they glide past
me. And how gracefully they glide, these ghosts! It is a
pleasure to watch them. It is a lesson in deportment. May
they never be laid! Of all my household pets, they are the
dearest to me. I am Duke of Strathsporran and Cairngorm,
Marquis of Sorby, and Earl Cairngorm, in the Peerage of
Scotland. In the glens of the hills about Strathsporran are
many noble and nimble stags. But I have never set foot
in my house there, for it is carpeted throughout with the

tartan of my clan. You seem to like tartan. What tartan is it you are wearing?'

Zuleika looked down at her skirt. 'I don't know,' she said. 'I got it in Paris.'

'Well,' said the Duke, 'it is very ugly. The Dalbraith tartan is harmonious in comparison, and has, at least, the excuse of history. If you married me, you would have the right to wear it. You would have many strange and fascinating rights. You would go to Court. I admit that the Hanoverian Court is not much. Still, it is better than nothing. At your presentation, moreover, you would be given the *entrée*. Is that nothing to you? You would be driven to Court in my state-coach. It is swung so high that the streetsters can hardly see its occupant. It is lined with rose-silk; and on its panels, and on its hammer-cloth, my arms are emblazoned—no one has ever been able to count the quarterings. You would be wearing the family jewels, reluctantly surrendered to you by my aunt. They are many and marvellous, in their antique settings. I don't want to brag. It humiliates me to speak to you as I am speaking. But I am heart-set on you, and to win you there is not a precious stone I would leave unturned. Conceive a *parure* all of white stones—diamonds, white sapphires, white topazes, tourmalines. Another, of rubies and amethysts, set in gold filigree. Rings that once were poison-combs on Florentine fingers. Red roses for your hair—every petal a hollowed ruby. Amulets and ape-buckles, zones and fillets. Aye! know that you would be weeping for wonder before you had seen a tithe of these gauds. Know, too, Miss Dobson, that in the Peerage of France I am Duc d'Etretat et de la Roche Guillaume. Louis Napoleon gave the title to my father for not cutting him in the Bois. I have a house in the Champs Elysées. There is a Swiss in its court-yard. He stands six-foot-seven in his stockings, and the chasseurs are hardly less tall than he. Wherever I go, there are two chefs in my retinue. Both are masters in their art, and furiously jealous of each other. When I compliment either of them on some dish, the other challenges him. They fight with rapiers, next morning, in the garden of whatever house I am occupying. I do not know whether you are greedy? If so, it may interest you to learn that I have a third chef, who makes only soufflés, and an Italian pastry-cook; to say nothing of a Spaniard for salads, an Englishwoman for roasts, and an Abyssinian for coffee. You found no trace of their handwork in the meal you have just had with me? No; for in Oxford it is a whim of mine—I may say a point of honour—to lead the ordinary life of an undergraduate. What I eat in this room is cooked by the heavy and unaided hand of Mrs Batch, my landlady. It is set before me by the unaided and—or are you in error?—loving hand of her daughter. Other ministers have I none here. I dispense with my private secretaries. I am unattended by a single valet. So simple a way of life repels you? You would never be called upon to share it. If you married me, I should take my name off the books of my College. I propose that we should spend our honeymoon at Baiae. I have a villa at Baiae. It is there that I keep my grandfather's collection of majolica. The sun shines there always. A long olive-grove secretes the garden from the sea. When you walk in the garden, you know the sea only in blue glimpses through the vacillating leaves. White-gleaming from the bosky shade of this grove are several goddesses. Do you care for Canova? I don't myself. If you do, these figures will appeal to you: they are in his best manner. Do you love the sea? This is not the only house of mine that looks out on it. On the coast of County Clare—am I not Earl of Enniskerry and Baron Shandrin in the Peerage of Ireland?—I have an ancient castle. Sheer from a rock stands it, and the sea has always raged up against its walls. Many ships lie wrecked under that loud implacable sea. But mine is a brave strong castle. No storm affrights it; and not the centuries, clustering houris, with their caresses can seduce it from its hard austerity. I have several titles which for the moment escape me. Baron Llffthwchl am I, and ... and ... but you can find them for yourself in Debrett. In me you behold a

Prince of the Holy Roman Empire, and a Knight of the Most Noble Order of the Garter. Look well at me! I am Hereditary Comber of the Queen's Lap-Dogs. I am young. I am handsome. My temper is sweet, and my character without blemish. In fine, Miss Dobson, I am a most desirable *parti*.'

'But,' said Zuleika, 'I don't love you.'

The Duke stamped his foot. 'I beg your pardon,' he said hastily. 'I ought not to have done that. But—you seem to have entirely missed the point of what I was saying.'

'No, I haven't,' said Zuleika.

'Then what,' cried the Duke, standing over her, 'what is your reply?'

Said Zuleika, looking up at him, 'My reply is that I think you are an awful snob.'

XII

OXFORD

CLEARLY IT WAS VAIN to seek distraction in my old College. I floated out into the untenanted meadows. Over them was the usual coverlet of white vapour, trailed from the Isis right up to Merton Wall. The scent of these meadows' moisture is the scent of Oxford. Even in hottest noon, one feels that the sun has not dried *them*. Always there is moisture drifting across them, drifting into the Colleges. It, one suspects, must have had much to do with the evocation of what is called the Oxford spirit—that gentlest spirit, so lingering and searching, so dear to them who as youths were brought into ken of it, so exasperating to them who were not. Yes, certainly, it is this mild, miasmal air, not less than the grey beauty and gravity of the buildings, that has helped Oxford to produce, and foster eternally, her peculiar race of artist-scholars, scholar-artists. The undergraduate, in his brief periods of residence, is too buoyant to be mastered by the spirit of the place. He does but salute it, and catch the manner. It is on him who stays to spend his maturity here that the spirit will in its fullness gradually descend. The buildings and their traditions keep astir in his mind whatsoever is gracious; the climate, enfolding and enfeebling him, lulling him, keeps him careless of the sharp, harsh, exigent realities of the outer world. Careless? Not utterly. These realities may be seen by him. He may study them, be amused or touched by them. But they cannot fire him. Oxford is too damp for that. The 'movements' made there have been no more than protests against the mobility of others. They have been without the dynamic quality implied in their name. They have been no more than the sighs of men gazing at what other men had left behind them; faint, impossible appeals to the god of retrogression, uttered for their own sake and ritual, rather than with any intent that they should be heard. Oxford, that lotus-land, saps the will-power, the power of action. But, in doing so, it clarifies the mind, makes larger the vision, gives, above all, that playful and caressing suavity of manner which comes of a conviction that nothing matters, except ideas, and that not even ideas are worth dying for, inasmuch as the ghosts of them slain seem worthy of yet more piously elaborate homage than can be given to them in their hey-day. If the Colleges could be transferred to the dry and bracing top of some hill, doubtless they would be more evidently useful to the nation. But let us be glad there is no engineer or enchanter to compass that task. *Egomet*, I would liefer have the rest of England subside into the sea than have Oxford set on a salubrious level. For there is nothing in England to be matched with what lurks in the vapours of these meadows, and in the shadows of these spires—that mysterious, inenubilable spirit, spirit of Oxford. Oxford! The very sight of the word printed, or sound of it spoken, is fraught for me with most actual magic.

Essay from

WORKS

Dandies and Dandies

[1896]

Essay from

MORE

Going Back to School

[1899]

DANDIES AND DANDIES

How very delightful Grego's drawings are! For all their mad perspective and crude colour, they have indeed the sentiment of style, and they reveal, with surer delicacy than does any other record, the spirit of Mr Brummell's day. Grego guides me, as Virgil Dante, through all the mysteries of that other world. He shows me those stiff-necked, over-hatted, wasp-waisted gentlemen, drinking Burgundy in the *Café des Milles Colonnes* or riding through the village of Newmarket upon their fat cobs or gambling at Crockford's. Grego's *Green Room of the Opera House* always delights me. The formal way in which Mlle Mercandotti is standing upon one leg for the pleasure of Lord Fife and Mr Ball Hughes; the grave regard directed by Lord Petersham towards that pretty little maid-a-mischief who is risking her rouge beneath the chandelier; the unbridled decorum of Mlle Hullin and the decorous debauchery of Prince Esterhazy in the distance, make altogether a quite enchanting picture. But, of the whole series, the most illuminative picture is certainly the *Ball at Almack's*. In the foreground stand two little figures, beneath whom, on the nether margin, are inscribed those splendid words, *Beau Brummell in Deep Conversation with the Duchess of Rutland*. The Duchess is a girl in pink, with a great wedge-comb erect among her ringlets, the Beau *très dégagé*, his head averse, his chin most supercilious upon his stock, one foot advanced, the gloved fingers of one hand caught lightly in his waistcoat; in fact, the very deuce of a pose.

In this, as in all known images of the Beau, we are struck by the utter simplicity of his attire. The 'countless rings' affected by D'Orsay, the many little golden chains, 'every

one of them slighter than a cobweb', that Disraeli loved
to insinuate from one pocket to another of his vest, would
have seemed vulgar to Mr Brummell. For is it not to his
fine scorn of accessories that we may trace that first aim
of modern dandyism, the production of the supreme effect
through means the least extravagant? In certain incon-
gruities of dark cloth, in the rigid perfection of his linen,
in the symmetry of his glove with his hand, lay the secret
of Mr Brummell's miracles. He was ever most economical,
most scrupulous of means. Treatment was everything with
him. Even foolish Grace and foolish Philip Wharton, in
their book about the beaux and wits of this period, speak
of his dressing-room as 'a studio in which he daily composed that elaborate portrait of himself which was to be
exhibited for a few hours in the clubrooms of the town'.
Mr Brummell was, indeed, in the utmost sense of the
word, an artist. No poet nor cook nor sculptor ever bore
that title more worthily than he.

And really, outside his art, Mr Brummell had a personality of almost Balzacian insignificance. There have
been dandies, like D'Orsay, who were nearly painters;
painters, like Mr Whistler, who wished to be dandies;
dandies, like Disraeli, who afterwards followed some less
arduous calling. I fancy Mr Brummell was a dandy, nothing
but a dandy, from his cradle to that fearful day when he
lost his figure and had to flee the country, even to that
distant day when he died, a broken exile, in the arms of
two *religieuses*. At Eton, no boy was so successful in
avoiding that strict alternative of study and athletics which
we force upon our youth. He once terrified a master,
named Parker, by asserting that he thought cricket 'foolish'. Another time, after listening to a reprimand from the
headmaster, he twitted that learned man with the asym-
metry of his neckcloth. Even in Oriel he could see little
charm, and was glad to leave it, at the end of his first year,
for a commission in the Tenth Hussars. Crack though the
regiment was—indeed, all the commissions were granted
by the Regent himself—young Mr Brummell could not

bear to see all his brother-officers in clothes exactly like his own; was quite as deeply annoyed as would be some god, suddenly entering a restaurant of many mirrors. One day, he rode upon parade in a pale-blue tunic, with silver epaulettes. The Colonel, apologising for the narrow system which compelled him to so painful a duty, asked him to leave the parade. The Beau saluted, trotted back to quarters and, that afternoon, sent in his papers. Henceforth he lived freely as a fop, in his maturity, should.

His *début* in the town was brilliant and delightful. Tales of his elegance had won for him there a precedent fame. He was reputed rich. It was known that the Regent desired his acquaintance. And thus, Fortune speeding the wheels of his cabriolet and Fashion running to meet him with smiles and roses in St James's, he might well, had he been worldly or a weakling, have yielded his soul to the polite follies. But he passed them by. Once he was settled in his suite, he never really strayed from his toilet-table, save for a few brief hours. Thrice every day of the year did he dress, and three hours were the average of his every toilet, and other hours were spent in council with the cutter of his coats or with the custodian of his wardrobe. A single, devoted life! To White's, to routs, to races, he went, it is true, not reluctantly. He was known to have played battledore and shuttlecock in a moonlit garden with Mr Previté and some other gentlemen. His elopement with a young Countess from a ball at Lady Jersey's was quite notorious. It was even whispered that he once, in the company of some friends, made as though he would wrench the knocker off the door of some shop. But these things he did, not, most certainly, for any exuberant love of life. Rather did he regard them as healthful exercise of the body and a charm against that dreaded corpulency which, in the end, caused his downfall. Some recreation from his work even the most strenuous artist must have; and Mr Brummell naturally sought his in that exalted sphere whose modish elegance accorded best with his temperament, the sphere of *le plus beau monde*. General Bucknall used to growl, from the window of the Guards' Club, that such a fellow was only fit to associate with tailors. But that was an old soldier's fallacy. The proper associates of an artist are they who practise his own art rather than they who—however honourably—do but cater for its practice. For the rest, I am sure that Mr Brummell was no lackey, as they have suggested. He wished merely to be seen by those who were best qualified to appreciate the splendour of his achievements. Shall not the painter show his work in galleries, the poet flit down Paternoster Row? Of rank, for its own sake, Mr Brummell had no love. He patronised all his patrons. Even to the Regent his attitude was always that of a master in an art to one who is sincerely willing and anxious to learn from him.

Indeed, English society is always ruled by a dandy, and the more absolutely ruled the greater that dandy be. For dandyism, the perfect flower of outward elegance, is the ideal it is always striving to realise in its own rather incoherent way. But there is no reason why dandyism should be confused, as it has been by nearly all writers, with mere social life. Its contact with social life is, indeed, but one of the accidents of an art. Its influence, like the scent of a flower, is diffused unconsciously. It has its own aims and laws, and knows none other. And the only person who ever fully acknowledged this truth in aesthetics is, of all persons most unlikely, the author of *Sartor Resartus*. That anyone who dressed so very badly as did Thomas Carlyle should have tried to construct a philosophy of clothes has always seemed to me one of the most pathetic things in literature. He in the Temple of Vestments! Why sought he to intrude, another Clodius, upon those mysteries and light his pipe from those ardent censers? What were his hobnails that they should mar the pavement of that delicate Temple? Yet, for that he betrayed one secret rightly heard there, will I pardon his sacrilege. 'A dandy', he cried through the mask of Teufelsdröck, 'is a clothes-wearing man, a man whose trade, office, and existence consists in the wearing of clothes. Every faculty of his soul, spirit, purse, and per-

son is heroically consecrated to this one object, the wearing of clothes wisely and well.' Those are true words. They
are, perhaps, the only true words in *Sartor Resartus*. And
I speak with some authority. For I found the key to that
empty book, long ago, in the lock of the author's empty
wardrobe. His hat, that is still preserved in Chelsea,
formed an important clue.

But (behold!) as we repeat the true words of Teufelsdröck, there comes Monsieur Barbey D'Aurevilly, that
gentle *moqueur*, drawling, with a wave of his hand, '*Les
esprits qui ne voient pas les choses que par leur plus petit
côté, ont imaginé que le Dandysme était surtout l'art de
la mise, une heureuse et audacieuse dictature en fait de
toilette et d'élégance extérieure. Très-certainement c'est
cela aussi, mois c'est bien davantage. Le Dandysme est
toute une manière d'être et l'on n'est pas que par le côté
matériellement visible. C'est une manière d'être entièrement composée de nuances, comme il arrive toujours dans
les sociétés très-vieilles et très-civilisées.*' It is a pleasure
to argue with so suave a subtlist, and we say to him that
this comprehensive definition does not please us. We say
we think he errs.

Not that Monsieur's analysis of the dandiacal mind is
worthless by any means. Nor, when he declares that
George Brummell was the supreme king of the dandies and
fut le dandysme même, can I but piously lay one hand
upon the rim of my hat, the other upon my heart. But it
is as an artist, and for his supremacy in the art of costume,
and for all he did to gain the recognition of costume as in
itself an art, and for that superb taste and subtle simplicity
of mode whereby he was able to expel, at length, the
Byzantine spirit of exuberance which had possessed St
James's and wherefore he is justly called the Father of
Modern Costume, that I do most deeply revere him. It is
not a little strange that Monsieur D'Aurevilly, the biographer who, in many ways, does seem most perfectly to
have understood Mr Brummell, should belittle to a mere
phase that which was indeed the very core of his existence.

To analyse the temperament of a great artist and then to
declare that his art was but a part—a little part—of his
temperament, is a foolish proceeding. It is as though a man
should say that he finds, on analysis, that gunpowder is
composed of potassium chloride (let me say), nitrate and
power of explosion. Dandyism is ever the outcome of a
carefully cultivated temperament, not part of the temperament itself. That *manière d'être, entièrement composée de
nuances,* was not more, as the writer seems to have supposed, than attributory to Mr Brummell's art. Nor is it
even peculiar to dandies. All delicate spirits, to whatever
art they turn, even if they turn to no art, assume an oblique
attitude towards life. Of all dandies, Mr Brummell did
most steadfastly maintain this attitude. Like the single-
minded artist that he was, he turned full and square towards his art and looked life straight in the face out of the
corners of his eyes.

It is not hard to see how, in the effort to give Mr Brummell his due place in history, Monsieur D'Aurevilly came
to grief. It is but strange that he should have fallen into a
rather obvious trap. Surely he should have perceived that,
so long as Civilisation compels her children to wear clothes,
the thoughtless multitude will never acknowledge dandyism to be an art. If considerations of modesty or hygiene
compelled every one to stain canvas or chip marble every
morning, painting and sculpture would in like manner be
despised. Now, as these considerations do compel every
one to envelop himself in things made of cloth and linen,
this common duty is confounded with that fair procedure,
elaborate of many thoughts, in whose accord the fop ac-
complishes his toilet, each morning afresh, Aurora speeding on to gild his mirror. Not until nudity be popular will
the art of costume be really acknowledged. Nor even then
will it be approved. Communities are ever jealous (quite
naturally) of the artist who works for his own pleasure,
not for theirs—more jealous by far of him whose energy
is spent only upon the glorification of himself alone.
Carlyle speaks of dandyism as a survival of 'the primeval

superstition, self-worship'. '*La vanité,*' are almost the first words of Monsieur D'Aurevilly, '*c'est un sentiment contre lequel tout le monde est impitoyable.*' Few remember that the dandy's vanity is far different from the crude conceit of the merely handsome man. Dandyism is, after all, one of the decorative arts. A fine ground to work upon is its first postulate. And the dandy cares for his physical endowments only in so far as they are susceptible of fine results. They are just so much to him as to the decorative artist is inilluminate parchment, the form of a white vase or the surface of a wall where frescoes shall be.

Consider the words of Count D'Orsay, spoken on the eve of some duel, 'We are not fairly matched. If I were to wound him in the face it would not matter; but if he were to wound me, *ce serait vraiment dommage!*' There we have a pure example of a dandy's peculiar vanity—'It would be a real pity!' They say that D'Orsay killed his man—no matter whom—in this duel. He never should have gone out. Beau Brummell never risked his dandyhood in these mean encounters. But D'Orsay was a wayward, excessive creature, too fond of life and other follies to achieve real greatness. The power of his predecessor, the Father of Modern Costume, is over us yet. All that is left of D'Orsay's art is a waistcoat and a handful of rings— vain relics of no more value for us than the fiddle of Paganini or the mask of Menischus! I think that in Carolo's painting of him, we can see the strength, that was the weakness, of *le jeune Cupidon*. His fingers are closed upon his cane as upon a sword. There is mockery in the in-constant eyes. And the lips, so used to close upon the wine-cup, in laughter so often parted, they do not seem im-mobile, even now. Sad that one so prodigally endowed as he was, with the three essentials of a dandy—physical dis-tinction, a sense of beauty and wealth or, if you prefer the term, credit—should not have done greater things. Much of his costume was merely showy or eccentric, without the rotund unity of the perfect fop's. It had been well had he lacked that dash and spontaneous gallantry that make him cut, it may be, a more attractive figure than Beau Brummell. The youth of St James's gave him a wonderful welcome. The flight of Mr Brummell had left them as sheep without a shepherd. They had even cried out against the inscrutable decrees of fashion and curtailed the height of their stocks. And (lo!) here, ambling down the Mall with tasselled cane, laughing in the window at White's or in Fop's Alley posturing, here, with the devil in his eyes and all the graces at his elbow, was D'Orsay, the prince paramount who should dominate London and should guard life from monotony by the daring of his whims. He accepted so many engagements that he often dressed very quickly both in the morning and at nightfall. His brilliant genius would sometimes enable him to appear faultless, but at other times not even his fine figure could quite dispel the shadow of a toilet too hastily conceived. Before long he took that fatal step, his marriage with Lady Harriet Gardner. The marriage, as we all know, was not a happy one, though the wedding was very pretty. It ruined the life of Lady Harriet and of her mother, the Blessington. It won the poor Count further still further from his art and sent him spinning here, there, and everywhere. He was continually at Clevedon, or Belvoir, or Welbeck, laughing gaily as he brought down our English partridges, or at Crockford's, smiling as he swept up our English guineas from the board. Holker declares that, excepting Mr Turner, he was the finest equestrian in London and describes how the mob would gather every morning round his door to see him descend, insolent from his toilet, and mount and ride away. Indeed, he surpassed us all in all the exercises of the body. He even essayed pre-eminence in the arts (as if his own art were insufficient to his vitality!) and was for ever penning impetuous verses for circulation among his friends. There was no great harm in this, perhaps. Even the handwriting of Mr Brummell was not unknown in the albums. But D'Orsay's painting of portraits is inexcusable. The æsthetic vision of a dandy should be bounded by his own mirror. A few crayon

sketches of himself—*dilectissimæ imagines*—are as much
as he should ever do. That D'Orsay's portraits, even his
much-approved portrait of the Duke of Wellington, are
quite amateurish, is no excuse. It is the process of painting
which is repellent; to force from little tubes of lead a
glutinous flamboyance and to defile, with the hair of a
camel therein steeped, taut canvas, is hardly the diversion
for a gentleman; and to have done all this for a man who
was admittedly a field-marshal . . .

I have often thought that this selfish concentration,
which is a part of dandyism, is also a symbol of that
Einsamkeit felt in greater or less degree by the practitioners
of every art. But, curiously enough, the very unity of his
mind with the ground he works on exposes the dandy to
the influence of the world. In one way dandyism is the
least selfish of all the arts. Musicians are seen and, except
for a price, not heard. Only for a price may you read what
poets have written. All painters are not so generous as
Mr Watts. But the dandy presents himself to the nation
whenever he sallies from his front door. Princes and
peasants alike may gaze upon his masterpieces. Now, any
art which is pursued directly under the eye of the public
is always far more amenable to fashion than is an art with
which the public is but vicariously concerned. Those stan-
dards to which artists have gradually accustomed it the
public will not see lightly set at naught. Very rigid, for
example, are the traditions of the theatre. If my brother
were to declaim his lines at the Haymarket in the floro-
tund manner of Macready, what a row there would be in
the gallery! It is only by the impalpable process of evolution that change comes to the theatre. Likewise in the
sphere of costume no swift rebellion can succeed, as was
exemplified by the Prince's effort to revive knee breeches.
Had his Royal Highness elected, in his wisdom, to wear
tight trousers strapped under his boots, 'smalls' might, in
their turn, have reappeared, and at length—who knows?
knee-breeches. It is only by the trifling addition or elimina-
tion, modification or extension, made by this or that dandy

and copied by the rest, that the mode proceeds. The young dandy will find certain laws to which he must conform. If he outrage them he will be hooted by the urchins of the street, not unjustly, for he will have outraged the slowly constructed laws of artists who have preceded him. Let him reflect that fashion is no bondage imposed by alien hands, but the last wisdom of his own kind, and that true dandyism is the result of an artistic temperament working upon a fine body within the wide limits of fashion. Through this habit of conformity, which it inculcates, the army has given us nearly all our finest dandies, from Alcibiades to Colonel Br★b★z★n *de nos jours*. Even Mr Brummell, though he defied his Colonel, must have owed some of his success to the military spirit. Any parent intending his son to be a dandy will do well to send him first into the army, there to learn humility, as did his archetype, Apollo, in the house of Admetus. A sojourn at one of the Public Schools is also to be commended. The University it were well to avoid.

Of course, the dandy, like any other artist, has moments when his own period, palling, inclines him to antique modes. A fellow-student once told me that, after a long vacation spent in touch with modern life, he had hammered at the little gate of Merton and felt of a sudden his hat assume plumes and an expansive curl, the impress of a ruff about his neck, the dangle of a cloak and a sword. I, too, have my Elizabethan, my Caroline moments. I have gone to bed Georgian and awoken Early Victorian. Even savagery has charmed me. And at such times I have often wished I could find in my wardrobe suitable costumes. But these modish regrets are sterile, after all, and comprimend. What boots it to defy the conventions of our time? The dandy is the 'child of his age', and his best work must be produced in accord with the age's natural influence. The true dandy must always love contemporary costume. In this age, as in all precedent ages, it is only the tasteless who cavil, being impotent to win from it fair results. How futile their voices are! The costume of the nineteenth century, as shadowed for us first by Mr Brummell, so quiet, so reasonable, and, I say emphatically, so beautiful; free from folly or affectation, yet susceptible to exquisite ordering; plastic, austere, economical, may not be ignored. I spoke of the doom of swift rebellions, but I doubt even if any soever gradual evolution will lead us astray from the general precepts of Mr Brummell's code. At every step in the progress of democracy those precepts will be strengthened. Every day their fashion is more secure, corroborate. They are acknowledged by the world. The barbarous costumes that in bygone days were designed by class-hatred, or hatred of race, are dying, very surely dying. The costermonger with his pearl-emblazoned coat has been driven even from that Variety Stage, whereon he sought a desperate sanctuary. The clinquant corslet of the Swiss girl just survives at *bals costumés*. I am told that the kilt is now confined entirely to certain of the soldiery and to a small cult of Scotch Archaïcists. I have seen men flock from the boulevards of one capital and from the avenues of another to be clad in Conduit Street. Even into Oxford, that curious little city, where nothing is ever born nor anything ever quite dies, the force of the movement has penetrated, insomuch that tasselled cap and gown of degree are rarely seen in the streets or colleges. In a place which was until recent times scarcely less remote, Japan, the white and scarlet gardens are trod by men who are shod in boots like our own, who walk—rather strangely still—in close-cut cloth of little colour, and stop each other from time to time, laughing to show how that they too can furl an umbrella after the manner of real Europeans.

It is very nice, this universal acquiescence in the dress we have designed, but, if we reflect, not wonderful. There are three apparent reasons, and one of them is æsthetic. So to clothe the body that its fineness be revealed and its meanness veiled has been the æsthetic aim of all costume, but before our time the mean had never been struck. The ancient Romans went too far. Muffled in the ponderous folds of a toga, Adonis might pass for Punchinello, Punchinello for Adonis. The ancient Britons, on the other hand, did not go far enough. And so it had been in all ages down to that bright morning when Mr Brummell, at his mirror, conceived the notion of trousers and simple coats. Clad according to his convention, the limbs of the weakling escape contempt, and the athlete is unobtrusive, and all is well. But there is also a social reason for the triumph of our costume—the reason of economy. That austerity, which has rejected from its toilet silk and velvet and all but a few jewels, has made more ample the wardrobes of Dives, and sent forth Irus nicely dressed among his fellows. And lastly there is a reason of psychology, most potent of all perhaps. Is not the costume of to-day, with its subtlety and sombre restraint, its quiet congruities of black and white and grey, supremely apt a medium for the expression of modern emotion and modern thought? That aptness, even alone, would explain its triumph. Let us be glad that we have so easy, yet so delicate, a mode of expression.

Yes! costume, dandiacal or not, is in the highest degree expressive, nor is there any type it may not express. It enables us to classify any 'professional man' at a glance, be he lawyer, leech or what not. Still more swift and obvious is its revelation of the work and the soul of those who dress, whether naturally or for effect, without reference to convention. The bowler of Mr Jerome K. Jerome is a perfect preface to all his works. The silk hat of Mr Whistler is a real *nocturne*, his linen a symphony *en blanc majeur*. To have seen Mr Hall Caine is to have read his soul. His flowing, formless cloak is as one of his own novels, twenty-five editions latent in the folds of it. Melodrama crouches upon the brim of his *sombrero*. His tie is a Publisher's Announcement. His boots are Copyright. In his hand he holds the staff of *The Family Herald.*

But the dandy, innowise violating the laws of fashion, can make more subtle symbols of his personality. More subtle these symbols are for the very reason that they are effected within the restrictions which are essential to an art. Chastened of all flamboyance, they are from most men occult, obvious, it may be, only to other artists or even only to him they symbolise. Nor will the dandy express merely a crude idea of his personality, as does, for example, Mr Hall Caine, dressing himself always and exactly after one pattern. Every day as his mood has changed since his last toilet, he will vary the colour, texture, form of his costume. Fashion does not rob him of free will. It leaves him liberty of all expression. Every day there is not one accessory, from the butterfly that alights above his shirt-front to the jewels planted in his linen, that will not symbolise the mood that is in him or the occasion of the coming day.

On this, the psychological side of foppery, I know not one so expert as him whom, not greatly caring for contemporary names, I will call Mr Le V. No hero-worshipper am I, but I cannot write without enthusiasm of his simple life. He has not spurred his mind to the quest of shadows nor vexed his soul in the worship of any gods. No woman has wounded his heart, though he has gazed gallantly into the eyes of many women, intent, I fancy, upon his own miniature there. Nor is the incomparable set of his trousers spoilt by the perching of any dear little child upon his knee. And so, now that he is stricken with seventy years, he knows none of the bitterness of eld, for his toilet-table is an imperishable altar, his wardrobe a quiet nursery and very constant harem. Mr Le V. has many disciples, young men who look to him for guidance in all that concerns costume, and each morning come, themselves tentatively clad, to watch the perfect procedure of his toilet and learn invaluable lessons. I myself, a lie-a-bed, often steal out, forgoing the best hours of the day abed, that I may attend that *levée*. The rooms of the Master are in St James's Street, and perhaps it were well that I should give some little record of them and of the manner of their use. In the first room the Master sleeps. He is called by one of his valets, at seven o'clock,

to the second room, where he bathes, is shampooed, is
manicured and, at length, is enveloped in a dressing-gown
of white wool. In the third room is his breakfast upon a
little table and his letters and some newspapers. Leisurely
he sips his chocolate, leisurely learns all that need be
known. With a cigarette he allows his temper, as informed by the news and the weather and what not, to
develop itself for the day. At length, his mood suggests,
imperceptibly, what colour, what form of clothes he shall
wear. He rings for his valet—'I will wear such and such
a coat, such and such a tie; my trousers shall be of this or
that tone; this or that jewel shall be radiant in the folds
of my tie.' It is generally near noon that he reaches the
fourth room, the dressing-room. The uninitiate can hardly
realise how impressive is the ceremonial there enacted. As
I write, I can see, in memory, the whole scene—the
room, severely simple, with its lemon walls and deep
wardrobes of white wood, the young fops, φιλομαθέστατοι
τινες τῶν νεανίσχων, ranged upon a long bench, rapt
in wonder, and, in the middle, now sitting, now standing, negligently, before a long mirror, with a valet at either
elbow, Mr Le V., our cynosure. There is no haste, no
faltering when once the scheme of the day's toilet has
been set. It is a calm toilet. A flower does not grow more
calmly.

Any of us, any day, may see the gracious figure of Mr
Le V., as he saunters down the slope of St James's. Long
may the sun irradiate the surface of his tilted hat! It is
comfortable to know that, though he die to-morrow, the
world will not lack a most elaborate record of his foppery.
All his life he has kept or, rather, the current valets have
kept for him, a *Journal de Toilette*. Of this there are now
fifty volumes, each covering the space of a year. Yes, fifty
springs have filled his button-hole with their violets; the
snow of fifty winters has been less white than his linen;
his boots have outshone fifty sequences of summer suns,
and the colours of all those autumns have faded in the
dry light of his apparel. The first page of each volume of

the *Journal de Toilette* bears the signature of Mr Le V. and of his two valets. Of the other pages each is given up, as in other diaries, to one day of the year. In ruled spaces are recorded there the cut and texture of the suit, the colour of the tie, the form of jewellery that was worn on the day the page records. No detail is omitted and a separate space is set aside for 'Remarks'. I remember that I once asked Mr Le V., half in jest, what he should wear on the Judgment Day. Seriously, and (I fancied) with a note of pathos in his voice, he said to me, 'Young man, you ask me to lay bare my soul to you. If I had been a saint I should certainly wear a light suit, with a white waistcoat and a flower, but I am no saint, sir, no saint. ... I shall probably wear black trousers or trousers of some very dark blue, and a frock-coat, tightly buttoned.' Poor old Mr Le V.! I think he need not fear. If there be a heaven for the soul, there must be other heavens also, where the intellect and the body shall be consummate. In both these heavens Mr Le V. will have his hierarchy. Of a life like his there can be no conclusion, really. Did not even Matthew Arnold admit that conduct of a cane is three-fourths of life?

Certainly Mr Le V. is a great artist, and his supremacy is in the tact with which he suits his toilet to his temperament. But the marvellous affinity of a dandy's mood to his daily toilet is not merely that it finds therein its perfect echo nor that it may even be, in reflex, thereby accentuated or made less poignant. For some years I had felt convinced that in a perfect dandy this affinity must reach a point, when the costume itself, planned with the finest sensibility, would change with the emotional changes of its wearer, automatically. But I felt that here was one of those boundaries, where the fields of art align with the fields of science, and I hardly dared to venture further. Moreover, the theory was not easy to verify. I knew that, except in some great emotional crisis, the costume could not palpably change its aspect. Here was an *impasse*; for the perfect dandy—the Brummell, the Mr Le V.—cannot afford to indulge in any great emotion outside his art; like Balzac, he has not time. The gods were good to me, however. One morning near the end of last July, they decreed that I should pass through Half Moon Street and meet there a friend who should ask me to go with him to his club and watch for the results of the racing at Goodwood. This club includes hardly any member who is not a devotee of the Turf, so that, when we entered it, the cloak-room displayed long rows of unburdened pegs—save where one hat shone. None but that illustrious dandy, Lord X., wears quite so broad a brim as this hat had. I said that Lord X. must be in the club.

'I conceive he is too nervous to be on the course,' my friend replied. 'They say he has plunged up to the hilt on to-day's running.'

His lordship was indeed there, fingering feverishly the sinuous ribands of the tape-machine. I sat at a little distance, watching him. Two results straggled forth within an hour, and, at the second of these, I saw with wonder Lord X.'s linen actually flush for a moment and then turn deadly pale. I looked again and saw that his boots had lost their lustre. Drawing nearer, I found that grey hairs had begun to show themselves in his raven coat. It was very painful and yet, to me, very gratifying. In the cloak-room, when I went for my own hat and cane, there was the hat with the broad brim, and (lo!) over its ironblue surface little furrows had been ploughed by Despair.

Rouen, 1896.

GOING BACK TO SCHOOL

THE OTHER EVENING, AT about seven o'clock, I was in a swift hansom. My hat was tilted at a gay angle, and, for all I was muffled closely, my gloves betokened a cere-

monious attire. I was smoking *la cigarette d'appetit*, and
was quite happy. Outside Victoria my cab was stopped
by a file of other cabs, that were following one another
in at the main entrance of the station. I noticed, on one
of them, a small hat-box, a newish trunk and a corded
playbox, and I caught one glimpse of a very small, pale
boy in a billicock-hat. He was looking at me through the
side-window. If Envy was ever inscribed on any face, it
was inscribed on the face of that very small, pale boy.
'There,' I murmured, 'but for the grace of God, goes Max
Beerbohm!'

My first thought, then, was for myself. I could not but
plume me on the contrast of my own state with his. But,
gradually, I became fulfilled with a very great compassion
for him. I understood the boy's Envy so well. It was
always the most bitter thing, in my own drive to the
station, to see other people, quite happy, as it seemed,
with no upheaval of their lives; people in cabs, who were
going out to dinner and would sleep in London; grown-
up people! Than the impotent despair of those drives—I
had exactly fifteen of them—I hope that I shall never
experience a more awful emotion. Those drives have
something, surely, akin with drowning. In their course the
whole of a boy's home-life passes before his eyes, every
phase of it standing out against the black curtain of his
future. The author of *Vice-Versa* has well analysed the
feeling, and he is right, I think, in saying that all boys, of
whatsoever temperament, are preys to it. Well do I
remember how, on the last day of the holidays, I used
always to rise early, and think that I had got twelve more
whole hours of happiness, and how those hours used to
pass me with mercifully slow feet. . . . Three more hours!
. . . Sixty more minutes! . . . Five! . . . I used to draw upon
my tips for a first-class ticket, that I might not be plunged
suddenly among my companions, with their hectic and
hollow mirth, their dreary disinterment of last term's
jokes. I used to revel in the thought that there were many
stations before G——. . . . The dreary walk, with my small

bag, up the hill! I was not one of those who made a rush for the few cabs. . . . The awful geniality of the House Master! The jugs in the dormitory! . . . Next morning, the bell that woke me! The awakening!

Not that I had any special reason for hating school! Strange as it may seem to my readers, I was not unpopular there. I was a modest, good-humoured boy. It is Oxford that has made me insufferable. At school, my character remained in a state of undevelopment. I had a few misgivings, perhaps. In some respects, I was always too young, in others, too old, for a perfect relish of the convention. As I hovered, in grey knickerbockers, on a cold and muddy field, round the outskirts of a crowd that was tearing itself limb from limb for the sake of a leathern bladder, I would often wish for a nice, warm room and a good game of hunt-the-slipper. And, when we sallied forth, after dark, in the frost, to the swimming-bath, my heart would steal back to the fireside in Writing School and the plot of Miss Braddon's latest novel. Often, since, have I wondered whether a Spartan system be really well for youths who are bound mostly for Capuan Universities. It is true, certainly, that this system makes Oxford or Cambridge doubly delectable. Undergraduates owe their happiness chiefly to the consciousness that they are no longer at school. The nonsense which was knocked out of them at school is all put gently back at Oxford or Cambridge. And the discipline to which they are subject is so slight that it does but serve to accentuate their real freedom. The sudden reaction is rather dangerous, I think, to many of them.

Even now, much of my own complacency comes of having left school. Such an apparition as that boy in the hansom makes me realise my state more absolutely. Why, after all, should I lavish my pity on him and his sorrows? *Dabit deus his quoque finem.* I am at a happier point in Nature's cycle. That is all. I have suffered every one of his ordeals, and I do not hesitate to assure him, if he chance to see this essay of mine, how glad I am that I do not happen to be his contemporary. I have no construe of Xenophon to prepare for to-morrow morning, nor any ode of Horace to learn, painfully, by heart. I assure him that I have no wish nor any need to master, as he has, at this moment, the intricate absurdities of that proposition in the second book of Euclid. I have no locker, with my surname printed on it and a complement of tattered school-books. I burnt all my school-books when I went up to Oxford. Were I to meet, now, any of those masters who are monsters to you, my boy, he would treat me even more urbanely, it may be, than I should treat him. When he sets you a hundred lines, you write them without pleasure, and he tears them up. When I, with considerable enjoyment and at my own leisure, write a hundred lines or so, they are printed for all the world to admire, and I am paid for them enough to keep you in pocket-money for many terms. I write at a comfortable table, by a warm fire, and occupy an arm-chair, whilst you are sitting on a narrow form. My boots are not made 'for school-wear', nor do they ever, like yours, get lost in a litter of other boots in a cold boot-room. In a word, I enjoy myself immensely. To-night, I am going to a theatre. Afterwards, I shall sup somewhere and drink wine. When I come home and go to bed, I shall read myself to sleep with some amusing book. . . . You will have torn yourself from your bed, at the sound of a harsh bell, have washed, quickly, in very cold water, have scurried off to Chapel, gone to first school and been sent down several places in your form, tried to master your next construe, in the interval of snatching a tepid breakfast, been kicked by a bigger boy, and had a mint of horrible experiences, long before I, your elder by a few years, have awakened, very gradually, to the tap of knuckles on the panel of my bedroom-door. I shall make a leisurely toilet. I shall descend to a warm breakfast, open one of the little budgets which my 'damned good-natured friend', Romeika, is always sending me, and glance at that morning paper which appeals most surely to my sense of humour. And when I have eaten well of all the dishes on the table, I shall light a cigarette. Through the haze of its fragrant smoke, I shall think of the happy day that is before me.

Essays from
YET AGAIN

The Humour of the Public
[1923]

The Naming of Streets
[1923]

'*The Ragged Regiment*'
[1923]

THE HUMOUR
OF THE PUBLIC

THEY OFTEN TELL ME that So-and-so has no sense of humour. Lack of this sense is everywhere held to be a horrid disgrace, nullifying any number of delightful qualities. Perhaps the most effective means of disparaging an enemy is to lay stress on his integrity, his erudition, his courage, the fineness of his head, the grace of his figure, his strength of purpose, which has overleaped all obstacles, his goodness to his parents, the kind word that he has for every one, his musical voice, his freedom from aught that in human nature is base; and then to say what a pity it is that he has no sense of humour. Perfection is not loved in this imperfect world; so that the more highly you extol any one, the more eagerly will your audience accept anything you may have to say against him. And what could match for deadliness the imputation of being without sense of humour? To convict a man of that lack is to strike him with one blow to a level with the beasts of the field—to kick him, once and for all, outside the human pale. What is it that mainly distinguishes us from the brute creation? That we walk erect? Some brutes are bipeds. That we do not slay one another? We do. That we build houses? So do they. That we remember and reason? So, again, do they. That we converse? They are chatterboxes, whose lingo we are not sharp enough to master. On no possible point of superiority can we preen ourselves, save this: that we can laugh, and that they, with one notable exception, cannot.

Belief in the general humorousness of the human race is the more deep-rooted for that every man is certain that he himself is not without sense of humour. A man will admit cheerfully that he does not know one tune from another, or that he cannot discriminate the vintages of wines. The blind beggar does not seek to benumb sympathy by telling his patrons how well they are looking. The deaf and dumb do not scruple to converse in signals. 'Have you no sense of beauty?' I said to a friend who in the Accademia of Florence suggested that we had stood long enough in front of the 'Primavera'. 'No!' was his simple, straightforward, quite unanswerable answer. But I have never heard a man assert that he had no sense of humour. And I take it that no such assertion ever was made. Moreover, were it made, it would be a lie. Every man laughs. Frequently or infrequently, the corners of his mouth are drawn up into his cheeks, and through his parted lips comes his own particular variety, soft or loud, of that noise which is called laughter. Frequently or infrequently, every man is amused by something. Every man has a sense of humour, but not every man the same sense. A may be incapable of smiling at what has convulsed B, and B may stare blankly when he hears what has rolled A off his chair. Jokes are so diverse that no one man can see them all. The very fact that he can see one kind is proof positive that certain other kinds will be invisible to him. And so egoistic in his judgment is the average man that he is apt to suspect of being humourless any one whose sense of humour squares not with his own. But the suspicion is always false, incomparably useful though it is in the form of an accusation.

Having no love for the public, I have often accused that body of having no sense of humour. Conscience pricks me to atonement. Let me withdraw my oft-made imputation, and show its hollowness by examining with you, reader (who are, of course, no more a member of the public than I am), what are the main features of that sense of humour which the public does undoubtedly possess.

The word 'public' must, like all collective words, be used with caution. When we speak of our hair, we should remember not only that the hairs on our heads are all numbered, but also that there is a *catalogue raisonné* in which every one of those hairs is shown to be in some respect unique. Similarly, let us not forget that 'public' denotes a collection not of identical units, but of units separable and (under close scrutiny) distinguishable one from another. I have said that not every man has the same sense of humour. I might have said truly that no two men have the same sense of humour, for that no two men have the same brain and heart and experience, by which things the sense of humour is formed and directed. One joke may go round the world tickling myriads but no two persons will be tickled in precisely the same way, to precisely the same degree. If the vibrations of inward or outward laughter could be (as some day, perhaps, they will be) scientifically registered, differences between them all would be made apparent to us. 'Oh,' is your cry, whenever you hear something that especially amuses you. 'I must tell that to' whomever you credit with a sense of humour most akin to your own. And the chances are that you will be disappointed by his reception of the joke. Either he will laugh less loudly than you hoped, or he will say something which reveals to you that it amuses him and you not in quite the same way. Or perhaps he will laugh so long and loudly that you are irritated by the suspicion that you have not yourself gauged the full beauty of it. In one of his books (I do not remember which, though they, too, I suppose, are all numbered) Mr Andrew Lang tells a story that has always delighted and always will delight me. He was in a railway-carriage, and his travelling-companions were two strangers, two silent ladies, middle-aged. The train stopped at Nuneaton. The two ladies exchanged a glance. One of them sighed, and said, 'Poor Eliza! She had reason to remember Nuneaton!' ... That is all. But how much! how deliciously and memorably much! How infinite a span of conjecture is in those dots which I have just made! And yet, would you believe me? Some of my most intimate friends, the people most like to myself, see little or nothing of the loveliness of that pearl of price. Perhaps you *would* believe me. That is the worst of it: one never knows. The most sensitive intelligence cannot predict how will be appraised its any treasure by its how near soever kin.

This sentence, which I admit to be somewhat mannered, has the merit of bringing me straight to the point at which I have been aiming; that, though the public is composed of distinct units, it may roughly be regarded as a single entity. Precisely because you and I have sensitive intelligences, we cannot postulate certainly anything about each other. The higher an animal be in grade, the more numerous and recondite are the points in which its organism differs from that of its peers. The lower the grade, the more numerous and obvious the points of likeness. By 'the public' I mean that vast number of human animals who are in the lowest grade of intelligence. (Of course, this classification is made without reference to social 'classes'. The public is recruited from the upper, the middle, and the lower class. That the recruits come mostly from the lower class is because the lower class is still the least well-educated. That they come in as high proportion from the middle class as from the less well-educated upper class, is because the 'young Barbarians', reared in a more gracious environment, often acquire a grace of mind which serves them as well as would mental keenness.) Whereas in the highest grade, to which you and I belong, the fact that a thing affects you in one way is no guarantee that it will not effect me in another, a thing which affects one man of the lowest grade in any particular way is likely to affect all the rest very similarly. The public's sense of humour may be regarded roughly as one collective sense.

It would be impossible for any one of *us* to define what are the things that amuse him. For him the wind of humour bloweth where it listeth. He finds his jokes in the unlikeliest places. Indeed, it is only there that he finds them at all. A thing that is labelled 'comic' chills his sense of humour instantly—perceptibly lengthens his face. A joke that has not a serious background, or some serious connexion, means nothing to him. Nothing to him, the crude jape of the professional jester. Nothing to him, the jangle of the bells in the wagged cap, the thud of the swung bladder. Nothing, the joke that hits him violently in the eye, or pricks him with a sharp point. The jokes that he loves are those quiet jokes which have no apparent point—the jokes which never can surrender their secret, and so can never pall. His humour is an indistinguishable part of his soul, and the things that stir it are indistinguishable from the world around him. But to the primitive and untutored public, humour is a harshly definite affair. The public can achieve no delicate process of discernment in humour. Unless a joke hits it in the eye, drawing forth a shower of illuminative sparks, all is darkness. Unless a joke be labelled 'Comic. Come! why don't you laugh?' the public is quite silent. Violence and obviousness are thus the essential factors. The surest way of making a thing obvious is to provide it in some special place, at some special time. It is thus that humour is provided for the public, and thus that it is easy for the student to lay his hand on materials for an analysis of the public's sense of humour. The obviously right plan for the student is to visit the music halls from time to time, and to buy the comic papers. Neither these halls nor these papers will amuse him directly through their art, but he will instruct himself better from them than from any other source, for they are the authentic sources of the public's laughter. Let him hasten to patronise them.

He will find that I have been there before him. The music halls I have known for many years. I mean, of course, the real old-fashioned music halls, not those depressing palaces where you see by grace of a biograph things that you have seen much better, and without a headache, in the street, and pitiable animals being forced to do things which Nature has forbidden them to do— things which we can do so very much better than they, without any trouble. Heaven defend me from those mean-

ingless palaces! But the little old music halls have always
attracted me by their unpretentious raciness, their quaint
monotony, the reality of the enjoyment on all those stolidly
rapt faces in the audience. Without that monotony there
would not be the same air of general enjoyment, the same
constant guffaws. That monotony is the secret of the success of music halls. It is not enough for the public to know
that everything is meant to be funny, that laughter is
craved for every point in every 'turn'. A new kind of
humour, however obvious and violent, might take the
public unawares, and be received in silence. The public
prefers always that the old well-tested and well-seasoned
jokes be cracked for it. Or rather, not the same old jokes,
but jokes on the same old subjects. The quality of the joke
is of slight import in comparison with its subject. It is the
matter, rather than the treatment, that counts, in the art
of the music hall. Some subjects have come to be recognised as funny. Two or three of them crop up in every
song, and before the close of the evening all of them
will have cropped up many times. I speak with authority,
as an earnest student of the music halls. Of comic papers
I know less. They have never allured me. They are not set
to music—an art for whose cheaper and more primitive
forms I have a very real sensibility; and I am not, as I
peruse one of them, privy to the public's delight: my copy
cannot be shared with me by hundreds of people whose
mirth is wonderful to see and hear. And the bare contents
are not such as to enchant me. However, for the purpose
of this essay, I did go to a bookstall and buy as many of
these papers as I could see—a terrific number, a terrific
burden to stagger away with.

I have gone steadily through them, one by one. My
main impression is of wonder and horror at the amount
of hebdomadal labour implicit in them. Who writes for
them? Who does the drawings for them—those thousands
of little drawings, week by week, so neatly executed? To
think that daily and nightly, in so many an English home,
in a room sacred to the artist, sits a young man inventing

and executing designs for *Chippy Snips*! To think how many a proud mother must be boasting to her friends: 'Yes, Edward is doing wonderfully well—more than fulfilling the hopes we always had of him. Did I tell you that the editor of *Natty Tips* has written asking him to contribute to his paper? I believe I have the letter on me. Yes, here it is,' etc., etc.! The awful thing is that many of the drawings in these comic papers are done with very real skill. Nothing is sadder than to see the hand of an artist wasted by alliance to a vacant mind, a common spirit. I look through these drawings, conceived all so tritely and stupidly, so hopelessly and helplessly, yet executed—many of them—so very well indeed, and I sigh over the haphazard way in which mankind is made. However, my concern is not with the tragedy of these draughtsmen, but with the specific forms taken by their humour. Some of them deal in a broad spirit with the world-comedy, limiting themselves to no set of funny subjects, finding inspiration in the habits and manners of men and women at large. 'HE WON HER' is the title appended to a picture of a young lady and gentleman seated in a drawing-room, and the libretto runs thus: '*Mabel:* Last night I dreamt of a most beautiful woman. *Harold:* Rather a coincidence. I dreamt of you, too, last night.' I have selected this as a typical example of the larger style. This style, however, occupies but a small space in the bulk of the papers that lie before me. As in the music halls so in these papers, the entertainment consists almost entirely of variations on certain ever-recurring themes. I have been at pains to draw up a list of these themes. I think it is exhaustive. If any fellow-student detect an omission, let him communicate with me. Meanwhile, here is my list:

Mothers-in-law
Hen-pecked husbands
Twins
Old maids
Jews

Frenchmen, Germans, Italians, Negroes (not Russians, or other foreigners of any denomination)
Fatness
Thinness
Long hair (worn by a man)
Baldness
Sea-sickness
Stuttering
Bad cheese
'Shooting the moon' (slang expression for leaving a lodging house without paying the bill).

You might argue that one week's budget of comic papers is no real criterion—that the recurrence of these themes may be fortuitous. My answer to that objection is that this list coincides exactly with a list which (before studying these papers) I had made of the themes commonest, during the past few years, in the music halls. This twin list, which results from separate study of the two chief forms of public entertainment, may be taken as a sure guide to the goal of our inquiry.

Let us try to find some unifying principle, or principles, among the variegated items. Take the first item—*Mothers-in-law*. Why should the public roar, as roar it does, at the mere mention of that relationship? There is nothing intrinsically absurd in the notion of a woman with a married daughter. It is probable that she will sympathise with her daughter in any quarrel that may arise between husband and wife. It is probable, also, that she will, as a mother, demand for her daughter more unselfish devotion than the daughter herself expects. But this does not make her ridiculous. The public laughs not at her, surely. It always respects a tyrant. It laughs at the implied concept of the oppressed son-in-law, who has to wage unequal warfare against two women. It is amused by the notion of his embarrassment. It is amused by suffering. This explanation covers, of course, the second item on my list—*Hen-pecked husbands*. It covers, also, the third and fourth items. The public is amused by the notion of a needy man put to double expense, and of a woman who has had no chance of fulfilling her destiny. The laughter at Jews, too, may be a survival of the old Jew-baiting spirit. Or this laughter may be explained by that fact which alone can explain why the public laughs at *Frenchmen, Germans, Italians, Negroes*. Jews, after all, are foreigners, strangers, and the public has never got used to them. The only apparent reason why it laughs at the notion of *Frenchmen, etc.*, is that they are unlike itself. (At the mention of *Russians and other foreigners* it does not laugh, because it has no idea what they are like: it has seen too few samples of them.)

So far, then, we have found two elements in the public's humour: delight in suffering, contempt for the unfamiliar. The former motive is the more potent. It accounts for the popularity of all these other items: *extreme fatness, extreme thinness, baldness, sea-sickness, stuttering*, and (as entailing distress for the landlady) *'shooting the moon'*. The motive of contempt for the unfamiliar accounts for *long hair (worn by a man)*. Remains one item unexplained. How can mirth possibly be evoked by the notion of *bad cheese*? Having racked my brains for the solution, I can but conjecture that it must be the mere ugliness of the thing. Why any one should be amused by mere ugliness I cannot conceive. Delight in cruelty, contempt for the unfamiliar, I can understand, though I cannot admire them. They are invariable elements in children's sense of humour, and it is natural that the public, as being unsophisticated, should laugh as children laugh. But any nurse will tell you that children are frightened by ugliness. Why, then, is the public amused by it? I know not. The laughter at *bad cheese* I abandon as a mystery. I pitch it among such other insoluble problems, as *Why does the public laugh when an actor and actress in a quite serious play kiss each other? Why does it laugh when a meal is eaten on the stage? Why does it laugh when any actor has to say 'damn'?*

If they cannot be solved soon, such problems never will be solved. For Mr Forster's Act will soon have had time to make apparent its effects; and the public will proudly display a sense of humour as sophisticated as our own.

THE NAMING
OF STREETS

'THE REBUILDING OF LONDON' proceeds ruthlessly apace. The humble old houses that dare not scrape the sky are being duly punished for their timidity. Down they come; and in their place are shot up new tenements, quick and high as rockets. And the little old streets, so narrow and exclusive, so shy and crooked—we are making an example of them, too. We lose our way in them, do we? —we whose time is money. Our omnibuses can't trundle through them, can't they? Very well, then. Down with them! We have no use for them. This is the age of 'noble arteries'.

'The Rebuilding of London' is a source of much pride and pleasure to most of London's citizens, especially to them who are county councillors, builders, contractors, navvies, glaziers, decorators, and so forth. There is but a tiny residue of persons who do not swell and sparkle. And of these glum bystanders at the carnival I am one. Our aloofness is mainly irrational, I suppose. It is due mainly to temperamental Toryism. We say, 'The old is better'. This we say to ourselves, every one of us feeling himself thereby justified in his attitude. But we are quite aware that such a postulate would not be accepted by the majority. For the majority, then, let us make some show of ratiocination. Let us argue that, forasmuch as London is an historic city, with many phases and periods behind her, and forasmuch as many of these phases and periods are enshrined in the aspect of her buildings, the constant rasure of these buildings is a disservice to the historian not less than to the mere sentimentalist, and that it will moreover (this is a more telling argument) filch from Englishmen the pleasant power of crowing over Americans, and from Americans the unpleasant necessity of balancing their pity for our present with envy of our past. After all, our past is our trump card. Our present is merely a bad imitation of what the Americans can do much better.

Ignoring as mere scurrility this criticism of London's present, but touched by my appeal to his pride in its history, the average citizen will reply, reasonably enough, to this effect: 'By all means let us have architectural evidence of our epochs—Caroline, Georgian, Victorian, what you will. But why should the Edvardian be ruled out? London is packed full of architecture already. Only by rasing much of its present architecture can we find room for commemorating duly the glorious epoch which we have just entered.' To this reply there are two rejoinders: (1) let special suburbs be founded by Edvardian buildings; (2) there are no really Edvardian buildings, and there won't be any. Long before the close of the Victorian Era our architects had ceased to be creative. They could not express in their work the spirit of their time. They could but evolve a medley of old styles, some foreign, some native, all inappropriate. Take the case of Mayfair. Mayfair has for some years been in a state of transition. The old Mayfair, grim and sombre, with its air of selfish privacy and *hauteur* and leisure, its plain bricked façades, so disdainful of show—was it not redolent of the century in which it came to being? Its wide pavements and narrow roads between—could not one see in them the time when by day gentlemen and ladies went out afoot, needing no vehicle to whisk them to a destination, and walked to and fro amply, needing elbow-room for their dignity and their finery, and by night were borne in chairs, singly? And those queer little places of worship, those stucco chapels, with their very secular little columns, their ample pews, and their negligible altars over which one saw the Lion and the Unicorn fighting, as who should say, for the Cross—did they not breathe all the inimitable Erastianism of their period? *In qua te quœro proseucha*, my Lady Powderbox? Alas! every one of your tabernacles is dust now—dust turned to mud by the tears of the ghost of the Rev. Charles Honeyman, and by my own tears ... I have strayed again into sentiment. Back to the point—which is that the new houses and streets in May-fair mean nothing. Let me show you Mount Street. Let me show you that airy stretch of sham antiquity, and defy you to say that it symbolises, how remotely soever, the spirit of its time. Mount Street is typical of the new May-fair. And the new Mayfair is typical of the new London. In the height of these new houses, in the width of these new roads, future students will find, doubtless, something characteristic of this pressing and bustling age. But from the style of the houses they will learn nothing at all. The style might mean anything; and means, therefore, nothing. Original architecture is a lost art in England. The Edvardian Era cannot be commemorated in its architecture.

Erection of new buildings robs us of the past and gives us in exchange nothing of the present. Consequently, the excuse put by me into the gaping mouth of the average Londoner cannot be accepted. I had no idea that my case was such a good one. Having now vindicated on grounds of patriotic utility that which I took to be a mere sentimental prejudice, I may be pardoned for dragging 'beauty' into the question. The new buildings are not only uninteresting through lack of temporal and local significance: they are also hideous. With all his learned eclecticism, the new architect seems unable to evolve a fake that shall be pleasing to the eye. Not at all pleasing is a mad hotch-potch of early Victorian hospital, Jacobean manor-house, Venetian palace, and bridecake in Gunter's best manner. Yet that, apparently, is the modern English architect's pet ideal. Even when he confines himself to one manner, the result (even if it be in itself decent) is made horrible by vicinity to the work of a rival who has been dabbling in some other manner. Every street in London is being converted into a battlefield of styles, all shrieking at one another, all murdering one another. The tumult may be exciting, especially to the architects, but it is not beautiful. It is not good to live in.

However, I am no propagandist. I am not sanguine enough to suppose that I could do anything to stop either the adulteration or the demolition of old streets. I do not wish to infect the public with my own misgivings. On the contrary, my motive for this essay is to inoculate the public with my own placid indifference in a certain matter which seems always to cause them painful anxiety. Whenever a new highway is about to be opened, the newspapers are filled with letters suggesting that it ought to be called by this or that beautiful name, or by the name of this or that national hero. I will show that a name cannot (in the long run) make any shadow of difference in our sentiment for the street that bears it, and that our sentiment is solely according to the character of the street itself; and, further, that a street does nothing at all to keep green the memory of one whose name is given to it.

For a street one name is as good as another. To prove this proposition, let me proceed by analogy of the names borne by human beings. Surnames and Christian names may alike be divided into two classes: (1) those which, being identical with words in the dictionary, connote some definite thing; (2) those which, connoting nothing, may or may not suggest something by their sound. Instances of Christian names in the first class are *Rose, Faith*; of surnames, *Lavender, Badger*; of Christian names in the second class, *Celia, Mary*; of surnames, *Jones, Vavasour*. Let us consider the surnames in the first class. You will say, off-hand, that *Lavender* sounds pretty, and that *Badger* sounds ugly. Very well. Now, suppose that Christian names connoting unpleasant things were sometimes conferred at baptisms. Imagine two sisters named *Nettle* and *Envy*. Off-hand, you will say that these names sound ugly, whilst *Rose* and *Faith* sound pretty. Yet, believe me, there is not, in point of actual sound, one pin to choose either between *Badger* and *Lavender*, or between *Rose* and *Nettle*, or between *Faith* and *Envy*. There is no such thing as a singly euphonious or a singly cacophonous name. There is no word which, by itself, sounds ill or well. In combination, names or words may be made to sound ill or well. A sentence can be musical or unmusical. But in detachment words are no more preferable one to another in their sound than are single notes of music. What you take to be beauty or ugliness of sound is indeed nothing but beauty or ugliness of meaning. You are pleased by the sound of such words as *gondola, vestments, chancel, ermine, manor-house*. They seem to be fraught with a subtle onomatopœia, severally suggesting by their sounds the grace or sanctity or solid comfort of the things which they connote. You murmur them luxuriously, dreamily. Prepare for a slight shock. *Scrofula, investments, cancer, vermin, warehouse*. Horrible words, are they not? But say *gondola—scrofula, vestments—investments*, and so on; and then lay your hand on your heart, and declare that the words in the first list are in mere sound prettier than the words in the second. Of course they are not. If gondola were a disease, and if scrofula were a beautiful boat peculiar to a beautiful city, the effect of each word would be exactly the reverse of what it is. This rule may be applied to all the other words in the two lists. And these lists might, of course, be extended to infinity. The appropriately beautiful or ugly sound of any word is an illusion wrought on us by what the word connotes. *Beauty* sounds as ugly as *ugliness* sounds beautiful. Neither of them has by itself any quality in sound.

It follows, then, that the Christian names and surnames in my first class sound beautiful or ugly according to what they connote. The sound of those in the second class depends on the extent to which it *suggests* any

known word more than another. Of course, there might
be a name hideous in itself. There might, for example, be
a Mr Griggsbiggmiggs. But there is not. And the fact that
I, after prolonged study of a *Postal Directory*, have been
obliged to use my imagination as factory for a name that
connotes nothing and is ugly in itself may be taken as
proof that such names do not exist actually. You cannot
stump me by citing Mr Matthew Arnold's citation of the
words 'Ragg is in custody', and his comment that 'there
was no Ragg by the Ilyssus'. 'Ragg' has not an ugly sound
in itself. Mr Arnold was jarred merely by its suggestion
of something ugly, a *rag*, and by the cold brutality of the
police-court reporter in witholding the prefix 'Miss' from
a poor girl who had got into trouble. If 'Ragg' had been
brought to his notice as the name of some illustrious old
family, Mr Arnold would never have dragged in the
Ilyssus. The name would have had for him a savour of
quaint distinction. The suggestion of a *rag* would never
have struck him. For it is a fact that whatever thing may
be connoted or suggested by a name is utterly overshadowed by the name's bearer (unless, as in the case of
poor 'Ragg', there is seen to be some connexion between
the bearer and the thing implied by the name). Roughly,
it may be said that all names connote their bearers, and
them only.

To have a 'beautiful' name is no advantage. To have
an 'ugly' name is no drawback. I am aware that this is a
heresy. In a famous passage, Bulwer Lytton propounded
through one of his characters a theory that 'it is not only
the effect that the sound of a name has on others which
is to be thoughtfully considered; the effect that his name
produces on the man himself is perhaps still more important. Some names stimulate and encourage the owner,
others deject and paralyse him.' And Bulwer himself, I
doubt not, believed that there was something in this
theory. It is natural that a novelist should. He is always
at great pains to select for his every puppet a name that
suggests to himself the character which he has ordained

for that puppet. In real life a baby get its surname by blind heredity, its other names by the blind whim of its parents, who know not at all what sort of person it will eventually become. And yet, when these babies grow up, their names seem every whit as appropriate as do the names of the romantic puppets. 'Obviously', thinks the novelist, 'these human beings must "grow to" their names; or else, we must be viewing them in the light of their names'. And the quiet ordinary people, who do not write novels, incline to his conjecture. How else can they explain the fact that every name seems to fit its bearer so exactly, to sum him or her up in a flash?

The true explanation, missed by them, is that a name derives its whole quality from its bearer, even as does a word from its meaning. The late Sir Redvers Buller, ταυρηδὸν ὑποβλέψας, was thought to be peculiarly well fitted with his name. Yet had it belonged not to him, but to (say) some gentle and thoughtful ecclesiastic, it would have seemed quite as inevitable. 'Gore' is quite as taurine as 'Buller', and yet does it not seem to us the right name for the author of *Lux Mundi*? In connexion with him, who is struck by its taurinity? What hint of ovinity would there have been for us if Sir Redver's surname had happened to be that of him who wrote the *Essays of Elia*? Conversely, 'Charles Buller' seems to us now an impossible *nom de vie* for Elia; yet it would have done just as well, really. Even 'Redvers Buller' would have done just as well. 'Walter Pater' meant for us—how perfectly!—the author of *Marius the Epicurean*, whilst the author of *All Sorts and Conditions of Men* was summed up for us, not less absolutely, in 'Walter Besant'. And yet, if the surnames of these two opposite Walters had been changed at birth, what difference would have been made? 'Walter Besant' would have signified a prose style sensuous in its severity, an exquisitely patient scholarship, an exquisitely sympathetic way of criticism. 'Walter Pater' would have signified no style, but an unslakable thirst for information, and a bustling human sympathy, and power

of carrying things through. Or take two names often found
in conjunction—Johnson and Boswell. Had the dear great
oracle been named Boswell, and had his young friend
been named Johnson, would the two names seem to us less
appropriate than they do? Should we suffer any greater
loss than if Salmon were Gluckstein, and Gluckstein
Salmon? Finally, take a case in which the same name
was borne by two very different characters. What name
could seem more descriptive of a certain illustrious Arch-
bishop of Westminster than 'Manning'? It seems the very
epitome of saintly astuteness. But for 'Cardinal' substitute
'Mrs' as its prefix, and, presto! it is equally descriptive of
that dreadful medio-Victorian murderess who in the dock
of the Old Bailey wore a black satin gown, and thereby
created against black satin a prejudice which has but lately
died. In itself black satin is a beautiful thing. Yet for many
years, by force of association, it was accounted loathsome.
Conversely, one knows that many quite hideous fashions
in costume have been set by beautiful women. Such instances of the subtle power of association will make clear
to you how very easily a name (being neither beautiful nor
hideous in itself) can be made hideous or beautiful by its
bearer—how inevitably it becomes for us a symbol of its
bearer's most salient qualities or defects, be they physical,
moral, or intellectual.

Streets are not less characteristic than human beings.
'Look!' cried a friend of mine, whom lately I found
studying a map of London, 'isn't it appalling? All these
streets—thousands of them—in this tiny compass! Think
of the miles and miles of drab monotony this map contains!' I pointed out to him (it is a thinker's penalty to be
always pointing things out to people) that his words were
nonsense. I told him that the streets on this map were no
more monotonous than the rivers on the map of England.
Just as there were no two rivers alike, every one of them
having its own speed, its own windings, depths, and shal-
lows, its own way with the reeds and grasses, so had every
street its own claim to an especial nymph, forasmuch as no

two streets had exactly the same proportions, the same habitual traffic, the same type of shops or houses, the same inhabitants. In some cases, of course, the difference between the 'atmosphere' of two streets is a subtle difference. But it is always there, not less definite to any one who searches for it than the difference between (say) Hill Street and Pont Street, High Street Kensington and High Street Notting Hill, Fleet Street and the Strand. I have here purposely opposed to each other streets that have obvious points of likeness. But what a yawning gulf of difference is between each couple! Hill Street, with its staid distinction, and Pont Street, with its eager, pushful 'smartness', its *air de petit parvenu*, its obvious delight in having been 'taken up'; High Street, Notting Hill, down-at-heels and unashamed, with a placid smile on its broad ugly face, and High Street, Kensington, with its traces of former beauty, and its air of neatness and self-respect, as befits one who in her day has been caressed by royalty; Fleet Street, that seething channel of business, and the Strand, that swollen river of business, on whose surface float so many aimless and unsightly objects. In every one of these thoroughfares my mood and my manner are differently affected. In Hill Street, instinctively, I walk very slowly—sometimes, even with a slight limp, as one recovering from an accident in the hunting-field. I feel very well-bred there, and, though not clever, very proud, and quick to resent any familiarity from those whom elsewhere I should regard as my equals. In Pont Street my demeanour is not so calm and measured. I feel less sure of myself, and adopt a slight swagger. In High Street, Kensington, I find myself dapper and respectable, with a timid leaning to the fine arts. In High Street, Notting Hill, I become frankly common. Fleet Street fills me with a conviction that if I don't make haste I shall be jeopardising the national welfare. The Strand utterly unmans me, leaving me with only two sensations: (1) a regret that I have made such a mess of my life; (2) a craving for alcohol. These are but a few instances. If I had time, I

could show you that every street known to me in London
has a definite effect on me, and that no two streets have
exactly the same effect. For the most part, these effects
differ in kind according only to the different districts and
their different modes of life; but they differ in detail
according to such specific little differences as exist between
such cognate streets as Bruton Street and Curzon Street,
Doughty Street and Great Russell Street. Every one of
my readers, doubtless, realises that he, too, is thus affected
by the character of streets. And I doubt not that for him,
as for me, the mere sound or sight of a street's name conjures up the sensation he feels when he passes through
that street. For him, probably, the name of every street
has hitherto seemed to be also its exact, inevitable symbol,
a perfect suggestion of its character. He has believed that
the grand or beautiful streets have grand or beautiful
names, the mean or ugly streets mean or ugly names. Let
me assure him that this is a delusion. The name of a
street, as of a human being, derives its whole quality
from its bearer.

'Oxford Street' sounds harsh and ugly. 'Manchester
Street' sounds rather charming. Yet 'Oxford' sounds
beautiful, and 'Manchester' sounds odious. 'Oxford' turns
our thoughts to that 'adorable dreamer, whispering from
her spires the last enchantments of the Middle Age'. An
uproarious monster, belching from its factory-chimneys
the latest exhalations of Hell—that is the image evoked
by 'Manchester'. But neither in 'Manchester Street' is
there for us any hint of that monster, nor in 'Oxford
Street' of that dreamer. The names have become part and
parcel of the streets. You see, then, that it matters not
whether the name given to a new street be one which in
itself suggests beauty, or one which suggests ugliness. In
point of fact, it is generally the most pitiable little holes
and corners that bear the most ambitiously beautiful
names. To any one who has studied London, such a title
as 'Paradise Court' conjures up a dark fetid alley, with
untidy fat women gossiping in it, untidy thin women

quarrelling across it, a host of haggard and shapeless children sprawling in its mud, and one or two drunken men propped against its walls. Thus, were there an official nomenclator of streets, he might be tempted to reject such names as in themselves signify anything beautiful. But his main principle would be to bestow whatever name first occurred to him, in order that he might save time for thinking about something that really mattered.

I have yet to fulfil the second part of my promise: show the futility of trying to commemorate a hero by making a street his namesake. By implication I have done this already. But, for the benefit of the less nimble among my readers, let me be explicit. Who, passing through the Cromwell Road, ever thinks of Cromwell, except by accident? What journalist ever thinks of Wellington in Wellington Street? In Marlborough Street, what police-man remembers Marlborough? In St James's Street, has any one ever fancied he saw the ghost of a pilgrim wrapped in a cloak, leaning on a staff? Other ghosts are there in plenty. The phantom chariot of Lord Petersham dashes down the slope nightly. Nightly Mr Ball Hughes appears in the bow-window of White's. At cock-crow Charles James Fox still emerges from Brooks's. Such men as these were indigenous to the street. Nothing will ever lay their ghosts there. But the ghost of St James—what should it do in that galley?... Of all the streets that have been named after famous men, I know but one whose namesake is suggested by it. In Regent Street you do sometimes think of the Regent; and that is not because the street is named after him, but because it was con-ceived by him, and was designed and built under his auspices, and is redolent of his character and his time. From this redolence I deduce that when a national hero is to be commemorated by a street we should ask him to design the street himself. Assuredly, the mere plastering-up of his name is no mnemonic.

'THE RAGGED REGIMENT'

——'COMMONLY CALLED "LONGSHANKS" on account
of his great height he was the first king crowned in the
Abbey as it now appears and was interred with great
pomp on St Simon's and St Jude's Day October 28th
1307 in 1774 the tomb was opened when the king's body
was found almost entire in the right hand was a richly
embossed sceptre and in the left'——

So much I gather as I pass one of the tombs on my way
to the Chapel of Abbot Islip. Anon the verger will have
stepped briskly forward, drawing a deep breath, with his
flock well to heel, and will be telling the secrets of the
next tomb on his tragic beat.

To be a verger in Westminster Abbey—what life could
be more unutterably tragic? We are, all of us, more or less
enslaved to sameness; but not all of us are saying, every
day, hour after hour, exactly the same thing, in exactly
the same place, in exactly the same tone of voice, to people
who hear it for the first time and receive it with a gasp
of respectful interest. In the name of humanity, I suggest
to the Dean and Chapter that they should relieve these
sad-faced men of their intolerable mission, and purchase
parrots. On every tomb, by every bust or statue, under
every memorial window, let a parrot be chained by the
ankle to a comfortable perch, therefrom to enlighten the
rustic and the foreigner. There can be no objection on the
ground of expense; for parrots live long. Vergers do not,
I am sure.

It is only the rustic and the foreigner who go to Westminster Abbey for general enlightenment. If you pause
beside any one of the verger-led groups, and analyse the
murmur emitted whenever the verger has said his say, you
will find the constituent parts of the sound to be such

phrases as 'Lor'!' 'Ach so!' 'Deary me!' 'Tiens!' and
'My!' 'My!' preponderates; for antiquities appeal with
greatest force to the race that has none of them; and it is
ever the Americans who hang the most tenaciously, in the
greatest numbers, on the vergers' tired lips. We of the
elder races are capable of taking antiquities as a matter
of course. Certainly, such of us as reside in London take
Westminster Abbey as a matter of course. A few of us
will be buried in it, but meanwhile we don't go to it, even
as we don't go to the Tower, or the Mint, or the Monu-
ment. Only for some special purpose do we go—as to
hear a sensational bishop preaching, or to see a monarch
anointed. And on these rare occasions we cast but a casual
glance at the Abbey—that close-packed chaos of beautiful
things and worthless vulgar things. That the Abbey should
be thus chaotic does not seem strange to us; for lack of
orderliness and discrimination is an essential characteristic
of the English genius. But to the Frenchman, with his
passion for symmetry and harmony, how very strange it
must all seem! How very whole-hearted a generalising
'Tiens!' must he utter when he leaves the edifice!

My own special purpose in coming is to see certain
old waxen effigies that are here.* A key grates in the lock
of a little door in the wall of (what I am told is) the North
Ambulatory; and up a winding wooden staircase I am
ushered into a tiny paven chamber. Not much light comes
through the very narrow and deeply embrased window,
and the space is so obstructed that I must pick my way
warily. All around are deep wooden cupboards, faced with
glass; and I become dimly aware that through each glass
some one is watching me. Like sentinels in sentry-boxes,
they fix me with their eyes, seeming as though they would
challenge me. How shall I account to them for my
presence? I slip my note-book into my pocket, and try, in
the dim light, to look as unlike a spy as possible. But I

* In its original form this essay had the good fortune to accompany two very romantic drawings by William Nicholson—one of
Queen Elizabeth's effigy, the other of Charles II's.

cannot, try as I will, acquit myself of impertinence. Who
am I that I should review this 'ragged regiment'? Who am
I that I should come peering in upon this secret conclave
of the august dead? Immobile and dark, very gaunt and
withered, these personages peer out at me with a malign
dignity, through the ages which separate me from them,
through the twilight in which I am so near to them.
Their eyes ...

Come, sir, their eyes are made of glass. It is quite
absurd to take wax-works seriously. Wax-works are not a
serious form of art. The aim of art is so to imitate life
as to produce in the spectator an illusion of life. Wax-
works, at best, can produce no such illusion. Don't pretend to be illuded. For its power to illude, an art depends
on its limitations. Art never can be life, but it may seem
to be so if it do but keep far enough away from life. A
statue may seem to live. A painting may seem to live.
That is because each is so far away from life that you do
not apply the test of life to it. A statue is of bronze or
marble, than either of which nothing could be less flesh-
like. A painting is a thing in two dimensions, whereas man
is in three. If sculptor or painter tried to dodge these
conventions, his labour would be undone. If a painter
swelled his canvas out and in according to the convexities
and concavities of his model, or if a sculptor overlaid his
material with authentic flesh-tints, then you would
demand that the painted or sculptured figure should
blink, or stroke its chin, or kick its foot in the air. That
it could do none of these things would rob it of all power
to illude you. An art that challenges life at close quarters
is defeated through the simple fact that it is not life. Wax-
works, being so near to life, having the exact proportions
of men and women, having the exact texture of skin and
hair and habiliments, must either be made animate or continue to be grotesque and pitiful failures. Lifelike? They?
Rather do they give you the illusion of death. They are
akin to photographs seen through stereoscopic lenses—
those photographs of persons who seem horribly to be

corpses, or, at least, catalepts; and ... You see, I have failed to cheer myself up. Having taken up a strong academic line, and set bravely out to prove to myself the absurdity of wax-works, I find myself at the point where I started, irrefutably arguing to myself that I have good reason to be frightened, here in the Chapel of Abbot Islip, in the midst of these, the Abbot's glowering and ghastly tenants. Catalepsy! death! that is the atmosphere I am breathing.

If I were writing in the past tense, I might pause here to consider whether this emotion were a genuine one or a mere figment for literary effect. As I am writing in the present tense, such a pause would be inartistic, and shall not be made. I must seem not to be writing, but to be actually on the spot, suffering. But then, you may well ask, why should I stay here, to suffer? why not beat a hasty retreat? The answer is that my essay would then seem skimpy; and that you, moreover, would know hardly anything about the wax-works. So I must ask you to imagine me fighting down my fears, and consoling myself with the reflection that here, after all, a sense of awe and oppression is just what one ought to feel—just what one comes for. At Madame Tussaud's exhibition, by which I was similarly afflicted some years ago, I had no such consolation. There my sense of fitness was outraged. The place was meant to be cheerful. It was brilliantly lit. A band was playing popular tunes. Downstairs there was even a restaurant. (Let fancy fondly dwell, for a moment, on the thought of a dinner at Madame Tussaud's: a few carefully-selected guests, and a menu well thought out; conversation becoming general; corks popping; quips flying; a sense of *bien-être*; 'thank you for a *most* delightful evening'. Madame's figures were meant to be agreeable and lively presentments. Her visitors were meant to have a thoroughly good time. But the Islip Chapel has no cheerful intent. It is, indeed, a place set aside, with all reverence, to preserve certain relics of a grim, yet not unlovely, old custom. These fearful images are no stock-in-trade of a showman; we are not invited to 'walk up' to them. They were fashioned with a solemn and wistful purpose. The reason of them lies in a sentiment which is as old as the world—lies in man's vain revolt from the prospect of death. If the soul must perish from the body, may not at least the body itself be preserved, somewhat in the semblance of life, and, for at least a while, on the face of the earth? By subtle art, with far-fetched spices, let the body survive its day and be (even though hidden beneath the earth) for ever. Nay more, since death cause it straightway to dwindle somewhat from the true semblance of life, let cunning artificers fashion it anew— fashion it as it was. Thus, in the earliest days of England, the kings, as they died, were embalmed, and their bodies were borne aloft upon their biers, to a sepulture long delayed after death. In later days, an image of every king that died was forthwith carved in wood, and painted according to his remembered aspect, and decked in his own robes, and, when they had sealed his tomb, the mourners, humouring, to the best of their power, his hatred of extinction, laid this image upon the tomb's slab; and left it so. In yet later days, the pretence became more realistic. The hands and the face were modelled in wax; and the figure stood upright, in some commanding pos- ture, on a valanced platform above the tomb. Nor were only the kings thus honoured. Every one who was interred in the Abbey, whether in virtue of lineage or of achieve- ments, was honoured thus. It was the fashion for every great lady to write in her will minute instructions as to the posture in which her image was to be modelled, and which of her gowns it was to be clad in, and with what of her jewellery it was to glitter. Men, too, used to in- dulge in such precautions. Of all the images thus erected in the Abbey, there remain but a few. The images had to take their chance, in days that were without benefit of police. Thieves, we may suppose, stripped the finery from many of them. Rebels, we know, broke in, less ignobly, and tore many of them limb from limb, as a protest against the governing classes. So only a poor remnant, a 'ragged regiment', has been rallied, at length, into the sanctuary of Islip's Chapel. Perhaps, if they were not so few, these images would not be so fascinating.

Yes, I am fascinated by them now. Terror has been toned to wonder. I am filled with a kind of wondering pity. My academic theory about wax-works has broken down utterly. These figures of kings, princes, duchesses, queens—all are real to me now, and all are pathetic, in the dignity of their fallen and forgotten greatness. With what majesty they wear their rusty velvets and faded silks, flaunting sere ruffles of point-lace, which at a touch now would be shivered like cobwebs! My heart goes out to them through the glass that divides us. I have an idea that they take pleasure in my propinquity. Even Queen Elizabeth, beholding whom, as she stands here, gaunt and imperious and appalling, I echo the words spoken by Philip's envoy, 'This woman is possessed of a hundred thousand devils'—even she herself, though she gazes askance into the air, seems to be conscious of my presence, and to be willing me to stay. It is a relief to meet the bourgeois eye of good Queen Anne. It has restored my common sense. 'These figures really are most curious, most interesting . . .' and anon I am asking intelligent questions about the contents of a big press, which, by special favour, has been unlocked for me.

Perhaps the most romantic thing in the Islip Chapel is this press. Herein, huddled one against another in dark recesses, lie the battered and disjected remains of the earlier effigies—the primitive wooden one. Edward I and Eleanor are known to be among them; and Henry VII and Elizabeth of York; and others not less illustrious. Which is which? By size and shape you can distinguish the men from the women; but beyond that is mere guess-work, be you never so expert. Time has broken and shuffled these erst so significant effigies till they have be-come as unmeaning for us as the bones in one of the old plague-pits. I feel that I ought to be more deeply moved than I am by this sad state of things. But—well, I seem to have exhausted my capacity for sentiment, and cannot rise to the level of my opportunity. Would that I were Thackeray! Dear gentleman, how promptly and copiously he would have wept and moralised here, in his grandest manner, with that perfect technical mastery which makes even now his tritest and shallowest sermons sound remarkable, his hollowest sentiment ring true! What a pity he never came to beat the muffled drum, on which he was so supreme a performer, around the Islip Chapel!

As I make my way down the stairs, I am trying to imagine what would have been the cadence of the final sentence in that essay by Thackeray. And, as I pass along the North Ambulatory, lo! there is the same verger with a new party; and I catch the words 'was interred with great pomp on St Simon's and St Jude's Day October 28 1307 in 1774 the tomb was opened when——'

Essays from

AND EVEN NOW

No. 2. The Pines
[1914]

Hosts and Guests
[1918]

Going Out for a Walk
[1918]

'A Clergyman'
[1918]

The Crime
[1920]

William and Mary
[1920]

'How Shall I Word It?'
[1910]

Laughter
[1920]

No. 2. THE PINES

[*Early in the year* 1914 *Mr Edmund Gosse told me he was asking certain of his friends to write for him a few words apiece in description of Swinburne as they had known or seen him at one time or another; and he was so good as to wish to include in this gathering a few words by myself. I found it hard to be brief without seeming irreverent. I failed in the attempt to make of my subject a snapshot that was not a grotesque. So I took refuge in an ampler scope. I wrote a reminiscential essay. From that essay I made an extract, which I gave to Mr Gosse. From that extract he made a quotation in his enchanting biography. The words quoted by him reappear here in the midst of the whole essay as I wrote it. I dare not hope they are unashamed of their humble surroundings.—M. B.*]

IN MY YOUTH THE suburbs were rather looked down on —I never quite knew why. It was held anomalous, and a matter for merriment, that Swinburne lived in one of them. For my part, had I known as a fact that Catullus was still alive, I should have been as ready to imagine him living in Putney as elsewhere. The marvel would have been merely that he lived. And Swinburne's survival struck as surely as could his have struck in me the chord of wonder.

Not, of course, that he had achieved a feat of longevity. He was far from the Psalmist's limit. Nor was he one of those men whom one associates with the era in which they happened to be young. Indeed, if there was one man belonging less than any other to Mid-Victorian days, Swinburne was that man. But by the calendar it was in those days that he had blazed—blazed forth with so unexampled a suddenness of splendour; and in the light of that conflagration all that he had since done, much and magnificent though this was, paled. The essential Swinburne was still the earliest. He was and would always be the flammiferous boy of the dim past—a legendary

creature, sole kin to the phœnix. It had been impossible that
he should ever surpass himself in the artistry that was from
the outset his; impossible that he should bring forth
rhythms lovelier and greater than those early rhythms, or
exercise over them a mastery more than—absolute. Also,
it had been impossible that the first wild ardour of spirit
should abide unsinkingly in him. Youth goes. And there
was not in Swinburne that basis on which a man may
in his maturity so build as to make good, in some degree,
the loss of what is gone. He was not a thinker: his mind
rose ever away from reason to rhapsody; neither was he
human. He was a king crowned but not throned. He was a
singing bird that could build no nest. He was a
youth who could not afford to age. Had he died young,
literature would have lost many glories; but none so great
as the glories he had already given, nor any such as we
should fondly imagine ourselves bereft of by his early
death. A great part of Keats' fame rests on our assumption
of what he *would* have done. But—even granting that
Keats may have had in him more than had Swinburne of
stuff for development—I believe that had he lived on we
should think of him as author of the poems that in fact
we know. Not philosophy, after all, not humanity, just
sheer joyous power of song, is the primal thing in poetry.
Ideas, and flesh and blood, are but reserves to be brought
up when the poet's youth is going. When the bird can no
longer sing in flight, let the nest be ready. After the king
has dazzled us with his crown, let him have something
to sit down on. But the session on throne or in nest is not
the divine period. Had Swinburne's genius been of the
kind that solidifies, he would yet at the close of the nineteenth century have been for us young men virtually—
though not so definitely as in fact he was—the writer of
Atalanta in Calydon and of *Poems and Ballads*.

Tennyson's death in '98 had not taken us at all by surprise. We had been fully aware that he was alive. He had
always been careful to keep himself abreast of the times.
Anything that came along—the Nebular Hypothesis at

one moment, the Imperial Institute at another—won mention from his Muse. He had husbanded for his old age that which he had long ago inherited: middle age. If in our mourning for him there really was any tincture of surprise, this was due to merely the vague sense that he had in the fullness of time died rather prematurely: his middle-age might have been expected to go on flourishing for ever. But assuredly Tennyson dead laid no such strain on our fancy as Swinburne living.

It is true that Swinburne did, from time to time, take public notice of current affairs; but what notice he took did but seem to mark his remoteness from them, from us. The Boers, I remember, were the theme of a sonnet which embarrassed even their angriest enemies in our midst. He likened them, if I remember rightly, to 'hellhounds foaming at the jaws'. This was by some people taken as a sign that he had fallen away from that high generosity of spirit which had once been his. To me it meant merely that he thought of poor little England writhing under the heel of an alien despotism, just as, in the days when he really was interested in such matters, poor little Italy had writhen. I suspect, too, that the first impulse to write about the Boers came not from the Muse within, but from Theodore Watts-Dunton without. . . . 'Now, Algernon, we're at war, you know—at war with the Boers. I don't want to bother you at all, but I do think, my dear old friend, you oughtn't to let slip this opportunity of,' etc., etc.

Some such hortation is easily imaginable by any one who saw the two old friends together. The first time I had this honour, this sight for lasting and affectionate memory, must have been in the Spring of '99. In those days Theodore Watts (he had but recently taken on the -Dunton) was still something of a gad-about. I had met him here and there, he had said in his stentorian tones pleasant things to me about my writing, I sent him a new little book of mine, and in acknowledging this he asked me to come down to Putney and 'have luncheon and meet Swinburne'. Meet Catullus!

On the day appointed 'I came as one whose feet half linger'. It is but a few steps from the railway-station in Putney High Street to No. 2. The Pines. I had expected a greater distance to the sanctuary—a walk in which to compose my mind and prepare myself for initiation. I laid my hand irresolutely against the gate of the bleak trim front-garden, I withdrew my hand, I went away. Out here were all the aspects of common modern life. In there was Swinburne. A butcher-boy went by, whistling. He was not going to see Swinburne. He could afford to whistle. I pursued my dilatory course up the slope of Putney, but at length it occurred to me that unpunctuality would after all be an imperfect expression of reverence, and I retraced my footsteps.

No. 2—prosaic inscription! But as that front-door closed behind me I had the instant sense of having slipped away from the harsh light of the ordinary and contemporary into the dimness of an odd, august past. Here, in this dark hall, the past was the present. Here loomed vivid and vital on the walls those women of Rossetti whom I had known but as shades. Familiar to me in small reproductions by photogravure, here they *themselves* were, life-sized, 'with curled-up lips and amorous hair' done in the original warm crayon, all of them intently looking down on me while I took off my overcoat—all wondering who was this intruder from posterity. That they hung in the hall, evidently no more than an overflow, was an earnest of packed plentitude within. The room I was ushered into was a back-room, a dining-room, looking on to a good garden. It was, in form and 'fixtures', an inalienably Mid-Victorian room, and held its stolid own in the riot of Rossettis. Its proportions, its window-sash bisecting the view of garden, its folding-doors (through which I heard the voice of Watts-Dunton booming mysteriously in the front room), its mantel-piece, its gas-brackets, all proclaimed that nothing ever would seduce them from their allegiance to Martin Tupper. 'Nor me from mine', said the sturdy cruet-stand on the long expanse of table-cloth. The voice of Watts-Dunton ceased suddenly, and a few moments later its owner appeared. He had been dictating, he explained. 'A great deal of work on hand just now—a great deal of work.'... I remember that on my subsequent visits he was always, at the moment of my arrival, dictating, and always greeted me with that phrase, 'A great deal of work on hand just now.' I used to wonder what work it was, for he published little enough. But I never ventured to inquire, and indeed rather cherished the mystery: it was a part of the dear little old man; it went with the something gnome-like about his swarthiness and chubbiness—went with the shaggy hair that fell over the collar of his eternally crumpled frock-coat, the shaggy eyebrows that overhung his bright little brown eyes, the shaggy moustache that hid his small round chin. It was a mystery inherent in the richly-laden atmosphere of The Pines. ...

While I stood talking to Watts-Dunton—talking as loudly as he, for he was very deaf—I enjoyed the thrill of suspense in watching the door through which would appear—Swinburne. I asked after Mr Swinburne's health. Watts-Dunton said it was very good: 'He always goes out for his long walk in the morning—wonderfully active. Active in mind, too. But I'm afraid you won't be able to get into touch with him. He's almost stone-deaf, poor fellow—almost stone-deaf now.' He changed the subject, and I felt I must be careful not to seem interested in Swinburne exclusively. I spoke of 'Aylwin'. The parlour-maid brought in the hot dishes. The great moment was at hand.

Nor was I disappointed. Swinburne's entry was for me a great moment. Here, suddenly visible in the flesh, was the legendary being and divine singer. Here he was, shutting the door behind him as might anybody else, and advancing—a strange small figure in grey, having an air at once noble and roguish, proud and skittish. My name was roared to him. In shaking his hand, I bowed low, of course—a bow *de cœur*; and he, in the old aristocratic manner, bowed equally low, but with such swiftness that we narrowly escaped concussion. You do not usually associate a man of genius, when you see one, with any social class; and, Swinburne being of an aspect so unrelated as it was to any species of human kind, I wondered the more that almost the first impression he made on me, or would make on any one, was that of a very great gentleman indeed. Not of an *old* gentleman, either. Sparse and straggling though the grey hair was that fringed the immense pale dome of his head, and venerably haloed though he was for me by his greatness, there was yet about him something—boyish? girlish? childish, rather; something of a beautifully well-bred child. But he had the eyes of a god, and the smile of an elf. In figure, at first glance, he seemed almost fat; but this was merely because of the way he carried himself, with his long neck strained so tightly back that he all receded from the waist upwards. I noticed afterwards that this deportment made the back of his jacket hang quite far away from his legs; and so small and sloping were his shoulders that the jacket seemed ever so likely to slip right off. I became aware, too, that when he bowed he did not unbend his back, but only his neck—the length of the neck accounting for the depth of the bow. His hands were tiny, even for his size, and they fluttered helplessly, touchingly, unceasingly.

Directly after my introduction, we sat down to the meal. Of course I had never hoped to 'get into touch with him' reciprocally. Quite apart from his deafness, I was too modest to suppose he could be interested in anything I might say. But—for I knew he had once been as high and copious a singer in talk as in verse—I had hoped to hear utterances from him. And it did not seem that my hope was to be fulfilled. Watts-Dunton sat at the head of the table, with a huge and very Tupperesque joint of roast mutton in front of him, Swinburne and myself close

up to him on either side. He talked only to me. This was
the more tantalising because Swinburne seemed as though
he were bubbling over with all sorts of notions. Not that
he looked at either of us. He smiled only to himself, and to
his plateful of meat, and to the small bottle of Bass's pale
ale that stood before him—ultimate allowance of one who
had erst clashed cymbals in Naxos. This small bottle he
eyed often and with enthusiasm, seeming to waver between
the rapture of broaching it now and the grandeur of having it to look forward to. It made me unhappy to see
what trouble he had in managing his knife and fork.
Watts-Dunton told me on another occasion that this
infirmity of the hands had been lifelong—had begun
before Eton days. The Swinburne family had been
alarmed by it and had consulted a specialist, who said
that it resulted from 'an excess of electric vitality', and
that any attempt to stop it would be harmful. So they
had let it be. I have known no man of genius who had
not to pay, in some affliction or defect either physical or
spiritual, for what the gods had given him. Here, in this
fluttering of his tiny hands, was a part of the price that
Swinburne had to pay. No doubt he had grown accustomed to it many lustres before I met him, and I need not
have felt at all unhappy at what I tried not to see. He,
evidently, was quite gay, in his silence—and in the world
that was for him silent. I had, however, the maddening
suspicion that he would have liked to talk. Why wouldn't
Watts-Dunton roar him an opportunity? I felt I had been
right perhaps in feeling that the lesser man was—no, not
jealous of the greater whom he had guarded so long and
with such love, but anxious that he himself should be as
fully impressive to visitors as his fine gifts warranted.
Not, indeed, that he monopolised the talk. He seemed to
regard me as a source of information about all the latest
'movements', and I had to shout banalities while he
munched his mutton—banalities whose one saving grace
for me was that they were inaudible to Swinburne. Had
I met Swinburne's gaze, I should have faltered. Now and

again his shining light-grey eyes roved from the table, darting this way and that—across the room, up at the ceiling, out of the window; only never at us. Somehow this aloofness gave no hint of indifference. It seemed to be, rather, a point in good manners—the good manners of a child 'sitting up to table', not 'staring', not 'asking questions', and reflecting great credit on its invaluable old nurse. The child sat happy in the wealth of its inner life; the child was content not to speak until it were spoken to; but, but, I felt it did want to be spoken to. And, at length, it *was*.

So soon as the mutton had been replaced by the apple-pie, Watts-Dutton leaned forward and 'Well, Algernon,' he roared, 'how was it on the Heath to-day?' Swinburne, who had meekly inclined his ear to the question, now threw back his head, uttering a sound that was like the cooing of a dove, and forthwith, rapidly, ever so musically, he spoke to us of his walk; spoke not in the strain of a man who had been taking his daily exercise on Putney Heath, but rather in that of a Peri who had at long last been suffered to pass through Paradise. And rather than that he spoke would I say that he cooingly and flutingly *sang* of his experience. The wonders of this morning's wind and sun and clouds were expressed in a flow of words so right and sentences so perfectly balanced that they would have seemed pedantic had they not been clearly as spontaneous as the wordless notes of a bird in song. The frail, sweet voice rose and fell, lingered, quickened, in all manner of trills and roulades. That he himself could not hear it, seemed to me the greatest loss his deafness inflicted on him. One would have expected this disability to mar the music; but it didn't; save that now and again a note would come out metallic and over-shrill, the tones were under good control. The whole manner and method had certainly a strong element of oddness; but no one incapable of condemning as unmanly the song of a lark would have called it affected. I had met young men of whose enunciation Swinburne's now reminded me. In

them the thing had always irritated me very much; and I
now became sure that it had been derived from people
who had derived it in old Balliol days from Swinburne
himself. One of the points familiar to me in such enunciation was the habit of stressing extremely, and lackadaisi-
cally dwelling on, some particular syllable. In Swinburne
this trick was delightful—because it wasn't a trick, but a
need of his heart. Well do I remember his ecstasy of
emphasis and immensity of pause when he described how
he had seen in a perambulator on the Heath to-day 'the
most BEAUT——iful babbie ever beheld by mortal eyes.'
For babies, as some of his latter volumes testify, he had
a sort of idolatry. After Mazzini had followed Landor
to Elysium, and Victor Hugo had followed Mazzini,
babies were what among live creatures most evoked
Swinburne's genius for self-abasement. His rapture about
this especial 'babbie' was such as to shake within me my
hitherto firm conviction that, whereas the young of the
brute creation are already beautiful at the age of five
minutes, the human young never begin to be so before the
age of three years. I suspect Watts-Dunton of having
shared my lack of innate enthusiasm. But it was one of
Swinburne's charms, as I was to find, that he took for
granted every one's delight in what he himself so fervidly
delighted in. He could as soon have imagined a man not
loving the very sea as not doting on the aspect of babies
and not reading at least one play by an Elizabethan or
Jacobean dramatist every day.

I forget whether it was at this my first meal or at another that he described a storm in which, one night years
ago, with Watts-Dunton, he had crossed the Channel.
The rhythm of his great phrases was as the rhythm of
those waves, and his head swayed in accordance to it like
the wave-rocked boat itself. He hymned in memory the
surge and darkness, the thunder and foam and phos-
phorescence—'You remember, Theodore? You remember
the PHOS——phorescence?'—all so beautifully and
vividly that I almost felt storm-bound and in peril of my

life. To disentangle one from another of the several occasions on which I heard him talk is difficult because the procedure was so invariable: Watts-Dunton always dictating when I arrived, Swinburne always appearing at the moment of the meal, always the same simple and substantial fare, Swinburne never allowed to talk before the meal was half over. As to this last point, I soon realised that I had been quite unjust in suspecting Watts-Dunton of selfishness. It was simply a sign of the care with which he watched over his friend's welfare. Had Swinburne been admitted earlier to the talk, he would not have taken his proper quantity of roast mutton. So soon, always, as he had taken that, the embargo was removed, the chance was given him. And, swiftly though he embraced the chance, and much though he made of it in the courses of apple-pie and of cheese, he seemed touchingly ashamed of 'holding forth'. Often, before he had said his really full say on the theme suggested by Watts-Dunton's loud interrogation, he would curb his speech and try to eliminate himself, bowing his head over his plate; and then, when he had promptly been brought in again, he would always try to atone for his inhibiting deafness by much reference and deference to all that we might otherwise have to say. 'I hope', he would coo to me, 'my friend Watts-Dunton, who'—and here he would turn and make a little bow to Watts-Dunton—'is himself a scholar, will bear me out when I say'—or 'I hardly know', he would flute to his old friend, 'whether Mr Beerbohm'—here a bow to me —'will agree with me in my opinion of' some delicate point in Greek prosody or some incident in an old French romance I had never heard of.

On one occasion, just before the removal of the mutton, Watts-Dunton had been asking me about an English translation that had been made of M. Rostand's 'Cyrano de Bergerac'. He then took my information as the match to ignite the Swinburnian tinder. 'Well, Algernon, it seems that "Cyrano de Bergerac"'—but this first spark was enough: instantly Swinburne was praising the works of Cyrano de Bergerac. Of M. Rostand he may have heard, but him he forgot. Indeed I never heard Swinburne mention a single contemporary writer. His mind ranged and revelled always in the illustrious or obscure past. To him the writings of Cyrano de Bergerac were as fresh as paint—as fresh as to me, alas, was the news of their survival. 'Of course, of course, you have read "L'Histoire Comique des Etats et des Empires de la Lune"?' I admitted, by gesture and facial expression, that I had not. Whereupon he reeled out curious extracts from that allegory—'almost as good as "Gulliver"'—with a memorable instance of the way in which the traveller to the moon was shocked by the conversation of the natives, and the natives' sense of propriety was outraged by the conversation of the traveller.

In life, as in (that for him more truly actual thing) literature, it was always the preterit that enthralled him. Of any passing events, of anything the newspapers were full of, never a word from him; and I should have been sorry if there had been. But I did, through the medium of Watts-Dunton, sometimes start him on topics that might have led him to talk of Rossetti and other old comrades. For me the names of those men breathed the magic of the past, just as it was breathed for me by Swinburne's presence. For him, I suppose, they were but a bit of the present, and the mere fact that they had dropped out of it was not enough to hallow them. He never mentioned them. But I was glad to see that he revelled as wistfully in the days just before his own as I in the days just before mine. He recounted to us things he had been told in his boyhood by an aged aunt, or great-aunt— 'one of the Ashburnhams'; how, for example, she had been taken by her mother to a county ball, a distance of many miles, and, on the way home through the frosty and snowy night, the family-coach had suddenly stopped: there was a crowd of dark figures in the way ... at which point Swinburne stopped too, before saying, with an ineffable smile and in a voice faint with appreciation, 'They were burying a suicide at the cross-roads.'

Vivid as this Hogarthian night-scene was to me, I saw beside it another scene: a great panelled room, a grim old woman in a high-backed chair, and, restless on a stool at her feet an extraordinary little nephew with masses of auburn hair and with tiny hands clasped in supplication —'Tell me more, Aunt Ashburnham, tell me more!'

And now, clearlier still, as I write in these after-years, do I see that dining-room of The Pines; the long white stretch of table-cloth, with Swinburne and Watts-Dunton and another at the extreme end of it; Watts-Dunton between us, very low down over his plate, very cosy and hirsute, and rather like the dormouse at that long tea-table which Alice found in Wonderland. I see myself sitting there wide-eyed, as Alice sat. And, had the hare been a great poet, and the hatter a great gentleman, and neither of them mad but each only very odd and vivacious, I might see Swinburne as a glorified blend of those two.

When the meal ended—for, alas! it was not, like that meal in Wonderland, unending—Swinburne would dart round the table, proffer his hand to me, bow deeply, bow to Watts-Dunton also, and disappear. 'He always walks in the morning, writes in the afternoon, and reads in the evening,' Watts-Dunton would say with a touch of tutorial pride in this regimen.

That parting bow of Swinburne to his old friend was characteristic of his whole relation to him. Cronies though they were, these two, knit together with bonds innumerable, the greater man was always *aux petits soins* for the lesser, treating him as a newly-arrived young guest might treat an elderly host. Some twenty years had passed since that night when, ailing and broken—thought to be nearly dying, Watts-Dunton told me—Swinburne was brought in a four-wheeler to The Pines. Regular private nursing-homes either did not exist in those days or were less in vogue than they are now. The Pines was to be a sort of private nursing-home for Swinburne. It was a good one. He recovered. He was most grateful to his friend and saviour. He made as though to depart, was persuaded to stay a little longer, and then a little longer than that. But I rather fancy that, to the last, he never did, in the fullness of his modesty and good manners, consent to regard his presence as a matter of course, or as anything but a terminable intrusion and obligation. His bow seemed always to convey that.

Swinburne having gone from the room, in would come the parlourmaid. The table was cleared, the fire was stirred, two leather arm-chairs were pushed up to the hearth. Watts-Dunton wanted gossip of the present. I wanted gossip of the great past. We settled down for a long, comfortable afternoon together.

Only once was the ritual varied. Swinburne (I was told before luncheon) had expressed a wish to show me his library. So after the meal he did not bid us his usual adieu, but with much courtesy invited us and led the way. Up the staircase he then literally bounded—three, literally three, stairs at a time. I began to follow at the same rate, but immediately slackened speed for fear that Watts-Dunton behind us might be embittered at sight of so much youth and legerity. Swinburne waited on the threshold to receive us, as it were, and pass us in. Watts-Dunton went and ensconced himself snugly in a corner. The sun had appeared after a grey morning, and it pleasantly flooded this big living-room whose walls were entirely lined with the mellow backs of books. Here, as host, among his treasures, Swinburne was more than ever attractive. He was as happy as was any mote in the sunshine about him; and the fluttering of his little hands, and feet too, was but as a token of so much felicity. He looked older, it is true, in the strong light. But these added years made only more notable his youngness of heart. An illustrious bibliophile among his books? A birthday child, rather, among his toys.

Proudly he explained to me the general system under which the volumes were ranged in this or that division of shelves. Then he conducted me to a chair near the window, left me there, flew away, flew up the rungs of a mahogany ladder, plucked a small volume, and in a twinkling was at my side: 'This, I *think*, will please you!' It did. It had a beautifully engraved title-page and a pleasing scent of old, old leather. It was *editio princeps* of a play by some lesser Elizabethan or Jacobean. 'Of course you know it?' my host fluted.

How I wished I could say that I knew it and loved it well! I revealed to him (for by speaking very loudly to-wards his inclined head I was able to make him hear) that I had not read it. He envied any one who had such pleasure in store. He darted to the ladder, and came back thrusting gently into my hands another volume of like date: 'Of course you know *this*?'

Again I had to confess that I did not, and to shout my appreciation of the fount of type, the margins, the bind-ing. He beamed agreement, and fetched another volume. Archly he indicated the title, cooing, 'You are a lover, of *this*, I hope?' And again I was shamed by my in-experience.

I did not pretend to know this particular play, but my tone implied that I had always been *meaning* to read it and had always by some mischance been prevented. For his sake as well as my own I did want to acquit myself passably. I wanted for him the pleasure of seeing his joys shared by a representative, however humble, of the common world. I turned the leaves caressingly, looking from them to him, while he dilated on the beauty of this and that scene in the play. Anon he fetched another volume, and another, always with the same faith that *this* was a favourite of mine. I quibbled, I evaded, I was very enthusiastic and uncomfortable. It was with intense relief that I beheld the title-page of yet another volume which (silently, this time) he laid before me—THE COUNTRY WENCH. '*This of course* I have read,' I heartily shouted.

Swinburne stepped back. 'You have? You have read it? Where?' he cried, in evident dismay.

Something was wrong. Had I *not*, I quickly wondered, read this play? 'Oh yes,' I shouted, 'I have read it.'

'But when? Where?' entreated Swinburne, adding that he had supposed it to be the sole copy extant.

I floundered. I wildly said I thought I must have read it years ago in the Bodleian.

'Theodore! Do you hear this? It seems that they have now a copy of *The Country Wench* in the Bodleian! Mr Beerbohm found one there—oh when? in what year?' he appealed to me.

I said it might have been six, seven, eight years ago. Swinburne knew for certain that no copy had been there *twelve* years ago, and was surprised that he had not heard of the acquisition. 'They might have told me,' he wailed.

I sacrificed myself on the altar of sympathy. I admitted that I might have been mistaken—must have been— must have confused this play with some other. I dipped into the pages and 'No,' I shouted, 'this I have *never* read.'

His equanimity was restored. He was up the ladder and down again, showing me further treasures with all pride and ardour. At length, Watts-Dunton, afraid that his old friend would tire himself, arose from his corner, and presently he and I went downstairs to the dining-room. It was in the course of our session together that there suddenly flashed across my mind the existence of a play called 'The Country Wife', by—wasn't it Wycherley? I had once read it—or read something about it. . . . But this matter I kept to myself. I thought I had appeared fool enough already.

I loved those sessions in that Tupperossettine dining-room, lair of solid old comfort and fervid old romanticism. Its odd duality befitted well its owner. The distinguished critic and poet, Rossetti's closest friend and Swinburne's, had been, for a while, in the dark ages, a solicitor; and one felt he had been a good one. His frock-coat, though the Muses had crumpled it, inspired confidence in his judgment of other things than verse. But let there be no mistake. He was no mere *bourgeois parnassien*, as his enemies insinuated. No doubt he had been very useful to men of genius, in virtue of qualities they lacked, but the secret of his hold on them was in his own rich nature. He was not only a born man of letters, he was a deeply emotional human being whose appeal was as much to the heart as to the head. The romantic Celtic mysticism of 'Aylwin', with its lack of fashionable Celtic nebulosity, lends itself, if you will, to laughter, though personally I saw nothing funny in it: it seemed to me, before I was in touch with the author, a work of genuine expression from within; and that it truly was so I presently knew. The mysticism of Watts-Dunton (who, once comfortably settled at the fireside, knew no reserve) was in contrast with the frock-coat and the practical abilities; but it was essential, and they were of the surface. For humorous Rossetti, I daresay, the very contrast made Theodore's company the more precious. He himself had assuredly been, and the memory of him still was, the master-fact in Watts-Dunton's life. 'Algernon' was as an adopted child, 'Gabriel' as a long-lost only brother. As he was to the outer world of his own day, so too to posterity Rossetti, the man, is conjectural and mysterious. We know that he was in his prime the most inspiring and splendid of companions. But we know this only by faith. The evidence is as vague as it is emphatic. Of the style and substance of not a few great talkers in the past we can piece together some more or less vivid and probably erroneous notion. But about Rossetti nothing has been recorded in such a way as to make him even faintly emerge. I suppose he had in him what reviewers seem to find so often in books: a quality that defies analysis. Listening to Watts-Dunton, I was always in hope that when next the long-lost turned up—for he was continually doing so—in the talk, I should *see* him, *hear* him, and share the rapture. But the revelation was not to be. You might think that to hear him called 'Gabriel' would have given me a sense of propinquity. But I felt no nearer to him than you feel to the Archangel who bears that name and no surname.

It was always when Watts-Dunton spoke carelessly, casually, of some to me illustrious figure in the past, that I had the sense of being wafted right into that past and plumped down in the very midst of it. When he spoke with reverence of this and that great man whom he had known, he did not thus waft and plump me; for I, too, revered those names. But I had the magical transition whenever one of the immortals was mentioned in the tone of those who knew him before he had put on immortality. Browning, for example, was a name deeply honoured by me. 'Browning, yes,' said Watts-Dunton, in the course of an afternoon, 'Browning,' and he took a sip of the steaming whisky-toddy that was a point in our day's ritual. 'I was a great diner-out in the old times. I used to dine out every night in the week. Browning was a great diner-out, too. We were always meeting. What a pity he went on writing all those plays! He hadn't any gift for drama—none. I never could understand why he took to play-writing.' He wagged his head, gazing regretfully into the fire, and added, 'Such a *clever* fellow, too!'

Whistler, though alive and about, was already looked to as a hierarch by the young. Not so had he been looked to by Rossetti. The thrill of the past was always strong in me when Watts-Dunton mentioned—seldom without a guffaw did he mention—'Jimmy Whistler'. I think he put in the surname because 'that fellow' had not behaved well to Swinburne. But he could not omit the nickname, because it was impossible for him to feel the right measure of resentment against 'such a funny fellow'. As heart-full of old hates as of old loves was Watts-Dunton, and I take it as high testimony to the charm of Whistler's quaintness that Watts-Dunton did not hate *him*. You may be aware that Swinburne, in '88, wrote for one of the monthly reviews a criticism of the 'Ten O'Clock' lecture. He paid courtly compliments to Whistler as a painter, but joined issue with his theories. Straightway there appeared in the *World* a little letter from Whistler, deriding 'one Algernon Swinburne—outside—Putney'. It was not in itself a very pretty or amusing letter; and still less so did it seem in the light of the facts which Watts-Dunton told me in some such words as these: 'After he'd published that lecture of his, Jimmy Whistler had me to dine with him at Kettner's or somewhere. He said, "Now, Theodore, I want you to do me a favour." He wanted to get me to get Swinburne to write an article about his lecture. I said, "No, Jimmy Whistler, I can't ask Algernon to do that. He's got a great deal of work on hand just now—a great deal of work. And besides, this sort of thing wouldn't be at all in his line." But Jimmy Whistler went on appealing to me. He said it would do him no end of good if Swinburne wrote about him. And—well, I half gave in: I said perhaps I *would* mention the matter to Algernon. And next day I did. I could see Algernon didn't want to do it at all. But—well, there, he said he'd do it to please *me*. And he did it. And then Jimmy Whistler published that letter. A very shabby trick—very shabby indeed.' Of course I do not vouch for the exact words in which Watts-Dunton told me this tale; but this was exactly the tale he told me. I expressed my astonishment. He added that of course he 'never wanted to see the fellow again after that, and never did.' But presently, after a long gaze into the coals, he emitted a chuckle, as for earlier memories of 'such a funny fellow'. One quite recent memory he had, too. 'When I took on the name of Dunton, I had a note from him. Just this, with his butterfly signature: *Theodore! What's Dunton?* That was very good—very good. ... But, of course,' he added gravely, 'I took no notice.' And no doubt, quite apart from the difficulty of finding an answer in the same vein, he did well in not replying. Loyalty to Swinburne forbade. But I see a certain pathos in the unanswered message. It was a message from the hand of an old jester, but also, I think, from the heart of

an old man—a signal waved jauntily, but in truth wistfully, across the gulf of years and estrangement; and one
could wish it had not been ignored.

Some time after Whistler died I wrote for one of the
magazines an appreciation of his curious skill in the art
of writing. Watts-Dunton told me he had heard of this
from Swinburne. 'I myself', he said, 'very seldom read the
magazines. But Algernon always has a look at them.'
There was something to me very droll, and cheery too, in
this picture of the illustrious recluse snatching at the
current issue of our twaddle. And I was immensely
pleased at hearing that my article had 'interested him very
much'. I inwardly promised myself that as soon as I
reached home I would read the article, to see just how it
might have struck Swinburne. When in due course I did
this, I regretted the tone of the opening sentences,
in which I declared myself 'no book-lover' and
avowed a preference for 'an uninterrupted view of my
fellow-creatures'. I felt that had I known my article would
meet the eye of Swinburne I should have cut out that
overture. I dimly remembered a fine passage in one of his
books of criticism—something (I preferred not to verify
it) about 'the dotage of duncedom which cannot perceive,
or the impudence of insignificance so presumptuous as to
doubt, that the elements of life and literature are in-
divisibly mingled one in another, and that he to whom
books are less real than life will assuredly find in men
and women as little reality as in his accursed crassness he
deserves to discover.' I quailed, I quailed. But mine is a
resilient nature, and I promptly reminded myself that
Swinburne's was a very impersonal one: he would not
think the less highly of me, for he never had thought about
me in any way whatsoever. All was well. I knew I could
revisit The Pines, when next Watts-Dunton should invite
me, without misgiving. And to this day I am rather proud
of having been mentioned, though not by name, and not
consciously, and unfavourably, by Swinburne.

I wonder that I cannot recall more than I do recall of

those hours at The Pines. It is odd how little remains to a man of his own past—how few minutes of even his memorable hours are not clean forgotten, and how few seconds in any one of those minutes can be recaptured. . . . I am middle-aged, and have lived a vast number of seconds. Subtract one-third of these, for one mustn't count sleep as life. The residual number is still enormous. Not a single one of those seconds was unimportant to me in its passage. Many of them bored me, of course; but even boredom is a positive state: one chafes at it and hates it; strange that one should afterwards forget it! And stranger still that of one's actual happinesses and un-happinesses so tiny and tattered a remnant clings about one! Of those hours at The Pines, of that past within a past, there was not a minute nor a second that I did not spend with pleasure. Memory is a great artist, we are told; she selects and rejects and shapes and so on. No doubt. Elderly persons would be utterly intolerable if they remembered *everything*. *Everything*, nevertheless, is just what they themselves would like to remember, and just what they would like to tell to *everybody*. But sure that the Ancient Mariner, though he remembered quite as much as his audience wanted to hear, and rather more, about the albatross and the ghastly crew, was inwardly raging at the sketchiness of his own mind; and believe me that his stopping only one of three was the merest oversight. I should like to impose on the world many tomes about The Pines.

But, scant though my memories are of the moments there, very full and warm in me is the whole fused memory of the two dear old men that lived there. I wish I had Watts-Dunton's sure faith in meetings beyond the grave. I am glad I do not disbelieve that people may so meet. I like to think that some day in Elysium I shall—not without diffidence—approach those two and re-introduce myself. I can see just how courteously Swinburne will bow over my hand, not at all remembering who I am. Watts-Dunton will remember me after a moment: 'Oh, to be sure, yes indeed! I've a great deal of work on hand just now—a great deal of work', but we shall sit down together on the asphodel, and I cannot but think we shall have whisky-toddy even there. He will not have changed. He will still be shaggy and old and chubby, and will wear the same frock-coat, with the same creases in it. Swinburne, on the other hand, will be quite, quite young, with a full mane of flaming auburn locks, and no clothes to hinder him from plunging back at any moment into the shining Elysian waters from which he will have just emerged. I see him skim lightly away into that element. On the strand is sitting a man of noble and furrowed brow. It is Mazzini, still thinking of Liberty. And anon the tiny young English amphibian comes ashore to fling himself dripping at the feet of the patriot and to carol the Republican ode he has composed in the course of his swim. 'He's wonderfully active—active in mind and body,' Watts-Dunton says to me. 'I come to the shore now and then, just to see how he's getting on. But I spend most of my time inland. I find I've so much to talk over with Gabriel. Not that he's quite the fellow he was. He always had rather a cult for Dante, you know, and now he's more than ever under the Florentine influence. He lives in a sort of monastery that Dante has here; and there he sits painting imaginary portraits of Beatrice, and giving them all to Dante. But he still has his great moments, and there's no one quite like him—no one. Algernon won't ever come and see him, because that fellow Mazzini's as Anti-Clerical as ever and makes a principle of having nothing to do with Dante. Look!—there's Algernon going into the water again! He'll tire himself out, he'll catch cold, he'll—' and here the old man rises and hurries down to the sea's edge. 'Now, Algernon,' he roars, 'I don't want to interfere with you, but I do think, my dear old friend,'—and then, with a guffaw, he breaks off, remembering that his friend is not deaf now nor old, and that here in Elysium, where no ills are, good advice is not needed.

HOSTS AND GUESTS

BEAUTIFULLY VAGUE THOUGH THE English language
is, with its meanings merging into one another as softly
as the facts of landscape in the moist English climate, and
much addicted though we always have been to ways of
compromise, and averse from sharp hard logical outlines,
we do not call a host a guest, nor a guest a host. The
ancient Romans did so. They, with a language that was
as lucid as their climate and was a perfect expression of
the sharp hard logical outlook fostered by that climate,
had but one word for those two things. Nor have their
equally acute descendants done what might have been
expected of them in this matter. *Hôte* and *ospite* and
héspide are as mysteriously equivocal as *hospes*. By
weight of all this authority I find myself being dragged to
the conclusion that a host and a guest must be the same
thing, after all. Yet in a dim and muzzy way, deep down
in my breast, I feel sure that they are different. Compromise, you see, as usual. I take it that strictly the two
things *are* one, but that our division of them is yet another instance of that sterling common-sense by which,
etc., etc.

I would go even so far as to say that the difference is
more than merely circumstantial and particular. I seem
to discern also a temperamental and general difference.
You ask me to dine with you in a restaurant, I say I shall
be delighted, you order the meal, I praise it, you pay for
it, I have the pleasant sensation of not paying for it; and
it is well that each of us should have a label according to
the part he plays in this transaction. But the two labels
are applicable in a larger and more philosophic way. In
every human being one or the other of these two instincts

is predominant: the active or passive instinct to offer hospitality, the negative or passive instinct to accept it. And either of these instincts is so significant of character that one might well say that mankind is divisible into two great classes: hosts and guests.

I have already (see third sentence of foregoing paragraph) somewhat prepared you for the shock of a confession which candour now forces from me. I am one of the guests. You are, however, so shocked that you will read no more of me? Bravo! Your refusal indicates that you have not a guestish soul. Here am I trying to entertain you, and you will not be entertained. You stand shouting that it is more blessed to give than to receive. Very well. For my part, I would rather read than write, any day. You shall write this essay for me. Be it never so humble, I shall give it my best attention and manage to say something nice about it. I am sorry to see you calming suddenly down. Nothing but a sense of duty to myself, and to guests in general, makes me resume my pen. I believe guests to be as numerous, really, as hosts. It may be that even you, if you examine yourself dispassionately, will find that you are one of them. In which case, you may yet thank me for some comfort. I think there are good qualities to be found in guests, and some bad ones in even the best hosts.

Our deepest instincts, bad or good, are those which we share with the rest of the animal creation. To offer hospitality, or to accept it, is but an instinct which man has acquired in the long course of his self-development. Lions do not ask one another to their lairs, nor do birds keep open nest. Certain wolves and tigers, it is true, have been so seduced by man from their natural state that they will deign to accept man's hospitality. But when you give a bone to your dog, does he run out and invite another dog to share it with him?—and does your cat insist on having a circle of other cats around her saucer of milk? Quite the contrary. A deep sense of personal property is common to all these creatures. Thousands of years hence they may have acquired some willingness to share things with their friends. Or rather, dogs may; cats, I think, not. Meanwhile, let us not be censorious. Though certain monkeys assuredly were of finer and more malleable stuff than any wolves or tigers, it was a very long time indeed before even we began to be hospitable. The cavemen did not entertain. It may be that now and again— say, towards the end of the Stone Age—one or another among the more enlightened of them said to his wife, while she plucked an eagle that he had snared the day before, 'That red-haired man who lives in the next valley seems to be a decent, harmless sort of person. And sometimes I fancy he is rather lonely. I think I will ask him to dine with us to-night,' and, presently going out, met the red-haired man and said to him, 'Are you doing anything to-night? If not, won't you dine with us? It would be a great pleasure to my wife. Only ourselves. Come just as you are.' 'That is most good of you, but,' stammered the red-haired man, 'as ill-luck will have it, I *am* engaged to-night. A long-standing, formal invitation. I wish I could get out of it, but I simply can't. I have a morbid conscientiousness about such things.' Thus we see that the will to offer hospitality was an earlier growth than the will to accept it. But we must beware of thinking these two things identical with the mere will to give and the mere will to receive. It is unlikely that the red-haired man would have refused a slice of eagle if it had been offered to him where he stood. And it is still more unlikely that his friend would have handed it to him. Such is not the way of hosts. The hospitable instinct is not wholly altruistic. There is pride and egoism mixed up with it, as I shall show.

Meanwhile, why did the red-haired man babble those excuses? It was because he scented danger. He was not by nature suspicious, but—what possible motive, except murder, could this man have for enticing him to that cave? Acquaintance in the open valley was all very well and pleasant, but a strange den after dark—no, no! You despise him for his fears? Yet these were not really so absurd as they may seem. As man progressed in civilisation, and grew to be definitely gregarious, hospitality became more a matter of course. But even then it was not above suspicion. It was not hedged around with those unwritten laws which make it the safe and eligible thing we know to-day. In the annals of hospitality there are many pages that make painful reading; many a great dark blot is there which the Recording Angel may wish, but will not be able, to wipe out with a tear.

If I were a host, I should ignore those tomes. Being a guest, I sometimes glance into them, but with more of horror, I assure you, than of malicious amusement. I carefully avoid those which treat of hospitality among barbarous races. Things done in the best periods of the most enlightened peoples are quite bad enough. The Israelites were the salt of the earth. But can you imagine a deed of colder-blooded treachery than Jael's? You would think it must have been held accursed by even the basest minds. Yet thus sang Deborah and Barak, 'Blessed above women shall Jael the wife of Heber the Kenite be, blessed shall she be among women in the tent.' And Barak, remember, was a gallant soldier, and Deborah was a prophetess who 'judged Israel at that time'. So much for the ideals of hospitality among the children of Israel.

Of the Homeric Greeks it may be said that they too were the salt of the earth; and it may be added that in their pungent and antiseptic quality there was mingled a measure of sweetness, not to be found in the children of Israel. I do not say outright that Odysseus ought not to have slain the suitors. That is a debatable point. It is true that they were guests under his roof. But he had not invited them. Let us give him the benefit of the doubt. I am thinking of another episode in his life. By what Circe did, and by his disregard of what she had done, a searching light is cast on the laxity of Homeric Greek notions as to what was due to guests. Odysseus was a clever, but not a bad man, and his standard of general

conduct was high enough. Yet, having foiled Circe in her
purpose to turn him into a swine, and having forced her
to restore his comrades to human shape, he did not let pass
the barrier of his teeth any such winged words as 'Now
will I bide no more under thy roof, Circe, but fare across
the sea with my dear comrades, even unto mine own
home, for that which thou didst was an evil thing, and
one not meet to be done unto strangers by the daughter
of a god.' He seems to have said nothing in particular, to
have accepted with alacrity the invitation that he and
his dear comrades should prolong their visit, and to have
prolonged it with them for a whole year, in the course
of which Circe bore him a son, named Telegonus. As
Matthew Arnold would have said, 'What a set!'

My eye roves, for relief, to those shelves where the
later annals are. I take down a tome at random. Rome in
the fifteenth century: civilisation never was more brilliant
than there and then, I imagine; and yet—no, I replace that
tome. I saw enough in it to remind me that the Borgias
selected and laid down rare poisons in their cellars with
as much thought as they gave to their vintage wines.
Extraordinary!—but the Romans do not seem to have
thought so. An invitation to dine at the Palazzo Borghese
was accounted the highest social honour. I am aware that
in recent books of Italian history there has been a tend-
ency to whiten the Borgias' characters. But I myself hold
to the old romantic black way of looking at the Borgias. I
maintain that though you would often in the fifteenth
century have heard the snobbish Roman say, in a would-be
off-hand tone, 'I am dining with the Borgias to-night', no
Roman ever was able to say, 'I dined last night with the
Borgias.'

To mankind in general Macbeth and Lady Macbeth
stand out as the supreme type of all that a host and hostess
should not be. Hence the marked coolness of Scotsmen
towards Shakespeare, hence the untiring efforts of that
proud and sensitive race to set up Burns in his stead.
It is a risky thing to offer sympathy to the proud and

sensitive, yet I must say that I think the Scots have a real grievance. The two actual, historic Macbeths were no worse than innumerable other couples in other lands that had not yet fully struggled out of barbarism. It is hard that Shakespeare happened on the story of that particular pair, and so made it immortal. But he meant no harm, and, let Scotsmen believe me, did positive good. Scotch hospitality is proverbial. As much in Scotland as in America does the English visitor blush when he thinks how perfunctory and niggard, in comparison, English hospitality is. It was Scotland that first formalised hospitality, made of it an exacting code of honour, with the basic principle that the guest must in all circumstances be respected and at all costs protected. Jacobite history bristles with examples of the heroic sacrifices made by hosts for their guests, sacrifices of their own safety and even of their own political convictions, for fear of infringing, however slightly, that sacred code of theirs. And what was the origin of all this noble pedantry? Shakespeare's 'Macbeth'.

Perhaps if England were a bleak and rugged country, like Scotland, or a new country, like America, the foreign visitor would be more overwhelmed with kindness here than he is. The landscapes of our country-side are so charming, London abounds in public monuments so redolent of history, so romantic and engrossing, that we are perhaps too apt to think the foreign visitor would have neither time nor inclination to sit dawdling in private dining-rooms. Assuredly there is no lack of hospitable impulse among the English. In what may be called mutual hospitality they touch a high level. The French, also the Italians, entertain one another far less frequently. In England the native guest has a very good time indeed—though of course he pays for it, in some measure, by acting as host too, from time to time.

In practice, no, there cannot be any absolute division of mankind into my two categories, hosts and guests. But psychologically a guest does not cease to be a guest when he gives a dinner, nor is a host not a host when he accepts one. The amount of entertaining that a guest need do is a matter wholly for his own conscience. He will soon find that he does not receive less hospitality for offering little; and he would not receive less if he offered none. The amount received by him depends wholly on the degree of his agreeableness. Pride makes an occasional host of him; but he does not shine in that capacity. Nor do hosts want him to assay it. If they accept an invitation from him, they do so only because they wish not to hurt his feelings. As guests they are fish out of water.

Circumstances do, of course, react on character. It is conventional for the rich to give, and for the poor to receive. Riches do tend to foster in you the instincts of a host, and poverty does create an atmosphere favourable to the growth of guestish instincts. But strong bents make their own way. Not all guests are to be found among the needy, nor all hosts among the affluent. For sixteen years after my education was, by courtesy, finished—from the age, that is, of twenty-two to the age of thirty-eight—I lived in London, seeing all sorts of people all the while; and I came across many a rich man who, like the master of the shepherd Corin, was 'of churlish disposition' and little recked 'to find the way to heaven by doing deeds of hospitality'. On the other hand, I knew quite poor men who were incorrigibly hospitable.

To such men, all honour. The most I dare claim for myself is that if I had been rich I should have been better than Corin's master. Even as it was, I did my best. But I had no authentic joy in doing it. Without the spur of pride I might conceivably have not done it at all. There recurs to me from among memories of my boyhood an episode that is rather significant. In my school, as in most others, we received now and again 'hampers' from home. At the mid-day dinner, in every house, we all ate to-gether; but at breakfast and supper we ate in four or five separate 'messes'. It was customary for the receiver of a hamper to share the contents with his mess-mates. On one occasion I received, instead of the usual variegated hamper, a box containing twelve sausage-rolls. It happened that when this box arrived and was opened by me there was no one around. Of sausage-rolls I was particularly fond. I am sorry to say that I carried the box up to my cubicle, and, having eaten two of the sausage-rolls, said nothing to my friends, that day, about the other ten, nor anything about them when, three days later, I had eaten them all—all, up there, alone.

Thirty years have elapsed, my school-fellows are scattered far and wide, the chance that this page may meet the eyes of some of them does not much dismay me; but I am glad there was no collective and contemporary judgment by them on my strange exploit. What defence could I have offered? Suppose I had said, 'You see, I am so essentially a guest,' the plea would have carried little weight. And yet it would not have been a worthless plea. On receipt of a hamper, a boy did rise, always, in the esteem of his mess-mates. His sardines, his marmalade, his potted meat, at any rate while they lasted, did make us think that his parents 'must be awfully decent' and that he was a not unworthy son. He had become our central figure, we expected him to lead the conversation, we liked listening to him, his jokes were good. With those twelve sausage-rolls I could have dominated my fellows for a while. But I had not a dominant nature. I never trusted myself as a leader. Leading abashed me. I was happiest in the comity of the crowd. Having received a hamper, I was always glad when it was finished, glad to fall back into the ranks. Humility is a virtue, and it is a virtue innate in guests.

Boys (as will have been surmised from my record of the effect of hampers) are all of them potential guests. It is only as they grow up that some of them harden into hosts. It is likely enough that if I, when I grew up, had been rich, my natural bent to guestship would have been diverted, and I too have become a (sort of) host. And perhaps I should have passed muster. I suppose I did pass

muster whenever, in the course of my long residence
in London, I did entertain friends. But the memory of
those occasions is not dear to me—especially not the
memory of those that were in the more distinguished
restaurants. Somewhere in the back of my brain, while
I tried to lead the conversation brightly, was always the
haunting fear that I had not brought enough money in
my pocket. I never let this fear master me. I never said
to any one 'Will you have a liqueur?'—always 'What
liqueur will you have?' But I postponed as far as possible the evil moment of asking for the bill. When I had,
in the proper casual tone (I hope and believe), at length
asked for it, I wished always it were not brought to me
folded on a plate, as though the amount were so hideously
high that I alone must be privy to it. So soon as it was laid
beside me, I wanted to know the worst at once. But I
pretended to be so occupied in talk that I was unaware
of the bill's presence; and I was careful to be always in
the middle of a sentence when I raised the upper fold and
took my not (I hope) frozen glance. In point of fact, the
amount was always much less than I had feared. Pessimism
does win us great happy moments.

Meals in the restaurants of Soho tested less severely the
pauper guest masquerading as host. But to them one
could not ask rich persons—nor even poor persons unless
one knew them very well. Soho is so uncertain that the
fare is often not good enough to be palmed off on even
one's poorest and oldest friends. A very magnetic host,
with a great gift for bluffing, might, no doubt, even in
Soho's worst moments, diffuse among his guests a conviction that all was of the best. But I never was good at
bluffing. I had always to let food speak for itself. 'It's
cheap' was the only pæan that in Soho's bad moments
ever occurred to me, and this of course I did not utter.
And *was* it so cheap, after all? Soho induces a certain
optimism. A bill there was always larger than I had
thought it would be.

Every one, even the richest and most munificent of

men, pays much by cheque more light-heartedly than he pays little in specie. In restaurants I should have liked always to give cheques. But in any restaurant I was so much more often seen as guest than as host that I never felt sure the proprietor would trust me. Only in my club did I know the luxury, or rather the painlessness, of entertaining by cheque. A cheque—especially if it is a club cheque, as supplied for the use of members, not a leaf torn out of his own book—makes so little mark on any man's imagination. He dashes off some words and figures, he signs his name (with that vague momentary pleasure which the sight of his own signature anywhere gives him), he walks away and forgets. Offering hospitality in my club, I was inwardly calm. But even there I did not glow (though my face and manner, I hoped, glowed). If my guest was by nature a guest, I managed to forget somewhat that I myself was a guest by nature. But if, as now and then happened, my guest was a true and habitual host, I did feel that we were in an absurdly false relation; and it was not without difficulty that I could restrain myself from saying to him, 'This is all very well, you know, but—frankly: your place is at the head of your own table.'

The host as guest is far, far worse than the guest as host. He never even passes muster. The guest, in virtue of a certain hability that is part of his natural equipment, can more or less ape the ways of a host. But the host, with his more positive temperament, does not even attempt the graces of a guest. By 'graces' I do not mean to imply anything artificial. The guest's manners are, rather, as wild flowers springing from good rich soil—the soil of genuine modesty and gratitude. He honourably wishes to please in return for the pleasure he is receiving. He wonders that people should be so kind to him, and, without knowing it, is very kind to *them*. But the host, as I said earlier in this essay, is a guest against his own will. That is the root of the mischief. He feels that it is more blessed, etc., and that he is conferring rather than accepting a favour. He does not adjust himself. He forgets his place. He leads the conversation. He tries genially to draw you out. He never comments on the goodness of the food or wine. He looks at his watch abruptly and says he must be off. He doesn't say he has had a delightful time. In fact, his place is at the head of his own table.

His own table, over his own cellar, under his own roof —it is only there that you see him at his best. To a club or restaurant he may sometimes invite you, but not there, not there, my child, do you get the full savour of his quality. In life or literature there has been no better host than Old Wardle. Appalling though he would have been as a guest in club or restaurant, it is hardly less painful to think of him as a host there. At Dingley Dell, with an ample gesture, he made you free of all that was his. He could not have given you a club or a restaurant. Nor, when you come to think of it, did he give you Dingley Dell. The place remained his. None knew better than Old Wardle that this was so. Hospitality, as we have agreed, is not one of the most deep-rooted instincts in man, whereas the sense of possession certainly is. Not even Old Wardle was a communist. 'This', you may be sure he said to himself, 'is *my* roof, these are *my* horses, that's a picture of *my* dear old grandfather.' And 'This', he would say to us, 'is *my* roof: sleep soundly under it. These are *my* horses: ride them. That's a portrait of *my* dear old grandfather: have a good look at it.' But he did not ask us to walk off with any of these things. Not even what he actually did give us would he regard as having passed out of his possession. 'That', he would muse if we were torpid after dinner, 'is *my* roast beef,' and 'That', if we staggered on the way to bed, 'is *my* cold milk punch.' 'But surely,' you interrupt me, 'to give and then not feel that one has given is the very best of all ways of giving.' I agree. I hope you didn't think I was trying to disparage Old Wardle. I was merely keeping my promise to point out that from among the motives of even the best hosts pride and egoism are not absent.

Every virtue, as we were taught in youth, is a mean between two extremes; and I think any virtue is the better understood by us if we glance at the vice on either side of it. I take it that the virtue of hospitality stands midway between churlishness and mere ostentation. Far to the left of the good host stands he who doesn't want to see anything of any one; far to the right, he who wants a horde of people to be always seeing something of *him*. I conjecture that the figure on the left, just discernible through my field-glasses, is that of old Corin's master. His name was never revealed to us, but Corin's brief account of his character suffices. 'Deeds of hospitality' is a dismal phrase that could have occurred only to the servant of a very dismal master. Not less tell-tale is Corin's idea that men who do these 'deeds' do them only to save their souls in the next world. It is a pity Shakespeare did not actually bring Corin's master on to the stage. One would have liked to see the old man genuinely touched by the charming eloquence of Rosalind's appeal for a crust of bread, and conscious that he would probably go to heaven if he granted it, and yet not quite able to grant it. Far away though he stands to the left of the good host, he has yet something in common with that third person discernible on the right—that speck yonder, which I believe to be Lucullus. Nothing that we know of Lucullus suggests that he was less inhuman than the churl of Arden. It does not appear that he had a single friend, nor that he wished for one. His lavishness was indiscriminate except in that he entertained only the rich. One would have liked to dine with him, but not even in the act of digestion could one have felt that he had a heart. One would have acknowledged that in all the material resources of his art he was a master, and also that he practised his art for sheer love of it, wishing to be admired for nothing but his mastery, and cocking no eye on any of those ulterior objects but for which some of the most prominent hosts would not entertain at all. But the very fact that he was an artist is repulsive. When hospitality becomes an art it loses its very soul. With this reflection I look away from Lucullus and, fixing my gaze on the middle ground, am the better able to appreciate the excellence of the figure that stands before me—the figure of Old Wardle. Some pride and egoism in that capacious breast, yes, but a great heart full of kindness, and ever a warm spontaneous welcome to the stranger in need, and to all old friends and young. Hark! he is shouting something. He is asking us both down to Dingley Dell. And you have shouted back that you will be delighted. Ah, did I not suspect from the first that you too were perhaps a guest?

But—I constrain you in the act of rushing off to pack your things—one moment: this essay has yet to be finished. We have yet to glance at those two extremes between which the mean is good guestship. Far to the right of the good guest, we descry the parasite; far to the left, the churl again. Not the same churl, perhaps. We do not know that Corin's master was ever sampled as a guest. I am inclined to call yonder speck Dante—Dante Alighieri, of whom we do know that he received during his exile much hospitality from many hosts and repaid them by writing how bitter was the bread in their houses, and how steep the stairs were. To think of dour Dante as a guest is less dispiriting only than to think what he would have been as a host had it ever occurred to him to entertain any one or anything except a deep regard for Beatrice; and one turns with positive relief to have a glimpse of the parasite—Mr Smurge, I presume, 'whose gratitude was as boundless as his appetite, and his presence as unsought as it appeared to be inevitable.' But now, how gracious and admirable is the central figure—radiating gratitude, but not too much of it; never intrusive, even within call; full of dignity, yet all amenable; quiet, yet lively; never echoing, ever amplifying; never contradicting, but often lighting the way to truth; an ornament, an inspiration, anywhere.

Such is he. But *who* is he? It is easier to confess a

defect than to claim a quality. I have told you that when I lived in London I was nothing as a host; but I will not claim to have been a perfect guest. Nor indeed was I. I was a good one, but, looking back, I see myself not quite in the centre—slightly to the left, slightly to the churlish side. I was rather *too* quiet, and I did sometimes contradict. And, though I always liked to be invited anywhere, I very often preferred to stay at home. If any one hereafter shall form a collection of the notes written by me in reply to invitations, I am afraid he will gradually suppose me to have been more in request than ever I really was, and to have been also a great invalid, and a great traveller.

GOING OUT FOR A WALK

IT IS A FACT that not once in all my life have I gone out for a walk. I have been taken out for walks; but that is another matter. Even while I trotted prattling by my nurse's side I regretted the good old days when I had, and wasn't, a perambulator. When I grew up it seemed to me that the one advantage of living in London was that nobody ever wanted me to come out for a walk. London's very drawbacks—its endless noise and hustle, its smoky air, the squalor ambushed everywhere in it—assured this one immunity. Whenever I was with friends in the country, I knew that at any moment, unless rain were actually falling, some man might suddenly say 'Come out for a walk!' in that sharp imperative tone which he would not dream of using in any other connexion. People seem to think there is something inherently noble and virtuous in the desire to go for a walk. Any one thus desirous feels that he has a right to impose his will on whomever he sees comfortably settled in an arm-chair, reading. It is easy to say simply 'No' to an old friend. In the case of a mere

acquaintance one wants some excuse. 'I wish I could, but'
—nothing ever occurs to me except 'I have some letters
to write.' This formula is unsatisfactory in three ways.
(1) It isn't believed. (2) It compels you to rise from your
chair, go to the writing-table, and sit improvising a letter
to somebody until the walkmonger (just not daring to call
you liar and hypocrite) shall have lumbered out of the
room. (3) It won't operate on Sunday mornings. 'There's
no post out till this evening' clinches the matter; and
you may as well go quietly.

Walking for walking's sake may be as highly laudable
and exemplary a thing as it is held to be by those who
practise it. My objection to it is that it stops the brain.
Many a man has professed to me that his brain never
works so well as when he is swinging along the high road
or over hill and dale. This boast is not confirmed by my
memory or anybody who on a Sunday morning has forced
me to partake of his adventure. Experience teaches me
that whatever a fellow-guest may have of power to instruct or to amuse when he is sitting on a chair, or standing on a hearth-rug, quickly leaves him when he takes
one out for a walk. The ideas that came so thick and fast
to him in any room, where are they now? where that
encyclopædic knowledge which he bore so lightly? where
the kindling fancy that played like summer lightning over
any topic that was started? The man's face that was so
mobile is set now; gone is the light from his fine eyes.
He says that A. (our host) is a thoroughly good fellow.
Fifty yards further on, he adds that A. is one of the best
fellows he has ever met. We tramp another furlong or so,
and he says that Mrs A. is a charming woman. Presently
he adds that she is one of the most charming women he
has ever known. We pass an inn. He reads vapidly aloud
to me: 'The King's Arms. Licensed to sell Ales and
Spirits.' I foresee that during the rest of the walk he will
read aloud any inscription that occurs. We pass a mile-
stone. He points at it with his stick, and says, 'Uxminster.
11 Miles.' We turn a sharp corner at the foot of a hill.

He points at the wall, and says, 'Drive Slowly.' I see far ahead, on the other side of the hedge bordering the high road, a small notice-board. He sees it too. He keeps his eye on it. And in due course 'Trespassers', he says, 'Will Be Prosecuted.' Poor man!—mentally a wreck.

Luncheon at the A.s', however, salves him and floats him in full sail. Behold him once more the life and soul of the party. Surely he will never, after the bitter lesson of this morning, go out for another walk. An hour later, I see him striding forth, with a new companion. I watch him out of sight. I know what he is saying. He is saying that I am rather a dull man to go a walk with. He will presently add that I am one of the dullest men he ever went a walk with. Then he will devote himself to reading out the inscriptions.

How comes it, this immediate deterioration in those who go walking for walking's sake? Just what happens? I take it that not by his reasoning faculties is a man urged to this enterprise. He is urged, evidently, by something in him that transcends reason; by his soul, I presume. Yes, it must be the soul that raps out the 'Quick march!' to the body.—'Halt! Stand at ease!' interposes the brain, and 'To what destination,' it suavely asks the soul, 'and on what errand, are you sending the body?'—'On no errand whatsoever,' the soul makes answer, 'and to no destination at all. It is just like you to be always on the look-out for some subtle ulterior motive. The body is going out because the mere fact of its doing so is a sure indication of nobility, probity, and rugged grandeur of character.' —'Very well, Vagula, have your own wayula! But I', says the brain, 'flatly refuse to be mixed up in this tomfoolery. I shall go to sleep till it is over.' The brain then wraps itself up in its own convolutions, and falls into a dreamless slumber from which nothing can rouse it till the body has been safely deposited indoors again.

Even if you go to some definite place, for some definite purpose, the brain would rather you took a vehicle; but it does not make a point of this; it will serve you well

enough unless you are going *for a walk*. It won't, while
your legs are vying with each other, do any deep thinking for you, nor even any close thinking; but it will do
any number of small odd jobs for you willingly—provided that your legs, also, are making themselves useful,
not merely bandying you about to gratify the pride of the
soul. Such as it is, this essay was composed in the course
of a walk, this morning. I am not one of those extremists
who must have a vehicle to every destination. I never
go out of my way, as it were, to avoid exercise. I take
it as it comes, and take it in great part. That vale-
tudinarians are always chattering about it, and indulg-
ing in it to excess, is no reason for despising it. I am
inclined to think that in moderation it is rather good for
one, physically. But, pending a time when no people wish
me to go and see them, and I have no wish to go and see
any one, and there is nothing whatever for me to do off
my own premises, I never will go out for a walk.

'A CLERGYMAN'

FRAGMENTARY, PALE, MOMENTARY; ALMOST no-
thing; glimpsed and gone; as it were, a faint human hand
thrust up, never to reappear, from beneath the rolling
waters of Time, he forever haunts my memory and solicits
my weak imagination. Nothing is told of him but that
once, abruptly, he asked a question, and received an
answer.

This was on the afternoon of April 7th, 1778, at
Streatham, in the well-appointed house of Mr Thrale.
Johnson, on the morning of that day, had entertained
Boswell at breakfast in Bolt Court, and invited him to
dine at Thrale Hall. The two took coach and arrived
early. It seems that Sir John Pringle had asked Boswell to
ask Johnson 'what were the best English sermons for

style'. In the interval before dinner, accordingly, Boswell reeled off the names of several divines whose prose might or might not win commendation. 'Atterbury?' he suggested. 'JOHNSON: Yes, Sir, one of the best. BOSWELL: Tillotson? JOHNSON: Why, not now. I should not advise any one to imitate Tillotson's style; though I don't know; I should be cautious of censuring anything that has been applauded by so many suffrages.—South is one of the best, if you except his peculiarities, and his violence, and sometimes coarseness of language.—Seed has a very fine style; but he is not very theological. Jortin's sermons are very elegant. Sherlock's style, too, is very elegant, though he has not made it his principal study.—And you may add Smalridge. BOSWELL: I like Ogden's Sermons on Prayer very much, both for neatness of style and subtility of reasoning. JOHNSON: I should like to read all that Ogden has written. BOSWELL: What I want to know is, what sermons afford the best specimen of English pulpit eloquence. JOHNSON: We have no sermons addressed to the passions, that are good for anything; if you mean that kind of eloquence. A CLERGYMAN, whose name I do not recollect: Were not Dodd's sermons addressed to the passions? JOHNSON: They were nothing, Sir, be they addressed to what they may.'

The suddenness of it! Bang!—and the rabbit that had popped from its burrow was no more.

I know not which is the more startling—the début of the unfortunate clergyman, or the instantaneousness of his end. Why hadn't Boswell told us there was a clergyman present? Well, we may be sure that so careful and acute an artist had some good reason. And I suppose the clergyman was left to take us unawares because just so did he take the company. Had we been told he was there, we might have expected that sooner or later he would join in the conversation. He would have had a place in our minds. We may assume that in the minds of the company around Johnson he had no place. He sat forgotten, over-looked; so that his self-assertion startled every one just as on Boswell's page it startles us. In Johnson's massive and magnetic presence only some very remarkable man, such as Mr Burke, was sharply distinguishable from the rest. Others might, if they had something in them, stand out slightly. This unfortunate clergyman may have had something in him, but I judge that he lacked the gift of seeming as if he had. That deficiency, however, does not account for the horrid fate that befell him. One of Johnson's strongest and most inveterate feelings was his veneration for the Cloth. To any one in Holy Orders he habitually listened with grave and charming deference. To-day moreover, he was in excellent good humour. He was at the Thrales', where he so loved to be; the day was fine; a fine dinner was in close prospect; and he had had what he always declared to be the sum of human felicity—a ride in a coach. Nor was there in the question put by the clergyman anything likely to enrage him. Dodd was one whom Johnson had befriended in adversity; and it had always been agreed that Dodd in his pulpit was very emotional. What drew the blasting flash must have been not the question itself, but the manner in which it was asked. And I think we can guess what that manner was.

Say the words aloud: 'Were not Dodd's sermons addressed to the passions?' They are words which, if you have any dramatic and histrionic sense, *cannot* be said except in a high, thin voice.

You may, from sheer perversity, utter them in a rich and sonorous baritone or bass. But if you do so, they sound utterly unnatural. To make them carry the conviction of human utterance, you have no choice: you must pipe them.

Remember, now, Johnson was very deaf. Even the people whom he knew well, the people to whose voices he was accustomed, had to address him very loudly. It is probable that this unregarded, young, shy clergyman, when at length he suddenly mustered courage to 'cut in', let his high, thin voice soar *too* high, insomuch that it was a kind of scream. On no other hypothesis can we account for the ferocity with which Johnson turned and rended him. Johnson didn't, we may be sure, mean to be cruel. The old lion, startled, just struck out blindly. But the force of paw and claws was not the less lethal. We have endless testimony to the strength of Johnson's voice; and the very cadence of those words, 'They were nothing, Sir, be they addressed to what they may', convince me that the old lion's jaws never gave forth a louder roar. Boswell does not record that there was any further conversation before the announcement of dinner. Perhaps the whole company had been temporarily deafened. But I am not bothering about *them*. My heart goes out to the poor dear clergyman exclusively.

I said a moment ago that he was young and shy; and I admit that I slipped those epithets in without having justified them to you by due process of induction. Your quick mind will have already supplied what I omitted. A man with a high, thin voice, and without power to impress any one with a sense of his importance, a man so null in effect that even the retentive mind of Boswell did not retain his very name, would assuredly not be a self-confident man. Even if he were not naturally shy, social courage would soon have been sapped in him, and would in time have been destroyed, by experience. That he had not yet given himself up as a bad job, that he still had faint wild hopes, is proved by the fact that he did snatch the opportunity for asking that question. He must, accordingly, have been young. Was he the curate of the neighbouring church? I think so. It would account for his having been invited. I see him as he sits there listening to the great Doctor's pronouncement on Atterbury and those others. He sits on the edge of a chair in the background. He has colourless eyes, fixed earnestly, and a face almost as pale as the clerical bands beneath his somewhat receding chin. His forehead is high and narrow, his hair mouse-coloured. His hands are clasped tight before him, the knuckles standing out sharply. This constriction does not mean that he is steeling himself to speak. He has no positive intention of speaking. Very much, nevertheless, is he wishing in the back of his mind that he *could* say something—something whereat the great Doctor would turn on him and say, after a pause for thought, 'Why yes, Sir. That is most justly observed' or 'Sir, this has never occurred to me. I thank you'—thereby fixing the observer for ever high in the esteem of all. And now in a flash the chance presents itself. 'We have', shouts Johnson, 'no sermons addressed to the passions, that are good for anything.' I see the curate's frame quiver with sudden impulse, and his mouth fly open, and—no, I can't bear it, I shut my eyes and ears. But audible, even so, is something shrill, followed by something thunderous.

Presently I re-open my eyes. The crimson has not yet faded from that young face yonder, and slowly down either cheek falls a glistening tear. Shades of Atterbury and Tillotson! Such weakness shames the Established Church. What would Jortin and Smalridge have said?— what Seed and South? And, by the way, who *were* they, these worthies? It is a solemn thought that so little is conveyed to us by names which to the palaeo-Georgians conveyed so much. We discern a dim, composite picture of a big man in a big wig and a billowing black gown, with a big congregation beneath him. But we are not anxious to hear what he is saying. We know it is all very elegant. We know it will be printed and be bound in finely-tooled full calf, and no palaeo-Georgian gentleman's library will be complete without it. Literate people in those days were comparatively few; but, bating that, one may say that sermons were as much in request as novels are to-day. I wonder, will mankind continue to be capricious? It is a very solemn thought indeed that no more than a hundred-and-fifty years hence the novelists of our time, with all their moral and political and sociological outlook and influence, will perhaps shine as indistinctly as do those old preachers, with all their elegance, now. 'Yes, Sir,' some great pundit may be telling

a disciple at this moment, 'Wells is one of the best. Gals-
worthy is one of the best, if you except his concern for
delicacy of style. Mrs Ward has a very firm grasp of
problems, but is not very creational.—Caine's books are
very edifying. I should like to read all that Caine has
written. Miss Corelli, too, is very edifying.—And you
may add Upton Sinclair.' 'What I want to know', says
the disciple, 'is, what English novels may be selected
as specially enthralling.' The pundit answers: 'We have
no novels addressed to the passions that are good for
anything, if you mean that kind of enthralment.' And
here some poor wretch (whose name the disciple will not
remember) inquires: 'Are not Mrs Glyn's novels addressed
to the passions?' and is in due form annihilated. Can it be
that a time will come when readers of this passage in our
pundit's Life will take more interest in the poor nameless
wretch than in all the bearers of those great names put
together, being no more able or anxious to discriminate
between (say) Mrs Ward and Mr Sinclair than we are to
set Ogden above Sherlock, or Sherlock above Ogden? It
seems impossible. But we must remember that things
are not always what they seem.

Every man illustrious in his day, however much he may
be gratified by his fame, looks with an eager eye to posterity
for a continuance of past favours, and would even live
the remainder of his life in obscurity if by so doing he
could insure that future generations would preserve a
correct attitude towards him forever. This is very natural
and human, but, like so many very natural and human
things, very silly. Tillotson and the rest need not, after
all, be pitied for our neglect of them. They either know
nothing about it, or are above such terrene trifles. Let us
keep our pity for the seething mass of divines who were *not*
elegantly verbose, and had no fun or glory while they
lasted. And let us keep a specially large portion for one
whose lot was so much worse than merely undistinguished. If that nameless curate had not been at the
Thrales' that day, or, being there, had kept the silence

that so well became him, his life would have been drab enough, in all conscience. But at any rate an unpromising career would not have been nipped in the bud. And that is what in fact happened, I'm sure of it. A robust man might have rallied under the blow. Not so our friend. Those who knew him in infancy had not expected that he would be reared. Better for him had they been right. It is well to grow up and be ordained, but not if you are delicate and very sensitive, and shall happen to annoy the greatest, the most stentorian and roughest of contemporary personages. 'A Clergyman' never held up his head or smiled again after the brief encounter recorded for us by Boswell. He sank into a rapid decline. Before the next blossoming of Thrale Hall's almond trees he was no more. I like to think that he died forgiving Dr Johnson.

THE CRIME

ON A BLEAK WET stormy afternoon at the outset of last year's Spring, I was in a cottage, all alone, and knowing that I must be all alone till evening. It was a remote cottage, in a remote country, and had been 'let furnished' by its owner. My spirits are easily affected by weather, and I hate solitude. And I dislike to be master of things that are not mine. 'Be careful not to break us,' say the glass and china. 'You'd better not spill ink on *me*,' growls the carpet. 'None of your dog's-earing, thumb-marking, back-breaking tricks *here*!' snarl the books.

The books in this cottage looked particularly disagreeable—horrid little upstarts of this and that scarlet or cerulean 'series' of 'standard' authors. Having gloomily surveyed them, I turned my back on them, and watched the rain streaming down the latticed window, whose panes seemed likely to be shattered at any moment by the wind.

I have known men who constantly visit the Central
Criminal Court, visit also the scenes where famous crimes
were committed, form their own theories of those crimes,
collect souvenirs of those crimes, and call themselves
Criminologists. As for me, my interest in crime is, alas,
merely morbid. I did not know, as those others would
doubtless have known, that the situation in which I found
myself was precisely of the kind most conducive to the
darkest deeds. I did not bemoan it, and think of Lear in
the hovel on the heath. The wind howled in the chimney,
and the rain had begun to sputter right down it, so that
the fire was beginning to hiss in a very sinister manner.
Suppose the fire went out! It looked as if it meant to.
I snatched the pair of bellows that hung beside it. I plied
them vigorously. 'Now mind!—not *too* vigorously. We
aren't yours!' they wheezed. I handled them more gently.
But I did not release them till they had secured me a
steady blaze.

I sat down before that blaze. Despair had been warded
off. Gloom, however, remained; and gloom grew. I felt
that I should prefer any one's thoughts to mine. I rose,
I returned to the books. A dozen or so of those which
were on the lowest of the three shelves were full-sized,
were octavo, looked as though they had been bought to be
read. I would exercise my undoubted right to read one
of them. Which of them? I gradually decided on a novel
by a well-known writer whose works, though I had several
times had the honour of meeting her, were known to me
only by repute.

I knew nothing of them that was not good. The lady's
'output' had not been at all huge, and it was agreed that
her 'level' was high. I had always gathered that the chief
characteristic of her work was its great 'vitality'. The
book in my hand was a third edition of her latest novel,
and at the end of it were numerous press-notices, at
which I glanced for confirmation. 'Immense vitality,' yes,
said one critic. 'Full', said another, 'of an intense vitality.'
'A book that will live,' said a third. How on earth did he

know that? I was, however, very willing to believe in the vitality of this writer for all present purposes. Vitality was a thing in which she herself, her talk, her glance, her gestures, abounded. She and they had been, I remembered, rather too much for me. The first time I met her, she said something that I lightly and mildly disputed. On no future occasion did I stem any opinion of hers. Not that she had been rude. Far from it. She had but in a sisterly, brotherly way, and yet in a way that was filially eager too, asked me to explain my point. I did my best. She was all attention. But I was conscious that my best, under her eye, was not good. She was quick to help me: she said for me just what I had tried to say, and proceeded to show me just why it was wrong. I smiled the gallant smile of a man who regards women as all the more adorable because logic is *not* their strong point, bless them! She asked—not aggressively, but strenuously, as one who dearly loves a joke—what I was smiling at. Altogether, a chastening encounter; and my memory of it was tinged with a feeble resentment. How she had scored! No man likes to be worsted in argument by a woman. And I fancy that to be vanquished by a feminine writer is the kind of defeat least of all agreeable to a man who writes. A 'sex war', we are often told, is to be one of the features of the world's future—women demanding the right to do men's work, and men refusing, resisting, counter-attacking. It seems likely enough. One can believe anything of the world's future. Yet one conceives that not all men, if this particular evil come to pass, will stand packed shoulder to shoulder against all women. One does not feel that the dockers will be very bitter against such women as want to be miners, or the plumbers frown much upon the would-be steeple-jills. I myself have never had my sense of fitness jarred, nor a spark of animosity roused in me, by a woman practising any of the fine arts—except the art of writing. That she should write a few little poems or *pensées*, or some impressions of a trip in a dahabieh as far as (say) Biskra, or even a short story or two, seems to me not wholly amiss, even though she do such things for publication. But that she should be an habitual, professional author, with a passion for her art, and a fountain-pen and an agent, and sums down in advance of royalties on sales in Canada and Australia, and a profound knowledge of human character, and an essentially sane outlook, is somehow incongruous with my notions—my mistaken notions, if you will—of what she ought to be.

'Has a profound knowledge of human character, and an essentially sane outlook' said one of the critics quoted at the end of the book that I had chosen. The wind and the rain in the chimney had not abated, but the fire was bearing up bravely. So would I. I would read cheerfully and without prejudice. I poked the fire and, pushing my chair slightly back, lest the heat should warp the book's covers, began Chapter I. A woman sat writing in a summer-house at the end of a small garden that overlooked a great valley in Surrey. The description of her was calculated to make her very admirable—a thorough *woman*, not strictly beautiful, but likely to be thought beautiful by those who knew her well; not dressed as though she gave much heed to her clothes, but dressed in a fashion that exactly harmonised with her special type. Her pen 'travelled' rapidly across the foolscap, and while it did so she was described in more and more detail. But at length she came to a 'knotty point' in what she was writing. She paused, she pushed back the hair from her temples, she looked forth at the valley; and now the landscape was described, but not at all exhaustively, it, for the writer soon overcame her difficulty, and her pen travelled faster than ever, till suddenly there was a cry of 'Mammy!' and in rushed a seven-year-old child, in conjunction with whom she was more than ever admirable; after which the narrative skipped back across eight years, and the woman became a girl, giving as yet no token of future eminence in literature but—I had an impulse which I obeyed almost before I was conscious of it.

Nobody could have been more surprised than I was at what I had done—done so neatly, so quietly and gently. The book stood closed, upright, with its back to me, just as on a book-shelf, behind the bars of the grate. There it was. And it gave forth, as the flames crept up the blue cloth sides of it, a pleasant though acrid smell. My astonishment had passed, giving place to an exquisite satisfaction. How pottering and fumbling a thing was even the best kind of written criticism! I understood the contempt felt by the man of action for the man of words. But what pleased me most was that at last, actually, I, at my age, I of all people, had committed a crime—was guilty of a crime. I had power to revoke it. I might write to my bookseller for an unburnt copy, and place it on the shelf where this one had stood—this gloriously glowing one. I would do nothing of the sort. What I had done I had done. I would wear forever on my conscience the white rose of theft and the red rose of arson. If hereafter the owner of this cottage happened to miss that volume —let him! If he were fool enough to write to me about it, would I share my grand secret with him? No. Gently, with his poker, I prodded that volume further among the coals. The all-but-consumed binding shot forth little tongues of bright colour—flamelets of sapphire, amethyst, emerald. Charming! Could even the author herself not admire them? Perhaps. Poor woman!—*I* had scored now, scored so perfectly that I felt myself to be almost a brute while I poked off the loosened black outer pages and led the fire on to pages that were but pale brown.

These were quickly devoured. But it seemed to me that whenever I left the fire to forage for itself it made little headway. I pushed the book over on its side. The flames closed on it, but presently, licking their lips, fell back, as though they had had enough. I took the tongs and put the book upright again, and raked it fore and aft. It seemed almost as thick as ever. With poker and tongs I carved it into two, three sections—the inner pages flashing white

as when they were sent to the binders. Strange! Afore-
time, a book was burnt now and again in the market-
place by the common hangman. Was he, I wondered, paid
by the hour? I had always supposed the thing quite easy
for him—a bright little, brisk little conflagration, and so
home. Perhaps other books were less resistant than this
one? I began to feel that the critics were more right than
they knew. Here was a book that had indeed an intense
vitality, and an immense vitality. It was a book that would
live—do what one might. I vowed it should not. I sub-
divided it, spread it, redistributed it. Ever and anon my
eye would be caught by some sentence or fragment of a
sentence in the midst of a charred page before the flames
crept over it. 'lways loathed you, bu', I remember; and
'ning. Tolstoi was right.' Who had always loathed whom?
And what, what, had Tolstoi been right about? I had
an absurd but genuine desire to know. Too late! Con-
found the woman!—she was scoring again. I furiously
drove her pages into the yawning crimson jaws of the
coals. Those jaws had lately been golden. Soon, to my
horror, they seemed to be growing grey. They seemed to
be closing—on nothing. Flakes of black paper, full-sized
layers of paper brown and white, began to hide them
from me altogether. I sprinkled a boxful of wax matches.
I resumed the bellows. I lunged with the poker. I held
a newspaper over the whole grate. I did all that inspiration
could suggest, or skill accomplish. Vainly. The fire went
out—darkly, dismally, gradually, quite out.

How she had scored again! But she did not know it. I
felt no bitterness against her as I lay back in my chair,
inert, listening to the storm that was still raging. I blamed
only myself. I had done wrong. The small room became
very cold. Whose fault was that but my own? I had done
wrong hastily, but had done it and been glad of it. I had
not remembered the words a wise king wrote long ago,
that the lamp of the wicked shall be put out, and that the
way of transgressors is hard.

WILLIAM AND MARY

MEMORIES, LIKE OLIVES, ARE an acquired taste. William and Mary (I give them the Christian names that were indeed theirs—the joint title by which their friends always referred to them) were for some years an interest in my life, and had a hold on my affection. But a time came when, though I had known and liked them too well ever to forget them, I gave them but a few thoughts now and then. How, being dead, could they keep their place in the mind of a young man surrounded with large and constantly renewed consignments of the living? As one grows older, the charm of novelty wears off. One finds that there is no such thing as novelty—or, at any rate, that one has lost the faculty for perceiving it. One sees every newcomer not as something strange and special, but as a ticketed specimen of this or that very familiar genius. The world has ceased to be remarkable; and one tends to think more and more often of the days when it was so very remarkable indeed.

I suppose that had I been thirty years older when first I knew him, William would have seemed to me little worthier of attention than a twopenny postage-stamp seems to-day. Yet, no: William really had some oddities that would have caught even an oldster's eye. In himself he was commonplace enough (as I, coeval though I was with him, soon saw). But in details of surface he was unusual. In them he happened to be rather ahead of his time. He was a socialist, for example. In 1890 there was only one other socialist in Oxford, and he not at all an undergraduate, but a retired chimney-sweep, named Hines, who made speeches, to which nobody, except perhaps William, listened, near the Martyrs' Memorial. And

William wore a flannel shirt, and rode a bicycle—very strange habits in those days, and very horrible. He was said to be (though he was short-sighted and wore glasses) a first-rate 'back' at football; but, as football was a thing frowned on by the rowing men, and coldly ignored by the bloods, his talent for it did not help him: he was one of the principal pariahs of our College; and it was rather in a spirit of bravado, and to show how sure of myself I was, that I began, in my second year, to cultivate his acquaintance.

We had little in common. I could not think Political Economy 'the most exciting thing in the world', as he used to call it. Nor could I without yawning listen to more than a few lines of Mr William Morris' interminable smooth Icelandic Sagas, which my friend, pious young socialist that he was, thought 'glorious'. He had begun to write an Icelandic Saga himself, and had already achieved some hundreds of verses. None of these pleased him, though to me they seemed very like his master's. I can see him now, standing on his hearth-rug, holding his MS close to his short-sighted eyes, declaiming the verses and trying, with many angular gestures of his left hand, to animate them—a tall, broad, raw-boned fellow, with long brown hair flung back from his forehead, and a very shabby suit of clothes. Because of his clothes and his socialism, and his habit of offering beer to a guest, I had at first supposed him quite poor; and I was surprised when he told me that he had from his guardian (his parents being dead) an allowance of £350, and that when he came of age he would have an income of £400. 'All out of dividends,' he would groan. I would hint that Mr Hines and similar zealots might disembarrass him of this load, if he asked them nicely. 'No,' he would say quite seriously, 'I can't do that,' and would read out passages from 'Fabian Essays' to show that in the present anarchical conditions only mischief could result from sporadic dispersal of rent. 'Ten, twelve years hence—' he would muse more hopefully. 'But by that time,' I would

say, 'you'll probably be married, and your wife mightn't
quite—', whereat he would hotly repeat what he had said
many times: that he would never marry. Marriage was an
anti-social anachronism. I think its survival was in some
part due to the machinations of Capital. Anyway, it was
doomed. Temporary civil contracts between men and
women would be the rule 'ten, twelve years hence'; pending which time the lot of any man who had civic sense
must be celibacy, tempered perhaps with free love.

Long before that time was up, nevertheless, William
married. One afternoon in the spring of '95 I happened
to meet him at a corner of Cockspur Street. I wondered
at the immense cordiality of his greeting; for our friendship, such as it was, had waned in our two final years at
Oxford. 'You look very flourishing, and', I said, 'you're
wearing a new suit!' 'I'm married,' he replied, obviously
without a twinge of conscience. He told me he had been
married just a month. He declared that to be married
was the most splendid thing in all the world; but he
weakened the force of this generalisation by adding that
there never was any one like his wife. 'You must see her,'
he said; and his impatience to show her proudly off to
some one was so evident, and so touching, that I could
but accept his invitation to go and stay with them for
two or three days—'why not next week?' They had taken
and furnished 'a sort of cottage' in ——shire, and this was
their home. He had 'run up for the day, on business—
journalism' and was now on his way to Charing Cross. 'I
know you'll like my wife,' he said at parting. 'She's—
well, she's glorious.'

As this was the epithet he had erst applied to 'Beowulf'
and to 'Sigurd the Volsung' it raised no high hopes. And
indeed, as I was soon to find, he had again misused it.
There was nothing glorious about his bride. Some people
might even have not thought her pretty. I myself did not,
in the flash of first sight. Neat, insignificant, pleasing,
was what she appeared to me, rather than pretty, and far
rather than glorious. In an age of fringes, her brow was

severely bare. She looked 'practical'. But an instant later, when she smiled, I saw that she was pretty, too. And presently I thought her delightful. William had met me in a 'governess cart', and we went to see him unharness the pony. He did this in a fumbling, experimental way, confusing the reins with the traces, and profiting so little by his wife's directions that she began to laugh. And her laugh was a lovely thing; quite a small sound, but exquisitely clear and gay, coming in a sequence of notes that neither rose nor fell, that were quite even; a trill of notes, and then another, and another, as though she were pulling repeatedly a little silver bell. . . . As I describe it, perhaps the sound may be imagined irritating. I can only say it was enchanting.

I wished she would go on laughing; but she ceased, she darted forward and (William standing obediently aside, and I helping unhelpfully) unharnessed the pony herself, and led it into its small stable. Decidedly, she was 'practical', but—I was prepared now to be lenient to any quality she might have.

Had she been feckless, no doubt I should have forgiven her that, too; but I might have enjoyed my visit less than I did, and might have been less pleased to go often again. I had expected to 'rough it' under William's roof. But everything thereunder, within the limits of a strict Arcadian simplicity, was well-ordered. I was touched, when I went to my bedroom, by the precision with which the very small maid had unpacked and disposed my things. And I wondered where my hostess had got the lore she had so evidently imparted. Certainly not from William. Perhaps (it only now strikes me) from a hand-book. For Mary was great at handbooks. She had handbooks about gardening, and others about poultry, and one about 'the stable', and others on cognate themes. From these she had filled up the gaps left in her education by her father, who was a widower and either a doctor or a solicitor—I forget which—in one of the smallest towns of an adjoining county. And I daresay she may have had, somewhere hidden away, a manual for young hostesses. If so, it must have been a good one. But to say this is to belittle Mary's powers of intuition. It was they, sharpened by her adoration of William, and by her intensity for everything around him, that made her so efficient a housewife.

If she possessed a manual for young house-hunters, it was assuredly not by the light of this that she had chosen the home they were installed in. The 'sort of cottage' had been vacant for many years—an unpromising and in-eligible object, a mile away from a village, and three miles away from a railway station. The main part of it was an actual cottage, of seventeenth-century workmanship; but a little stuccoed wing had been added to each side of it, in 1850 or thereabouts, by an eccentric old gentleman who at that time chose to make it his home. He had added also the small stable, a dairy, and other appanages. For these, and for garden, there was plenty of room, as he had purchased and enclosed half an acre of the sur-rounding land. Those two stuccoed, very Victorian wings of his, each with a sash-window above and a French window below, consorted queerly with the old red brick and the latticed panes. And the long wooden veranda that he had invoked did not unify the trinity. But one didn't want it to. The wrongness had a character all its own. The wrongness was right—at any rate after Mary had hit on it for William. As a spinster, she would, I think, have been happiest in a trim modern villa. But it was a belief of hers that she had married a man of strange genius. She had married him for himself, not for his genius; but this added grace in him was a thing to be reckoned with, ever so much; a thing she must coddle to the utmost in a proper setting. She was a year older than he (though, being so small and slight, she looked several years younger), and in her devotion the maternal instinct played a great part. William, as I have already conveyed to you, was not greatly gifted. Mary's instinct, in this one matter, was at fault. But endearingly, rightly at fault. And, as William *was* outwardly odd, wasn't it well that his home should be so, too? On the inside, comfort was what Mary always aimed at for him, and achieved.

The ground floor had all been made one room, into which you stepped straight from the open air. Quite a long big room (or so it seemed, from the lowness of the ceiling), and well-freshened in its antiquity, with rush-mats here and there on the irregular red tiles, and very white whitewash on the plaster between the rafters. This was the dining-room, drawing-room, and general focus throughout the day, and was called simply the Room. William had a 'den' on the ground floor of the left wing; and there, in the mornings, he used to write a great deal. Mary had no special place of her own: her place was wherever her duties needed her. William wrote reviews of books for the *Daily* ——. He did also creative work. The vein of poetry in him had worked itself out—or rather, it expressed itself for him in Mary. For technical purposes, the influence of Ibsen had superseded that of Morris. At the time of my first visit, he was writing an extraordinarily gloomy play about an extraordinarily un-happy marriage. In subsequent seasons (Ibsen's disc hav-ing been somehow eclipsed for him by George Gissing's) he was usually writing novels in which every one—or do I exaggerate?—had made a disastrous match. I think Mary's belief in his genius had made him less diffident than he was at Oxford. He was always emerging from his den, with fresh pages of MS, into the Room. 'You don't mind?' he would say, waving his pages, and then would shout 'Mary!' She was always promptly forth-coming—sometimes from the direction of the kitchen, in a white apron, sometimes from the garden, in a blue one. She never looked at him while he read. To do so would have been lacking in respect for his work. It was on this that she must concentrate her whole mind, privileged auditor that she was. She sat looking straight before her, with her lips slightly compressed, and her

hands folded on her lap. I used to wonder that there had
been that first moment when I did not think her pretty.
Her eyes were of a very light hazel, seeming all the lighter
because her hair was of so dark a brown; and they were
beautifully set in a face of that 'pinched oval' kind which
is rather rare in England. Mary as listener would have
atoned to me for any defects there may have been in dear
old William's work. Nevertheless, I sometimes wished this
work had some comic relief in it. Publishers, I believe,
shared this wish; hence the eternal absence of William's
name from among their announcements. For Mary's sake,
and his, I should have liked him to be 'successful'. But at
any rate he didn't need money. He didn't need, in addition
to what he had, what he made by his journalism. And as
for success—well, didn't Mary think him a genius? And
wasn't he Mary's husband? The main reason why I
wished for light passages in what he read to us was that
they would have been cues for Mary's laugh. This was a
thing always new to me. I never tired of that little bell-
like euphony; those funny little lucid and level trills.

There was no stint of that charm when William was
not reading to us. Mary was in no awe of him, apart from
his work, and in no awe at all of me: she used to laugh
at us both, for one thing and another—just the same
laugh as I had first heard when William tried to unharness
the pony. I cultivated in myself whatever amused her in
me; I drew out whatever amused her in William; I never
let slip any of the things that amused her in herself.
'Chaff' is a great bond; and I should have enjoyed our
bouts of it even without Mary's own special *obbligato*.
She used to call me (for I was very urban in those days)
the Gentleman from London. I used to call her the Brave
Little Woman. Whatever either of us said or did could
be twisted easily into relation to those two titles; and our
bouts, to which William listened with a puzzled, benevolent smile, used to cease only because Mary regarded me
as a possible purveyor of what William, she was sure,
wanted and needed, down there in the country, alone

with her: intellectual conversation, after his work. She
often, I think, invented duties in garden or kitchen so that
he should have this stimulus, or luxury, without hind-
rance. But when William was alone with me it was about
her that he liked to talk, and that I myself liked to talk
too. He was very sound on the subject of Mary; and so
was I. And if, when I was alone with Mary, I seemed to
be sounder than I was on the subject of William's wonderfulness, who shall blame me?

Had Mary been a mother, William's wonderfulness
would have been less greatly important. But he was her
child as well as her lover. And I think, though I do not
know, she believed herself content that this should
always be, if so it were destined. It was not destined so.
On the first night of a visit I paid them in April, 1899,
William, when we were alone, told me news. I had been
vaguely conscious, throughout the evening, of some
change; conscious that Mary had grown gayer, and less
gay—somehow different, somehow remote. William said
that her child would be born in September, if all went
well. 'She's immensely happy,' he told me. I realised
that she was indeed happier than ever. . . . 'And of
course it would be a wonderful thing, for both of us',
he said presently, 'to have a son—or a daughter.' I asked
him which he would rather it were, a son or a daughter.
'Oh, either,' he answered wearily. It was evident that he
had misgivings and fears. I tried to reason him out of
them. He did not, I am thankful to say, ever let Mary
suspect them. *She* had no misgivings. But it was destined
that her child should live only for an hour, and that she
should die in bearing it.

I had stayed again at the cottage in July, for some days.
At the end of that month I had gone to France, as was
my custom, and a week later had written to Mary. It was
William that answered this letter, telling me of Mary's
death and burial. I returned to England next day. William
and I wrote to each other several times. He had not left

his home. He stayed there, 'trying', as he said in a grotesque and heart-rending phrase, 'to finish a novel.' I saw him in the following January. He wrote to me from the Charing Cross Hotel, asking me to lunch with him there. After our first greetings, there was a silence. He wanted to talk of—what he could not talk of. We stared helplessly at each other, and then, in the English way, talked of things at large. England was engaged in the Boer War. William was the sort of man whom one would have expected to be violently Pro-Boer. I was surprised at his fervour for the stronger side. He told me he had tried to enlist, but had been rejected on account of his eyesight. But there was, he said, a good chance of his being sent out, almost immediately, as one of the *Daily* ——'s special correspondents. 'And then', he exclaimed, 'I shall see something of it.' I had a presentiment that he would not return, and a belief that he did not want to return. He did not return. Special correspondents were not so carefully shepherded in that war as they have since been. They were more at liberty to take risks, on behalf of the journals to which they were accredited. William was killed a few weeks after he had landed at Cape Town.

And there came, as I have said, a time when I did not think of William and Mary often; and then a time when I did more often think of them. And especially much did my mind hark back to them in the late autumn of last year; for on the way to the place I was staying at I had passed the little railway station whose name had always linked itself for me with the names of those two friends. There were but four intervening stations. It was not a difficult pilgrimage that I made some days later—back towards the past, for that past's sake and honour. I had thought I should not remember the way, the three miles of way, from the station to the cottage; but I found my- self remembering it perfectly, without a glance at the finger-posts. Rain had been falling heavily, driving the late leaves off the trees; and everything looked rather sodden and misty, though the sun was now shining. I had known this landscape only in spring, summer, early autumn. Mary had held to a theory that at other seasons I could not be acclimatised. But there were groups of trees that I knew even without their leaves; and farm-houses and small stone bridges that had not at all changed. Only what mattered was changed. Only what mattered was gone. Would what I had come to see be there still? In comparison with what it had held, it was not much. But I wished to see it, melancholy spectacle though it must be for me if it were extant, and worse than melan-choly if it held something new. I began to be sure it had been demolished, built over. At the corner of the lane that had led to it, I was almost minded to explore no further, to turn back. But I went on, and suddenly I was at the four-barred iron gate, that I remembered, between the laurels. It was rusty, and was fastened with a rusty pad-lock, and beyond it there was grass where a winding 'drive' had been. From the lane the cottage never had been visible, even when these laurels were lower and sparser than they were now. Was the cottage still standing? Presently, I climbed over the gate, and walked through the long grass, and—yes, there was Mary's cottage; still there; William's and Mary's cottage. Trite enough, I have no doubt, were the thoughts that possessed me as I stood gazing. There is nothing new to be thought about the evanescence of human things; but there is always much to be felt about it by one who encounters in his maturity some such intimate instance and reminder as confronted me, in that cold sunshine, across that small wilderness of long rank wet grass and weeds.

Incredibly woebegone and lonesome the house would have looked even to one for whom it contained no memo-ries; all the more because in its utter dereliction it looked so durable. Some of the stucco had fallen off the walls of the two wings; thick flakes of it lay on the discoloured roof of the veranda, and thick flakes of it could be seen lying in the grass below. Otherwise, there were few signs of actual decay. The sash-window and the French window of each wing were shuttered, and, from where I was standing the cream-coloured paint of those shutters behind the glass looked almost fresh. The latticed windows between had all been boarded up from within. The house was not to be let perish soon.

I did not want to go nearer to it; yet I did go nearer, step by step, across the wilderness, right up to the edge of the veranda itself, and within a yard of the front-door.

I stood looking at that door. I had never noticed it in the old days, for then it had always stood open. But it asserted itself now, master of the threshold.

It was a narrow door—narrow even for its height, which did not exceed mine by more than two inches or so; a door that even when it was freshly painted must have looked mean. How much meaner now, with its paint all faded and mottled, cracked and blistered! It had no knocker, not even a slit for letters. All that it had was a large-ish key-hole. On this my eyes rested; and presently I moved to it, stooped down to it, peered through it. I had a glimpse of—darkness impenetrable.

Strange it seemed to me, as I stood back, that there the Room was, the remembered Room itself, separated from me by nothing but this unremembered door ... and a quarter of a century, yes. I saw it all, in my mind's eye, just as it had been: the way the sunlight came into it through this same doorway and through the lattices of these same four windows; the way the little bit of a staircase came down into it, so crookedly yet so confidently; and how uneven the tiled floor was, and how low the rafters were, and how littered the whole place was with books brought in from his den by William, and how bright with flowers brought in by Mary from her garden. The rafters, the stairs, the tiles, were still existing, changeless in despite of cobwebs and dust and darkness, all quite changeless on the other side of the door, so near to me. I wondered how I should feel if by some enchantment the door slowly turned on its hinges, letting in light. I should not enter, I felt, not even look, so much must I hate to see those inner things lasting when all that had given to them a meaning was gone from them, taken away from them, finally. And yet, why blame them for their survival? And how know that *nothing* of the past ever came to them, revisiting, hovering? Something— sometimes—perhaps? One knew so little. How not be tender to what, as it seemed to me, perhaps the dead loved?

So strong in me now was the wish to see again all those things, to touch them and, as it were, commune with them, and so queerly may the mind be wrought upon in a solitude among memories, that there were moments when I almost expected that the door would obey my will. I was recalled to a clearer sense of reality by something which I had not before noticed. In the door-post to the right was a small knob of rusty iron—mocking reminder that to gain admission to a house one does not 'will' the door: one rings the bell—unless it is rusty and has quite obviously no one to answer it; in which case one goes away. Yet I did not go away. The movement that I made, in despite of myself, was towards the knob itself. But, I hesitated, suppose I did what I half meant to do, and there were no sound. That would be ghastly. And surely there *would* be no sound. And if sound there were, wouldn't that be worse still? My hand drew back, wavered, suddenly closed on the knob. I heard the scrape of the wire—and then, from somewhere within the heart of the shut house, a tinkle.

It had been the weakest, the puniest of noises. It had been no more than is a fledgling's first attempt at a twitter. But I was not judging it by its volume. Deafening peals from steeples had meant less to me than that one single note breaking the silence—in there. In there, in the dark, the bell that had answered me was still quivering, I supposed, on its wire. But there was no one to answer *it*, no footstep to come hither from those recesses, making prints in the dust. Well, *I* could answer it; and again my hand closed on the knob, unhesitatingly this time, pulling further. That was my answer; and the rejoinder to it was more than I had thought to hear—a whole quick sequence of notes, faint but clear, playful, yet poignantly sad, like a trill of laughter echoing out of the past, or even merely out of this neighbouring darkness. It was so like something I had known, so recognisable and, oh, recognising, that I was lost in wonder. And long must I have remained standing at that door, for I heard the sound often, often. I must have rung again and again, tenaciously, vehemently, in my folly.

'HOW SHALL I WORD IT?'

IT WOULD SEEM THAT I am one of those travellers for whom the railway bookstall does not cater. Whenever I start on a journey, I find that my choice lies between well-printed books which I have no wish to read, and well-written books which I could not read without permanent injury to my eyesight. The keeper of the bookstall, seeing me gaze vaguely along his shelves, suggests that I should take *Fen Country Fanny*, or else *The Track of Blood* and have done with it. Not wishing to hurt his feelings, I refuse these works on the plea that I have read them. Whereon he, divining despite me that I am a superior person, says 'Here is a nice little handy edition of More's *Utopia*' or 'Carlyle's *French Revolution*' and again I make some excuse. What pleasure could I get from trying to cope with a masterpiece printed in diminutive grey-ish type on a semi-transparent little grey-ish page? I relieve the bookstall of nothing but a newspaper or two.

The other day, however, my eye and fancy were caught by a book entitled *How Shall I Word It?* and sub-entitled 'A Complete Letter Writer for Men and Women'. I had never read one of these manuals, but had often heard that there was a great and constant 'demand' for them. So I demanded this one. It is no great fun in itself. The writer is no fool. He has evidently a natural talent for writing letters. His style is, for the most part, discreet and easy. If you were a young man writing 'to Father of Girl he wishes to Marry' or 'thanking Fiancée for Present' or 'reproaching Fiancée for being a Flirt', or if you were a mother 'asking Governess her Qualifications' or 'replying to Undesirable Invitation for her Child', or indeed if you were in any other one of the crises which this book is designed to alleviate, you might copy out and post the specially-provided letter without making yourself ridiculous in the eyes of its receiver—unless, of course, he or she also possessed a copy of the book. But— well, can you conceive any one copying out and posting one of these letters, or even taking it as the basis for composition? You cannot. That shows how little you know of your fellow-creatures. Not you nor I can plumb the abyss at the bottom of which such humility is pos- sible. Nevertheless, as we know by that great and con- stant 'demand', there the abyss is, and there multitudes are at the bottom of it. Let's peer down.... No, all is darkness. But faintly, if we listen hard, is borne up to us a sound of the scratching of innumerable pens—pens whose wielders are all trying, as the author of this hand- book urges them, to 'be original, fresh, and interesting' by dint of more or less strict adherence to sample.

Giddily you draw back from the edge of the abyss. Come!—here is a thought to steady you. The mysterious great masses of helpless folk for whom *How Shall I Word It?* is written are sound at heart, delicate in feel- ing, anxious to please, most loth to wound. For it must be presumed that the author's style of letter-writing is informed as much by a desire to give his public what it needs, and will pay for, as by his own beautiful nature; and in the course of all the letters that he dictates you will find not one harsh word, not one ignoble thought or unkind insinuation. In all of them, though so many are for the use of persons placed in the most trying circumstances, and some of them are for persons writhing under a sense of intolerable injury, sweetness and light do ever reign. Even 'yours truly, Jacob Langton', in his 'letter to his Daughter's Mercenary Fiancée', mitigates the sternness of his tone by the remark that his 'task is inexpressibly painful'. And he, Mr Langton, is the one writer who lets the post go out on his wrath. When Horace Masterton, of Thorpe Road, Putney, receives from Miss Jessica Weir, of Fir Villa, Blackheath, a letter 'declaring her Change of Feelings', does he upbraid her? No; 'it was honest and brave of you to write to me so straightforwardly and at the back of my mind I know you have done what is best. . . . I give you back your freedom only at your desire. God bless you, dear.' Not less admirable is the behaviour, in similar case, of Cecil Grant (14, Glover Street, Streatham). Suddenly, as a bolt from the blue, comes a letter from Miss Louie Hawke (Elm View, Deerhurst), breaking off her betrothal to him. Haggard, he sits down to his desk; his pen traverses the notepaper—calling down curses on Louie and on all her sex? No; 'one cannot say good-bye for ever without deep regret to days that have been so full of happiness. I must thank you sincerely for all your great kindness to me. . . . With every sincere wish for your future happiness,' he bestows complete freedom on Miss Hawke. And do not imagine that in the matter of self-control and sympathy, of power to understand all and pardon all, the men are lagged behind by the women. Miss Leila Johnson (The Manse, Carlyle) has observed in Leonard Wace (Dover Street, Saltburn) a certain coldness of demeanour; yet 'I do not blame you; it is probably your nature'; and Leila in her sweet forbearance is typical of all the other pained women in these pages: she is but one of a crowd of heroines.

Face to face with all this perfection, the not perfect reader begins to crave some little outburst of wrath, of hatred or malice, from one of these imaginary ladies and gentlemen. He longs for—how shall he word it?—a glimpse of some bad motive, of some little lapse from dignity. Often, passing by a pillar-box, I have wished I could unlock it and carry away its contents, to be studied at my leisure. I have always thought such a haul would abound in things fascinating to a student of human nature. One night, not long ago, I took a waxen impression of the lock of the pillar-box nearest to my house, and had a key made. This implement I have as yet lacked either the courage or the opportunity to use. And now I think I shall throw it away. . . . No, I shan't. I refuse, after all, to draw my inference that the bulk of the British public writes always in the manner of this handbook. Even if they all have beautiful natures they must sometimes be sent slightly astray by inferior impulses, just as are you and I.

And, if err they must, surely it were well they should know how to do it correctly and forcibly. I suggest to our author that he should sprinkle his next edition with a few less righteous examples, thereby both purging his book of its monotony and somewhat justifying its sub-title. Like most people who are in the habit of writing things to be printed, I have not the knack of writing really good letters. But let me crudely indicate the sort of thing that our manual needs. . . .

LETTER FROM POOR MAN
TO OBTAIN MONEY FROM RICH ONE

*[The English law is particularly hard on what is called blackmail. It is therefore essential that the applicant should write nothing that might afterwards be twisted to incriminate him.—*ED.*]*

DEAR SIR,

To-day, as I was turning out a drawer in my attic, I came across a letter which by a curious chance fell into my hands some years ago, and which, in the stress of grave pecuniary embarrassment, had escaped my memory. It is a letter written by yourself to a lady, and the date shows it to have been written shortly after your marriage. It is of a confidential nature, and might, I fear, if it fell into the wrong hands, be cruelly misconstrued. I would wish you to have the satisfaction of destroying it in person. At first I thought of sending it on to you by post. But I know how happy you are in your domestic life; and probably your wife and you, in your perfect mutual trust, are in the habit of opening each other's letters. Therefore, to avoid risk, I would prefer to hand the document to you personally. I will not ask you to come to my attic, where I could not offer you such hospitality as is due to a man of your wealth and position. You will be so good as to meet me at 3.0 A.M. (sharp) to-morrow (Thursday) beside the tenth lamp-post to the left on the Surrey side of Waterloo Bridge; at which hour and place we shall not be disturbed.

I am, dear Sir,

Your faithfully,

JAMES GRIDGE.

LETTER FROM YOUNG MAN
REFUSING TO PAY HIS TAILOR'S BILL

Mr Eustace Davenant has received the half-servile, half-insolent screed which Mr Yardley has addressed to him. Let Mr Yardley cease from crawling on his knees and shaking his fist. Neither this posture nor this gesture can wring one bent farthing from the pockets of Mr Davenant, who was a minor at the time when that series of ill-made suits was supplied to him and will hereafter, as in the past, shout (without prejudice) from the house-tops that of all the tailors in London Mr Yardley is at once the most grasping and the least competent.

LETTER TO THANK AUTHOR
FOR INSCRIBED COPY OF BOOK

DEAR MR EMANUEL FLOWER,

It was kind of you to think of sending me a copy of

your new book. It would have been kinder still to think
again and abandon that project. I am a man of gentle
instincts, and do not like to tell you that 'A Flight into
Arcady' (of which I have skimmed a few pages, thus wasting two or three minutes of my not altogether worthless
time) is trash. On the other hand, I am determined that
you shall not be able to go around boasting to your friends,
if you have any, that this work was not condemned,
derided, and dismissed by your sincere well-wisher,
WREXFORD CRIPPS.

LETTER TO MEMBER OF PARLIAMENT
UNSEATED AT GENERAL ELECTION

DEAR MR POBSBY-BURFORD,

Though I am myself an ardent Tory, I cannot but
rejoice in the crushing defeat you have just suffered in
West Odgetown. There are moments when political conviction is overborne by personal sentiment; and this is one
of them. Your loss of the seat that you held is the more
striking by reason of the splendid manner in which the
northern and eastern divisions of Odgetown have been
wrested from the Liberal Party. The great bulk of the
newspaper-reading public will be puzzled by your extinction in the midst of our party's triumph. But then, the
great mass of the newspaper-reading public has not met
you. I have. You will probably not remember me. You
are the sort of man who would not remember anybody
who might not be of some definite use to him. Such, at
least, was one of the impressions you made on me when
I met you last summer at a dinner given by our friends
the Pelhams. Among the other things in you that struck
me were the blatant pomposity of your manner, your
appalling flow of cheap platitudes, and your hoggish lack
of ideas. It is such men as you that lower the tone of
public life. And I am sure that in writing to you thus I
am but expressing what is felt, without distinction of
party, by all who sat with you in the late Parliament.

The one person in whose behalf I regret your withdrawal into private life is your wife, whom I had the pleasure of taking in to the aforesaid dinner. It was evident to me that she was a woman whose spirit was well-nigh broken by her conjunction with you. Such remnants of cheerfulness as were in her I attributed to the Parliamentary duties which kept you out of her sight for so very many hours daily. I do not like to think of the fate to which the free and independent electors of West Odgetown have just condemned her. Only, remember this: chattel of yours though she is, and timid and humble, she despises you in her heart.

> I am, dear Mr Pobsby-Burford,
>> Yours very truly,
>>> HAROLD THISTLAKE.

LETTER FROM YOUNG LADY IN ANSWER
TO INVITATION FROM OLD SCHOOLMISTRESS

MY DEAR MISS PRICE,

How awfully sweet of you to ask me to stay with you for a few days but how *can* you think I may have forgotten you for of course I think of you so very often and of the three ears I spent at your school because it is such a joy not to be there any longer and if one is at all down it bucks one up derectly to remember that *thats* all over atanyrate and that one has enough food to nurrish one and not that awful monottany of life and not the petty fogging daily tirrany you went in for and I can imagin no greater thrill and luxury in a way than to come and see the whole dismal grind still going on but without me being in it but this would be *rather* beastly of me wouldn't it so please dear Miss Price dont expect me and do excuse mistakes of English Composition and Spelling and etcetra in your affectionate old pupil,

> EMILY THÉRÈSE LYNN-ROYSTON.

ps, I often rite to people telling them where I was edducated and highly reckomending you.

LETTER IN ACKNOWLEDG-
MENT OF WEDDING PRESENT

DEAR LADY AMBLESHAM,

Who gives quickly, says the old proverb, gives twice. For this reason I have purposely delayed writing to you, lest I should appear to thank you more than once for the small, cheap, hideous present you sent me on the occasion of my recent wedding. Were you a poor woman, that little bowl of ill-imitated Dresden china would convict you of tastelessness merely; were you a blind woman, of nothing but an odious parsimony. As you have normal eyesight and more than normal wealth, your gift to me proclaims you at once a Philistine and a miser (or rather did so proclaim you until, less than ten seconds after I had unpacked it from its wrappings of tissue paper, I took it to the open window and had the satisfaction of seeing it shattered to atoms on the pavement). But stay! I perceive a possible flaw in my argument. Perhaps you were guided in your choice by a definite wish to insult me. I am sure, on reflection, that this was so. *I shall not forget.*

Yours, etc.,

CYNTHIA BEAUMARSH.

PS. My husband asks me to tell you to warn Lord Amblesham to keep out of his way or to assume some disguise so complete that he will not be recognised by him and horsewhipped.

PPS. I am sending copies of this letter to the principal London and provincial newspapers.

LETTER FROM . . .

But enough! I never thought I should be so strong in this line. I had not foreseen such copiousness and fatal fluency. Never again will I tap these deep dark reservoirs in a character that had always seemed to me, on the whole, so amiable.

LAUGHTER

M. BERGSON, IN HIS well-known essay on this theme
says ... well, he says many things; but none of these,
though I have just read them, do I clearly remember, nor
am I sure that in the act of reading I understood any of
them. That is the worst of these fashionable philosophers
—or rather, the worst of me. Somehow I never manage to
read them till they are just going out of fashion, and even
then I don't seem able to cope with them. About twelve
years ago, when every one suddenly talked to me about
Pragmatism and William James, I found myself moved
by a dull but irresistible impulse to try Schopenhauer, of
whom, years before that, I had heard that he was the
easiest reading in the world, and the most exciting and
amusing. I wrestled with Schopenhauer for a day or so,
in vain. Time passed; M. Bergson appeared 'and for his
hour was lord of the ascendant'; I tardily tackled William
James. I bore in mind, as I approached him, the testi-
monials that had been lavished on him by all my friends.
Alas, I was insensible to his thrillingness. His gaiety did
not make me gay. His crystal clarity confused me dread-
fully. I could make nothing of William James. And now,
in the fullness of time, I have been floored by M. Bergson.

It distresses me, this failure to keep pace with the leaders
of thought as they pass into oblivion. It makes me wonder
whether I am, after all, an absolute fool. Yet surely I am
not that. Tell me of a man or a woman, a place or an
event, real or fictitious: surely you will find me a fairly
intelligent listener. Any such narrative will present to me
some image, and will stir me to not altogether fatuous
thoughts. Come to me in some grievous difficulty: I will
talk to you like a father, even like a lawyer. I'll be hanged

if I haven't a certain mellow wisdom. But if you are by way of weaving theories as to the nature of things in general, and if you want to try those theories on some one who will luminously confirm them or powerfully rend them, I must, with a hang-dog air, warn you that I am not your man. I suffer from a strong suspicion that things in general cannot be accounted for through any formula or set of formulæ, and that any one philosophy, howsoever new, is no better than another. That is in itself a sort of philosophy, and I suspect it accordingly; but it has for me the merit of being the only one I can make head or tail of. If you try to expound any other philosophic system to me, you will find not merely that I can detect no flaw in it (except the one great flaw just suggested), but also that I haven't, after a minute or two, the vaguest notion of what you are driving at. 'Very well,' you say, 'instead of trying to explain all things all at once, I will explain some little, simple, single thing.' It was for sake of such shorn lambs as myself, doubtless, that M. Bergson sat down and wrote about—Laughter. But I have profited by his kindness no more than if he had been treating of the Cosmos. I cannot tread even a limited space of air. I have a gross satisfaction in the crude fact of being on hard ground again, and I utter a coarse peal of—Laughter.

At least, I say I do so. In point of fact, I have merely smiled. Twenty years ago, ten years ago, I should have laughed, and have professed to you that I had merely smiled. A very young man is not content to be very young, nor even a young man to be young: he wants to share the dignity of his elders. There is no dignity in laughter, there is much of it in smiles. Laughter is but a joyous surrender, smiles give token of mature criticism. It may be that in the early ages of this world there was far more laughter than is to be heard now, and that æons hence laughter will be obsolete, and smiles universal—every one, always, mildly, slightly, smiling. But it is less useful to speculate as to mankind's past and future than to observe men. And you will have observed with me in the club-room that young men at most times look solemn, whereas old men or men of middle age mostly smile; and also that those young men do often laugh loud and long among themselves, while we others—the gayest and best of us in the most favourable circumstances—seldom achieve more than our habitual act of smiling. Does the sound of that laughter jar on us? Do we liken it to the crackling of thorns under a pot? Let us do so. There is no cheerier sound. But let us not assume it to be the laughter of fools because we sit quiet. It is absurd to disapprove of what one envies, or to wish a good thing were no more because it has passed out of our possession.

But (it seems that I must begin every paragraph by questioning the sincerity of what I have just said) *has* the gift of laughter been withdrawn from me? I protest that I do still, at the age of forty-seven, laugh often and loud and long. But not, I believe, so long and loud and often as in my less smiling youth. And I am proud, nowadays, of laughing, and grateful to any one who makes me laugh. That is a bad sign. I no longer take laughter as a matter of course. I realise, even after reading M. Bergson on it, how good a thing it is. I am qualified to praise it.

As to what is most precious among the accessories to the world we live in, different men hold different opinions. There are people whom the sea depresses, whom mountains exhilarate. Personally, I want the sea always—some not populous edge of it for choice; and with it sunshine, and wine, and a little music. My friend on the mountain yonder is of tougher fibre and sterner outlook, disapproves of the sea's laxity and instability, has no ear for music and no palate for the grape, and regards the sun as a rather enervating institution, like central heating in a house. What he likes is a grey day and the wind in his face; crags at a great altitude; and a flask of whisky. Yet I think that even he, if we were trying to determine from what inner sources mankind derives the greatest pleasure in life, would agree with me that only the emotion of love

takes higher rank than the emotion of laughter. Both these
emotions are partly mental, partly physical. It is said that
the mental symptoms of love are wholly physical in origin.
They are not the less ethereal for that. The physical
sensations of laughter, on the other hand, are reached by
a process whose starting-point is in the mind. They are
not the less 'gloriously of our clay'. There is laughter that
goes so far as to lose all touch with its motive, and to
exist only, grossly, in itself. This is laughter at its best. A
man to whom such laughter has often been granted may
happen to die in a work-house. No matter. I will not
admit that he has failed in life. Another man, who has
never laughed thus, may be buried in Westminster Abbey,
leaving more than a million pounds overhead. What then?
I regard him as a failure.

Nor does it seem to me to matter one jot how such
laughter is achieved. Humour may rollick on high planes
of fantasy or in depths of silliness. To many people it
appeals only from those depths. If it appeal to them
irresistibly, they are more enviable than those who are
sensitive only to be mastered and dissolved by it. Laughter
is a thing to be rated according to its own intensity.

Many years ago I wrote an essay in which I poured
scorn on the fun purveyed by the music halls, and on the
great public for which that fun was quite good enough. I
take that callow scorn back. I fancy that the fun itself was
better than it seemed to me, and might not have displeased me if it had been wafted to me in private, in
presence of a few friends. A public crowd, because of a
lack of broad impersonal humanity in me, rather insulates
than absorbs me. Amidst the guffaws of a thousand
strangers I become unnaturally grave. If these people
were the entertainment, and I the audience, I should
be sympathetic enough. But to be one of them is a position that drives me spiritually aloof. Also, there is to me
something rather dreary in the notion of going anywhere
for the specific purpose of being amused. I prefer that
laughter shall take me unawares. Only so can it master

and dissolve me. And in this respect, at any rate, I am not peculiar. In music halls and such places, you may hear loud laughter, but—not see silent laughter, not see strong men weak, helpless, suffering, gradually convalescent, dangerously relapsing. Laughter at its greatest and best is not there.

To such laughter nothing is more propitious than an occasion that demands gravity. To have good reason for not laughing is one of the surest aids. Laughter rejoices in bonds. If music halls were schoolrooms for us, and the comedians were our schoolmasters, how much less talent would be needed for giving us how much more joy! Even in private and accidental intercourse, few are the men whose humour can reduce us, be we never so susceptible, to paroxysms of mirth. I will wager that nine tenths of the world's best laughter is laughter *at*, not *with*. And it is the people set in authority over us that touch most surely our sense of the ridiculous. Freedom is a good thing, but we lose through it golden moments. The schoolmaster to his pupils, the monarch to his courtiers, the editor to his staff—how priceless they are! Reverence is a good thing, and part of its value is that the more we revere a man, the more sharply are we struck by anything in him (and there is always much) that is incongruous with his greatness. And herein lies one of the reasons why as we grow older we laugh less. The men we esteemed so great are gathered to their fathers. Some of our coevals may, for aught we know, be very great, but good heavens! we can't esteem *them* so.

Of extreme laughter I know not in any annals a more satisfying example than one that is to be found in Moore's *Life of Byron*. Both Byron and Moore were already in high spirits when, on an evening in the spring of 1813, they went 'from some early assembly' to Mr Rogers' house in St James's Place and were regaled there with an impromptu meal. But not high spirits alone would have led the two young poets to such excess of laughter as made the evening so very memorable. Luckily they both venerated Rogers (strange as it may seem to us) as the greatest of living poets. Luckily, too, Mr Rogers was ever the kind of man, the coldly and quietly suave kind of man, with whom you don't take liberties, if you can help it— with whom, if you *can't* help it, to take liberties is in itself a most exhilarating act. And he had just received a presentation copy of Lord Thurloe's latest book, *Poems on Several Occasions.* The two young poets found in this elder's Muse much that was so execrable as to be delightful. They were soon, as they turned the pages, held in throes of laughter, laughter that was but intensified by the endeavours of their correct and nettled host to point out the genuine merits of his friend's work. And then suddenly—oh joy—'we lighted', Moore records, 'on the discovery that our host, in addition to his sincere approbation of some of this book's contents, had also the motive of gratitude for standing by its author, as one of the poems was a warm and, I need not add, well-deserved panegyric on himself. We were, however'—the narrative has an added charm from Tom Moore's demure care not to offend or compromise the still-surviving Rogers—'too far gone in nonsense for even this eulogy, in which we both so heartily agreed, to stop us. The opening line of the poem was, as well as I can recollect, "When Rogers o'er this labour bent;" and Lord Byron undertook to read it aloud;—but he found it impossible to get beyond the first two words. Our laughter had now increased to such a pitch that nothing could restrain it. Two or three times he began; but no sooner had the words "When Rogers" passed his lips, than our fit burst out afresh,—till even Mr Rogers himself, with all his feeling of our injustice, found it impossible not to join us; and we were, at last, all three in such a state of inextinguishable laughter, that, had the author himself been of our party, I question much whether he could have resisted the infection.' The final fall and disolution of Rogers, Rogers behaving as badly as either of them, is all that was needed to give perfection to this heart-warming scene. I like to think that on a certain night in spring, year after year, three ghosts revisit that old room and (without, I hope, inconvenience to Lord Northcliffe, who may happen to be there) sit rocking and writhing in the grip of that old shared rapture. Uncanny? Well, not more so than would have seemed to Byron and Moore and Rogers the notion that more than a hundred years away from them was some one joining in their laughter—as *I* do.

Alas, I cannot join in it more than gently. To imagine a scene, however vividly, does not give us the sense of being, or even of having been, present at it. Indeed, the greater the glow of the scene reflected, the sharper is the pang of our realisation that we were *not* there, and of our annoyance that we weren't. Such a pang comes to me with special force whenever my fancy posts itself outside the Temple's gate in Fleet Street, and there, at a late hour of the night of May 10th, 1773, observes a gigantic old man laughing wildly, but having no one with him to share and aggrandise his emotion. Not that he is alone; but the young man beside him laughs only in politeness and is inwardly puzzled, even shocked. Boswell has a keen, an exquisitely keen, scent for comedy, for the fun that is latent in fine shades of character; but imaginative burlesque, anything that borders on lovely nonsense, he was not formed to savour. All the more does one revel in his account of what led up to the moment when Johnson 'to support himself, laid hold of one of the posts at the side of the foot pavement, and sent forth peals so loud that in the silence of the night his voice seemed to resound from Temple Bar to Fleet Ditch.'

No evening ever had an unlikelier ending. The omens were all for gloom. Johnson had gone to dine at General Paoli's, but was so ill that he had to leave before the meal was over. Later he managed to go to Mr Chambers' rooms in the Temple. 'He continued to be very ill' there, but gradually felt better, and 'talked with a noble enthusiasm of keeping up the representation of respectable families', and was great on 'the dignity and propriety of male suc-

cession'. Among his listeners, as it happened, was a
gentleman for whom Mr Chambers had that day drawn
up a will devising his estate to his three sisters. The news
of this might have been expected to make Johnson violent
in wrath. But no, for some reason he grew violent only in
laughter, and insisted thenceforth on calling that gentleman The Testator and chaffing him without mercy. 'I
daresay he thinks he has done a mighty thing. He won't
stay till he gets home to his seat in the country, to produce this wonderful deed; he'll call up the landlord of the
first inn on the road; and after a suitable preface upon
mortality and the uncertainty of life, will tell him that he
should not delay in making his will; and Here, Sir, will he
say, is *my* will, which I have just made, with the assistance
of one of the ablest lawyers in the kingdom; and he will
read it to him. He believes he has made this will; but he
did not make it; you, Chambers, made it for him. I hope
you have had more conscience than to make him say
"being of sound understanding!" ha, ha, ha! I hope he
has left me a legacy. I'd have his will turned into verse,
like a ballad.' These flights annoyed Mr Chambers, and
are recorded by Boswell with the apology that he wishes
his readers to be 'acquainted with the slightest occasional
characteristics of so eminent a man'. Certainly, there is
nothing ridiculous in the fact of a man making a will.
But this is the measure of Johnson's achievement. He
had created gloriously much out of nothing at all. There
he sat, old and ailing and unencouraged by the company,
but soaring higher and higher in absurdity, more and
more rejoicing, and still soaring and rejoicing after he
had gone out into the night with Boswell, till at last in
Fleet Street his paroxysms were too much for him and he
could no more. Echoes of that huge laughter come ringing down the ages. But is there also perhaps a note of
sadness for us in them? Johnson's endless sociability came
of his inherent melancholy: he could not bear to be alone;
and his very mirth was but a mode of escape from the
dark thoughts within him. Of these the thought of death

was the most dreadful to him, and the most insistent. He
was for ever wondering how death would come to him,
and how he would acquit himself in the extreme moment.
A later but not less devoted Anglican, meditating on his
own end, wrote in his diary that 'to die in church appears
to be a great euthanasia, but not', he quaintly and touchingly added, 'at a time to disturb worshippers.' Both the
sentiment here expressed and the reservation drawn would
have been as characteristic of Johnson as they were of
Gladstone. But to die of laughter—this, too, seems to me
a great euthanasia; and I think that for Johnson to have
died thus, that night in Fleet Street, would have been a
grand ending to 'a life radically wretched'. Well, he was
destined to outlive another decade; and, selfishly, who
can wish such a life as his, or such a Life as Boswell's,
one jot shorter?

Strange, when you come to think of it, that of all the
countless folk who have lived before our time on this
planet not one is known in history or in legend as having
died of laughter. Strange, too, that not to one of all the
characters in romance has such an end been allotted. Has
it ever struck you what a chance Shakespeare missed
when he was finishing the Second Part of King Henry
the Fourth? Falstaff was not the man to stand cowed and
bowed while the new young king lectured him and cast
him off. Little by little, as Hal proceeded in that por-
tentous allocution, the humour of the situation would have
mastered old Sir John. His face, blank with surprise at
first, would presently have glowed and widened, and his
whole bulk have begun to quiver. Lest he should miss one
word, he would have mastered himself. But the final
words would have been the signal for release of all the
roars pent up in him; the welkin would have rung; the
roars, belike, would have gradually subsided in dreadful
rumblings of more than utterable or conquerable mirth.
Thus and thus only might his life have been rounded
off with dramatic fitness, *secundum ipsius naturam*. He

never should have been left to babble of green fields and die 'an it had been any christom child'.

Falstaff is a triumph of comedic creation because we are kept laughing equally at and with him. Nevertheless, if I had the choice of sitting with him at the Boar's Head or with Johnson at the Turk's, I shouldn't hesitate for an instant. The agility of Falstaff's mind gains much of its effect by contrast with the massiveness of his body; but in contrast with Johnson's equal agility is Johnson's moral as well as physical bulk. His sallies 'tell' the more startlingly because of the noble weight of character behind them: they are the better because *he* makes them. In Falstaff there isn't this final incongruity and element of surprise. Falstaff is but a sublimated sample of 'the funny man'. We cannot, therefore, laugh so greatly with him as with Johnson. (Nor even *at* him; because we are not tickled so much by the weak points of a character whose points are all weak ones; also because we have no reverence trying to impose restraint upon us.) Still, Falstaff has indubitably the power to convulse us. I don't mean we ever are convulsed in reading Henry the Fourth. No printed page, alas, can thrill us to extremities of laughter. These are ours only if the mirthmaker be a living man whose jests we hear as they come fresh from his own lips. All I claim for Falstaff is that he would be able to convulse us if he were alive and accessible. Few, as I have said, are the humorists who can induce this state. To master and dissolve us, to give us the joy of being worn down and tired out with laughter, is a success to be won by no man save in virtue of a rare staying-power. Laughter becomes extreme only if it be consecutive. There must be no pauses for recovery. Touch-and-go humour, however happy, is not enough. The jester must be able to grapple his theme and hang on to it, twisting it this way and that, and making it yield magically all manner of strange and precious things, one after another, without pause. He must have invention keeping pace with utterance. He must be inexhaustible. Only so can he exhaust us.

I have a friend whom I would praise. There are many other of my friends to whom I am indebted for much laughter; but I do believe that if all of them sent in their bills to-morrow and all of them overcharged me not a little, the total of all those totals would be less appalling than that which looms in my own vague estimate of what I owe to Comus. Comus I call him here in observance of the line drawn between public and private virtue, and in full knowledge that he would of all men be the least glad to be quite personally thanked and laurelled in the market-place for the hours he has made memorable among his cronies. No one is so diffident as he, no one so self-postponing. Many people have met him again and again without faintly suspecting 'anything much' in him. Many of his acquaintances—friends, too—relatives, even—have lived and died in the belief that he was quite ordinary. Thus is he the more greatly valued by his cronies. Thus do we pride ourselves on possessing some curious right quality to which alone he is responsive. But it would seem that either this asset of ours or its effect on him is intermittent. He can be dull and null enough with us sometimes—a mere asker of questions, or drawer of comparisons between this and that brand of cigarettes, or full expatiator on the merits of some new patent razor. A whole hour and more may be wasted in such humdrum and darkness. And then—something will have happened. There has come a spark in the murk; a flame now, presage of a radiance: Comus has begun. His face is a great part of his equipment. A cast of it might be somewhat akin to the comic masks of the ancients; but no cast could be worthy of it; mobility is the essence of it. It flickers and shifts in accord to the matter of his discourse; it contracts and it expands; is there anything its elastic can't express? Comus would be eloquent even were he dumb. And he is mellifluous. His voice, while he develops an idea or conjures up a scene, takes on a peculiar richness and unction.

If he be describing an actual scene, voice and face are adaptable to those of the actual persons therein. But it is not in such mimicry that he excels. As a reporter he has rivals. For the most part, he moves on a higher plane than that of mere fact: he imagines, he creates, giving you not a person, but a type, a synthesis, and not what anywhere has been, but what anywhere might be—what, as one feels, for all the absurdity of it, just would be. He knows his world well, and nothing human is alien to him, but certain skeins of life have a special hold on him, and he on them. In his youth he wished to be a clergy-man; and over the clergy of all grades and denominations his genius hovers and swoops and ranges with a special mastery. Lawyers he loves less; yet the legal mind seems to lie almost as wide-open to him as the sacerdotal; and the legal manner in all its phases he can unerringly burlesque. In the minds of journalists, diverse journalists, he is not less thoroughly at home, so that of the wild contingencies imagined by him there is none about which he cannot reel off an oral 'leader' or 'middle' in the like-liest style, and with as much ease as he can preach a High Church or Low Church sermon on it. Nor are his impro-visations limited by prose. If a theme call for nobler treat-ment, he becomes an unflagging fountain of ludicrously adequate blank-verse. Or again, he may deliver himself in rhyme. There is no form of utterance that comes amiss to him for interpreting the human comedy, or for broadening the farce into which that comedy is turned by him. No-thing can stop him when once he is in the vein. No appeals move him. He goes from strength to strength while his audience is more and more piteously debilitated.

What a gift to have been endowed with! What a power to wield! And how often I have envied Comus! But this envy of him has never taken root in me. His mind laughs, doubtless, at his own conceptions; but not his body. And if you tell him something that you have been sure will convulse him you are likely to be rewarded with no more than a smile betokening that he sees the point.

Incomparable laughter-giver, he is not much a laugher. He is vintner, not toper. I would therefore not change places with him. I am well content to have been his beneficiary during thirty years, and to be so for as many more as may be given us.

Parodies from

A CHRISTMAS
GARLAND

[1912]

*The Mote in
the Middle Distance*

P.C., X, 36

*Some Damnable
Errors about Christmas*

Scruts

Endeavour

The Feast

THE MOTE IN
THE MIDDLE DISTANCE
by H*nry J*m*s

IT WAS WITH THE sense of a, for him, very memorable
something that he peered now into the immediate future,
and tried, not without compunction, to take that period
up where he had, prospectively, left it. But just where
the deuce *had* he left it? The consciousness of dubiety
was, for our friend, not, this morning, quite yet clean-
cut enough to outline the figures on what she had called
his 'horizon', between which and himself the twilight
was indeed of a quality somewhat intimidating. He had
run up, in the course of time, against a good number
of 'teasers'; and the function of teasing them back—
of, as it were, giving them, every now and then, 'what
for'—was in him so much a habit that he would have
been at a loss had there been, on the face of it, nothing
to lose. Oh, he always had offered rewards, of course—
had ever so liberally pasted the windows of his soul with
staring appeals, minute descriptions, promises that knew
no bounds. But the actual recovery of the article—the
business of drawing and crossing the cheque, blotched
though this were with tears of joy—had blankly appeared
to him rather in the light of a sacrilege, casting, he
sometimes felt, a palpable chill on the fervour of the next
quest. It was just this fervour that was threatened as,
raising himself on his elbow, he stared at the foot of his
bed. That his eyes refused to rest there for more than
the fraction of an instant, may be taken—*was*, even then,
taken by Keith Tantalus—as a hint of his recollection
that after all the phenomenon wasn't to be singular. Thus
the exact repetition, at the foot of Eva's bed, of the

shape pendulous at the foot of *his* was hardly enough to account for the fixity with which he envisaged it, and for which he was to find, some years later, a motive in the (as it turned out) hardly generous fear that Eva had already made the great investigation 'on her own'. Her very regular breathing presently reassured him that, if she *had* peeped into 'her' stocking, she must have done so in sleep. Whether he should wake her now, or wait for their nurse to wake them both in due course, was a problem presently solved by a new development. It was plain that his sister was now watching him between her eyelashes. He had half expected that. She really was— he had often told her that she really was—magnificent; and her magnificence was never more obvious than in the pause that elapsed before she all of a sudden remarked, 'They so very indubitably *are*, you know!'

It occurred to him as befitting Eva's remoteness, which was a part of Eva's magnificence, that her voice emerged somewhat muffled by the bedclothes. She was ever, indeed, the most telephonic of her sex. In talking to Eva you always had, as it were, your lips to the receiver. If you didn't try to meet her fine eyes, it was that you simply couldn't hope to: there were too many dark, too many buzzing and bewildering and all frankly not negotiable leagues in between. Snatches of other voices seemed often to interlude themselves in the parley; and your loyal effort not to overhear these was complicated by your fear of missing what Eva might be twittering. 'Oh, you certainly haven't, my dear, the trick of propinquity!' was a thrust she had once parried by saying that, in that case, *he* hadn't—to which his unspoken rejoinder that she had caught her tone from the peevish young women at the Central seemed to him (if not perhaps in the last, certainly in the last but one, analysis) to lack finality. With Eva, he had found, it was always safest to 'ring off'. It was with a certain sense of his rashness in the matter, therefore, that he now, with an air of feverishly 'holding the line', said, 'Oh, as to that!'

Had *she*, he presently asked himself, 'rung off'? It was characteristic of our friend—was indeed 'him all over'—that his fear of what she was going to say was as nothing to his fear of what she might be going to leave unsaid. He had, in his converse with her, been never so conscious as now of the intervening leagues; they had never so insistently beaten the drum of his ear; and he caught himself in the act of awfully computing, with a certain statistical passion, the distance between Rome and Boston. He has never been able to decide which of these points he was psychically the nearer to at the moment when Eva, replying, 'Well, one does, anyhow, leave a margin for the pretex, you know!' made him, for the first time in his life, wonder whether she were not more magnificent than even he had ever given her credit for being. Perhaps it was to test this theory, or perhaps merely to gain time, that he now raised himself to his knees, and, leaning with outstretched arm towards the foot of his bed, made as though to touch the stocking which Santa Claus had, overnight, left dangling there. His posture, as he stared obliquely at Eva, with a sort of beaming defiance, recalled to him something seen in an 'illustration'. This reminiscence, however—if such it was, save in the scarred, the poor dear old woebegone and so very beguilingly *not* refractive mirror of the moment—took a peculiar twist from Eva's behaviour. She had, with startling suddenness, sat bolt upright, and looked to him as if she were overhearing some tragedy at the other end of the wire, where, in the nature of things, she was unable to arrest it. The gaze she fixed on her extravagant kinsman was of a kind to make him wonder how he contrived to remain, as he beautifully did, rigid. His prop was possibly the reflection that flashed on him that, if *she* abounded in attenuations, well, hang it all, so did *he*! It was simply a difference of plane. Readjust the 'values', as painters say, and there you were! He was to feel that he was only too crudely 'there' when, leaning further forward, he laid a chubby forefinger on the stocking, causing that receptacle to rock ponderously to and fro. This effect was more expected than the tears which started to Eva's eyes and the intensity with which 'Don't you', she exclaimed, 'see?'

'The mote in the middle distance?' he asked. 'Did you ever, my dear, know me to see anything else? I tell you it blocks out everything. It's a cathedral, it's a herd of elephants, it's the whole habitable globe. Oh, it's, believe me, of an obsessiveness!' But his sense of the one thing it *didn't* block out from his purview enabled him to launch at Eva a speculation as to just how far Santa Claus had, for the particular occasion, gone. The gauge, for both of them, of this seasonable distance seemed almost blatantly suspended in the silhouettes of the two stockings. Over and above the basis of (presumably) sweetmeats in the toes and heels, certain extrusions stood for a very plenary fulfilment of desire. And since Eva *had* set her heart on a doll of ample proportions and practicable eyelids—*had* asked that most admirable of her sex, their mother, for it with not less directness than he himself had put into his demand for a sword and helmet—her coyness now struck Keith as lying near to, at indeed a hardly measurable distance from, the border line of his patience. If she didn't *want* the doll, why the deuce had she made such a point of getting it? He was perhaps on the verge of putting this question to her, when, waving her hand to include both stockings, she said, 'Of course, my dear, you *do* see. There they are, and you know I know you know we wouldn't, either of us, dip a finger into them.' With a vibrancy of tone that seemed to bring her voice quite close to him, 'One doesn't', she added, 'violate the shrine —pick the pearl from the shell!'

Even had the answering question 'Doesn't one just?' which for an instant hovered on the tip of his tongue, been uttered, it could not have obscured for Keith the change which her magnificence had wrought in him. Something, perhaps, of the bigotry of the convert was already discernible in the way that, averting his eyes, he said, 'One doesn't even peer.' As to whether, in the years that have elapsed since he said this, either of our friends (now adult) has, in fact, 'peered', is a question which, whenever I call at the house, I am tempted to put to one or other of them. But any regret I may feel in my invariable failure to 'come up to the scratch' of yielding to this temptation is balanced, for me, by my impression—my sometimes all but throned and anointed certainty—that the answer, if vouchsafed, would be in the negative.

P.C., X, 36
by R*d**rd K*pl*ng

Then it's collar 'im tight,
  In the name o' the Lawd!
'Ustle 'im, shake 'im till 'e's sick!
  Wot, 'e *would*, would 'e? Well,
  Then yer've got ter give him 'im 'Ell,
An' it's trunch, trunch, truncheon does the trick.
                          POLICE STATION DITTIES.

I HAD SPENT CHRISTMAS EVE at the Club, listening to a grand pow-wow between certain of the choicer sons of Adam. Then Slushby had cut in. Slushby is one who writes to newspapers and is theirs obediently 'HUMANI-TARIAN'. When Slushby cuts in, men remember they have to be up early next morning.

Sharp round a corner on the way home, I collided with something firmer than the regulation pillar-box. I righted myself after the recoil and saw some stars that were very pretty indeed. Then I perceived the nature of the obstruction.

'Evening, Judlip,' I said sweetly, when I had collected my hat from the gutter. 'Have I broken the law, Judlip? If so, I'll go quiet.'

'Time yer was in bed,' grunted X, 36. 'Yer Ma'll be lookin' out for yer.'

This from the friend of my bosom! It hurt. Many were the night-beats I had been privileged to walk with Judlip, imbibing curious lore that made glad the civilian heart of me. Seven whole 8×5 inch note-books had I pitmanised to the brim with Judlip. And now to be repulsed as one of the uninitiated! It hurt horrid.

There is a thing called Dignity. Small boys sometimes stand on it. Then they have to be kicked. Then they get down, weeping. I don't stand on Dignity.

'What's wrong, Judlip?' I asked, more sweetly than ever. 'Drawn a blank to-night?'

'Yuss. Drawn a blank blank blank. 'Aven't 'ad so much as a kick at a lorst dorg. Christmas Eve ain't wot it was.' I felt for my note-book. 'Lawd! I remembers the time when the drunks and disorderlies down this street was as thick as flies on a flypaper. One just picked 'em orf with one's finger and thumb. A bloomin' battew, that's wot it wos.'

'The night's yet young, Judlip,' I insinuated, with a jerk of my thumb at the flaring windows of the 'Rat and Blood Hound'. At that moment the saloon-door swung open, emitting a man and woman who walked with linked arms and exceeding great care.

Judlip eyed them longingly as they tacked up the street. Then he sighed. Now, when Judlip sighs the sound is like unto that which issues from the vent of a Crosby boiler when the cog-gauges are at 260° F.

'Come, Judlip!' I said. 'Possess your soul in patience. You'll soon find some one to make an example of. Meanwhile'—I threw back my head and smacked my lips— 'the usual, Judlip?'

In another minute I emerged through the swingdoor, bearing a furtive glass of that same 'usual', and nipped down the mews where my friend was wont to await these little tokens of esteem.

'To the Majesty of the Law, Judlip!'

When he had honoured the toast, I scooted back
with the glass, leaving him wiping the beads off his
beard-bristles. He was in his philosophic mood when I
rejoined him at the corner.

'Wot am I?' he said, as we paced along. 'A bloomin'
cypher. Wot's the sarjint? 'E's got the Inspector over
'im. Over above the Inspector there's the Sooprintendent.
Over above 'im's the old red-tape-masticatin' Yard. Over
above that there's the 'Ome Sec. Wot's 'e? A cypher,
like me. Why?' Judlip looked up at the stars. 'Over
above 'im's We Dunno Wot. Somethin' wot issues its
horders an' regulations an' divisional injunctions, in-
scrootable like, but p'remptory; an' we 'as ter see as
'ow they're carried out, not arskin' no questions, but
each man goin' about 'is dooty.'

' " 'Is dooty",' said I, looking up from my notebook.
'Yes, I've got that.'

'Life ain't a bean-feast. It's a 'arsh reality. An' them
as makes it a bean-feast 'as got to be 'arshly dealt with
accordin'. That's wot the Force is put 'ere for from
Above. Not as 'ow we ain't fallible. We makes our mistakes. An' when we makes 'em we sticks to 'em. For the
honour o' the Force. Which same is the jool Britannia
wears on 'er bosom as a charm against hanarchy. That's
wot the brarsted old Beaks don't understand. Yer remember Smithers of our Div.?'

I remembered Smithers—well. As fine, upstanding,
square-toed, bullet-headed, clean-living a son of a gun
as ever perjured himself in the box. There was nothing
of the softy about Smithers. I took off my billicock to
Smithers' memory.

'Sacrificed to public opinion? Yuss,' said Judlip, pausing at a front door and flashing his 45 c.p. down the slot
of a two-grade Yale. 'Sacrificed to a parcel of screamin'
old women wot ort ter 'ave gorn down on their knees an'
thanked Gawd for such a protector. 'E'll be out in another 'alf year. Wot'll 'e do then, pore devil? Go a bust
on 'is conduc' money an' throw in 'is lot with them same

hexperts wot 'ad a 'oly terror of 'im.' Then Judlip swore
gently.

'What should you do, O Great One, if ever it were
your duty to apprehend him?'

'Do? Why, yer blessed innocent, yer don't think I'd
shirk a fair clean cop? Same time, I don't say as 'ow I
wouldn't 'andle 'im tender like, for sake o' wot 'e wos.
Likewise cos 'e'd be a stiff customer to tackle. Likewise
'cos——'

He had broken off, and was peering fixedly upwards
at an angle of 85° across the moonlit street. "'Ullo!' he
said in a hoarse whisper.

Striking an average between the direction of his eyes—
for Judlip, when on the job, has a soul-stirring squint—I
perceived some one in the act of emerging from a chim-
ney-pot.

Judlip's voice clove the silence. 'Wot are yer doin' hup
there?'

The person addressed came to the edge of the parapet.
I saw then that he had a hoary white beard, a red ulster
with the hood up, and what looked like a sack over his
shoulder. He said something or other in a voice like a
concertina that has been left out in the rain.

'I dessay,' answered my friend. 'Just you come down,
an' we'll see about that.'

The old man nodded and smiled. Then—as I hope to
be saved—he came floating gently down through the
moonlight, with the sack over his shoulder and a young
fir-tree clasped to his chest. He alighted in a friendly
manner on the curb beside us.

Judlip was the first to recover himself. Out went his
right arm, and the airman was slung round by the scruff
of the neck, spilling his sack in the road. I made a bee-
line for his shoulder-blades. Burglar or no burglar, he was
the best airman out, and I was muchly desirous to know
the precise nature of the apparatus under his ulster. A
backhander from Judlip's left caused me to hop quickly
aside. The prisoner was squealing and whimpering. He

didn't like the feel of Judlip's knuckles at his cervical vertebræ.

'Wot was yer doin' hup there?' asked Judlip, tightening the grip.

'I'm S-Santa Claus, Sir. P-please, Sir, let me g-go.'

'Hold him,' I shouted. 'He's a German!'

'It's my dooty ter caution yer that wotever yer say now may be used in hevidence against yer, yer old sinner. Pick up that there sack, an' come along o' me.'

The captive snivelled something about peace on earth, good will toward men.

'Yuss,' said Judlip. 'That's in the Noo Testament, ain't it? The Noo Testament contains some uncommon nice readin' for old gents an' young ladies. But it ain't included in the librery o' the Force. We confine ourselves to the Old Testament—O.T., 'ot. An' 'ot you'll get it. Hup with that sack, an' quick march!'

I have seen worse attempts at a neck-wrench, but it was just not slippery enough for Judlip. And the kick that Judlip then let fly was a thing of beauty and a joy for ever.

'Frog's-march him!' I shrieked, dancing. 'For the love of Heaven, frog's-march him!'

Trotting by Judlip's side to the Station, I reckoned it out that if Slushby had not been at the Club I should not have been here to see. Which shows that even Slushbys are put into this world for a purpose.

SOME DAMNABLE
ERRORS ABOUT CHRISTMAS
by G. K. Ch*st*rt*n

THAT IT IS HUMAN to err is admitted by even the most positive of our thinkers. Here we have the great difference between latter-day thought and the thought of the past. If Euclid were alive to-day (and I daresay he is) he would not say, 'The angles at the base of an isosceles triangle are equal to one another.' He would say, 'To me (a very frail and fallible being, remember) it does somehow seem that these two angles have a mysterious and awful equality to one another.' The dislike of schoolboys for Euclid is unreasonable in many ways; but fundamentally it is entirely reasonable. Fundamentally it is the revolt from a man who was either fallible and therefore (in pretending to infallibility) an imposter, or infallible and therefore not human.

Now, since it is human to err, it is always in reference to those things which arouse in us the most human of all our emotions—I mean the emotion of love—that we conceive the deepest of our errors. Suppose we met Euclid on Westminster Bridge, and he took us aside and confessed to us that whilst he regarded parallelograms and rhomboids with an indifference bordering on contempt, for isosceles triangles he cherished a wild romantic devotion. Suppose he asked us to accompany him to the nearest music-shop, and there purchased a guitar in order that he might worthily sing to us the radiant beauty and the radiant goodness of isosceles triangles. As men we should, I hope, respect his enthusiasm, and encourage his enthusiasm, and catch his enthusiasm. But as seekers after truth we should be compelled to regard with a dark suspicion, and to check with the most anxious care, every fact that he told us about isosceles triangles. For adoration involves a glorious obliquity of vision. It involves more than that. We do not say of Love that he is short-sighted. We do not say of Love that he is myopic. We do not say of Love that he is astigmatic. We say quite simply, Love is blind. We might go further and say, Love is deaf. That would be a profound and obvious truth. We might go further still and say, Love is dumb. But that would be a profound and obvious lie. For love is always an extraordinarily fluent talker. Love is a wind-bag, filled with a gusty wind from Heaven.

It is always about the thing that we love most that we

talk most. About this thing, therefore, our errors are
something more than our deepest errors: they are our
most frequent errors. That is why for nearly two thousand
years mankind has been more glaringly wrong on the subject of Christmas than on any other subject. If mankind
had hated Christmas, he would have understood it from
the first. What would have happened then, it is impossible
to say. For that which is hated, and therefore is perse-
cuted, and therefore grows brave, lives on for ever, whilst
that which is understood dies in the moment of our understanding of it—dies, as it were, in our awful grasp. Between the horns of this eternal dilemma shivers all the
mystery of the jolly visible world, and of that still jollier
world which is invisible. And it is because Mr Shaw and
the writers of his school cannot, with all their splendid
sincerity and acumen, perceive that he and they and all
of us are impaled on those horns as certainly as the
sausages I ate for breakfast this morning had been impaled
on the cook's toasting-fork—it is for this reason, I say,
that Mr Shaw and his friends seem to me to miss the
basic principle that lies at the root of all things human
and divine. By the way, not all things that are divine are
human. But all things that are human are divine. But to
return to Christmas.

I select at random two of the more obvious fallacies that
obtain. One is that Christmas should be observed as a
time of jubilation. This is (I admit) quite a recent idea.
It never entered into the tousled heads of the shepherds
by night, when the light of the angel of the Lord shone
about them and they arose and went to do homage to the
Child. It never entered into the heads of the Three Wise
Men. They did not bring their gifts as a joke, but as an
awful oblation. It never entered into the heads of the
saints and scholars, the poets and painters, of the Middle
Ages. Looking back across the years, they saw in that
dark and ungarnished manger only a shrinking woman,
a brooding man, and a child born to sorrow. The philo-
maths of the eighteenth century, looking back, saw

nothing at all. It is not the least of the glories of the
Victorian Era that it rediscovered Christmas. It is not the
least of the mistakes of the Victorian Era that it supposed
Christmas to be a feast.

The splendour of the saying 'I have piped unto you,
and you have not danced; I have wept with you, and you
have not mourned' lies in the fact that it might have been
uttered with equal truth by any man who had ever piped
or wept. There is in the human race some dark spirit of
recalcitrance, always pulling us in the direction contrary
to that in which we are reasonably expected to go. At a
funeral, the slightest thing, not in the least ridiculous at
any other time, will convulse us with internal laughter.
At a wedding, we hover mysteriously on the brink of tears.
So it is with the modern Christmas. I find myself in agreement with the cynics in so far that I admit that Christmas, as now observed, tends to create melancholy. But the
reason for this lies solely in our own misconception.
Christmas is essentially a *dies iræ*. If the cynics will only
make up their minds to treat it as such, even the saddest
and most atrabilious of them will acknowledge that he
has had a rollicking day.

This brings me to the second fallacy. I refer to the
belief that 'Christmas comes but once a year'. Perhaps
it does, according to the calendar—a quaint and interesting compilation, but of little or no practical value to anybody. It is not the calendar, but the Spirit of Man that
regulates the recurrence of feasts and fasts. Spiritually,
Christmas Day recurs exactly seven times a week. When
we have frankly acknowledged this, and acted on this, we
shall begin to realise the Day's mystical and terrific
beauty. For it is only every-day things that reveal themselves to us in all their wonder and their splendour. A
man who happens one day to be knocked down by a
motor-bus merely utters a curse and instructs his solicitor;
but a man who has been knocked down by a motor-bus
every day of the year will have begun to feel that he is
taking part in an august and soul-cleansing ritual. He will

await the diurnal stroke of fate with the same lowly and pious joy as animated the Hindoos awaiting Juggernaut. His bruises will be decorations, worn with the modest pride of the veteran. He will cry aloud, in the words of the late W. E. Henley, 'My head is bloody but unbowed.' He will add, 'My ribs are broken but unbent.'

I look for the time when we shall wish one another a Merry Christmas every morning; when roast turkey and plum-pudding shall be the staple of our daily dinner, and the holly shall never be taken down from the walls, and every one will always be kissing every one else under the mistletoe. And what is right as regards Christmas is right as regards all other so-called anniversaries. The time will come when we shall dance round the Maypole every morning before breakfast—a meal at which hot-cross buns will be a standing dish—and shall make April fools of one another every day before noon. The profound significance of All Fools' Day—the glorious lesson that we are all fools—is too apt at present to be lost. Nor is justice done to the sublime symbolism of Shrove Tuesday —the day on which all sins are shriven. Every day pancakes shall be eaten either before or after the plum-pudding. They shall be eaten slowly and sacramentally. They shall be fried over fires tended and kept for ever bright by Vestals. They shall be tossed to the stars.

I shall return to the subject of Christmas next week.

SCRUTS
by Arn*ld B*nn*tt

I

EMILY WRACKGARTH STIRRED THE Christmas pudding till her right arm began to ache. But she did not cease for that. She stirred on till her right arm grew so numb that it might have been the right arm of some girl at the other end of Bursley. And yet something deep down in her whispered 'It is *your* right arm! And you can do what you like with it!'

She did what she liked with it. Relentlessly she kept it moving till it reasserted itself as the arm of Emily Wrackgarth, prickling and tingling as with red-hot needles in every tendon from wrist to elbow. And still Emily Wrackgarth hardened her heart.

Presently she saw the spoon no longer revolving, but wavering aimlessly in the midst of the basin. Ridiculous! This must be seen to! In the down of dark hairs that connected her eyebrows there was a marked deepening of that vertical cleft which, visible at all times, warned you that here was a young woman not to be trifled with. Her brain despatched to her hand a peremptory message —which miscarried. The spoon wabbled as though held by a baby. Emily knew that she herself as a baby had been carried into this very kitchen to stir the Christmas pudding. Year after year, as she grew up, she had been allowed to stir it 'for luck'. And those, she reflected, were the only cookery lessons she ever got. How like Mother!

Mrs Wrackgarth had died in the past year, of a complication of ailments.* Emily still wore on her left shoulder that small tag of crape which is as far as the Five Towns go in the way of mourning. Her father had died in the year previous to that, of a still more curious and enthralling complication of ailments.† Jos, his son, carried on the Wrackgarth Works, and Emily kept house for Jos. She with her own hand had made this pudding. But for her this pudding would not have been. Fantastic! Utterly incredible! And yet so it was. She was grown-up. She was mistress of the house. She could make or unmake puddings at will. And yet she was Emily Wrackgarth. Which was absurd.

She would not try to explain, to reconcile. She abandoned herself to the exquisite mysteries of existence. And

* See *The History of Sarah Wrackgarth*, pp. 345-482.
† See *The History of Sarah Wrackgarth*, pp. 231-344.

yet in her abandonment she kept a sharp look-out on herself, trying fiercely to make head or tail of her nature. She thought herself a fool. But the fact that she thought so was for her a proof of adult sapience. Odd! She gave herself up. And yet it was just by giving herself up that she seemed to glimpse sometimes her own inwardness. And these bleak revelations saddened her. But she savoured her sadness. It was the wine of life to her. And for her sadness she scorned herself, and in her conscious scorn she recovered her self-respect.

It is doubtful whether the people of southern England have even yet realised how much introspection there is going on all the time in the Five Towns.

Visible from the window of the Wrackgarths' parlour was that colossal statue of Commerce which rears itself aloft at the point where Oodge Lane is intersected by Blackstead Street. Commerce, executed in glossy Doulton-ware by some sculptor or sculptors unknown, stands pointing her thumb over her shoulder towards the chimneys of far Hanbridge. When I tell you that the circumference of that thumb is six inches, and the rest to scale, you will understand that the statue is one of the prime glories of Bursley. There were times when Emily Wrackgarth seemed to herself as vast and as lustrously impressive as it. There were other times when she seemed to herself as trivial and slavish as one of those performing fleas she had seen at the Annual Ladies' Evening Fête organised by the Bursley Mutual Burial Club. Extremist!

She was now stirring the pudding with her left hand. The ingredients had already been mingled indistinguishably in that rich, undulating mass of tawniness which proclaims perfection. But Emily was determined to give her left hand, not less than her right, what she called 'a doing'. Emily was like that.

At mid-day, when her brother came home from the Works, she was still at it.

'Brought those scruts with you?' she asked, without looking up.

'That's a fact,' he said, dipping his hand into the sagging pocket of his coat.

It is perhaps necessary to explain what scruts are. In the daily output of every potbank there are a certain proportion of flawed vessels. These are cast aside by the foreman, with a lordly gesture, and in due course are hammered into fragments. These fragments, which are put to various uses, are called scruts; and one of the uses they are put to is a sentimental one. The dainty and luxurious Southerner looks to find in his Christmas pudding a wedding-ring, a gold thimble, a threepenny-bit, or the like. To such fal-lals the Five Towns would say fie. A Christmas pudding in the Five Towns contains nothing but suet, flour, lemon-peel, cinnamon, brandy, almonds, raisins—and two or three scruts. There is a world of poetry, beauty, romance, in scruts—though you have to have been brought up on them to appreciate it. Scruts have passed into the proverbial philosophy of the district. 'Him's a pudden with more scruts than raisins to 'm' is a criticism not infrequently heard. It implies respect, even admiration. Of Emily Wrackgarth herself people often said, in reference to her likeness to her father, 'Her's a scrut o' th' owd basin.'

Jos had emptied out from his pocket on to the table a good three dozen of scruts. Emily laid aside her spoon, rubbed the palms of her hands on the bib of her apron, and proceeded to finger these scruts with the air of a connoisseur, rejecting one after another. The pudding was a small one, designed merely for herself and Jos, with remainder to 'the girl'; so that it could hardly accommodate more than two or three scruts. Emily knew well that one scrut is as good as another. Yet she did not want her brother to feel that anything selected by him would necessarily pass muster with her. For his benefit she ostentatiously wrinkled her nose.

'By the by,' said Jos, 'you remember Albert Grapp? I have asked him to step over from Hanbridge and help eat our snack on Christmas Day.'

Emily gave Jos one of her looks. 'You've asked that Mr Grapp?'

'No objection, I hope? He's not a bad sort. And he's considered a bit of a ladies' man, you know.'

She gathered up all the scruts and let them fall in a rattling shower on the exiguous pudding. Two or three fell wide of the basin. These she added.

'Steady on!' cried Jos. 'What's that for?'

'That's for your guest,' replied his sister. 'And if you think you're going to palm me off on to him, or on to any other young fellow, you're a fool, Jos Wrackgarth.'

The young man protested weakly, but she cut him short.

'Don't think', she said, 'I don't know what you've been after, just of late. Cracking up one young sawny and then another on the chance of me marrying him! I never heard of such goings on. But here I am, and here I'll stay, as sure as my name's Emily Wrackgarth, Jos Wrackgarth!'

She was the incarnation of the adorably feminine. She was exquisitely vital. She exuded at every pore the pathos of her young undirected force. It is difficult to write calmly about her. For her, in another age, ships would have been launched and cities besieged. But brothers are a race apart, and blind. It is a fact that Jos would have been glad to see his sister 'settled'—preferably in one of the other four Towns.

She took up the spoon and stirred vigorously. The scruts grated and squeaked together around the basin, while the pudding feebly wormed its way up among them.

II

Albert Grapp, ladies' man though he was, was humble of heart. Nobody knew this but himself. Not one of his fellow clerks in Clither's Bank knew it. The general theory in Hanbridge was 'Him's got a stiff opinion o' hisself'. But this arose from what was really a sign of humility in him. He made the most of himself. He had, for instance, a way of his own in the matter of dressing. He always wore a voluminous frockcoat, with a pair of neatly-striped vicuna trousers, which he placed every night under his mattress, thus preserving in perfection the crease down the centre of each. His collar was of the highest, secured in front with an aluminium stud, to which was attached by a patent loop a natty bow of dove-coloured sateen. He had two caps, one of blue serge, the other of shepherd's plaid. These he wore on alternative days. He wore them in a way of his own—well back from his forehead, so as not to hide his hair, and with the peak behind. The peak made a sort of half-moon over the back of his collar. Through a fault of his tailor, there was a yawning gap between the back of his collar and the collar of his coat. Whenever he shook his head, the peak of his cap had the look of a live thing trying to investigate this abyss. Dimly aware of the effect, Albert Grapp shook his head as seldom as possible.

On wet days he wore a mackintosh. This, as he did not yet possess a great-coat, he wore also, but with less glory, on cold days. He had hoped there might be rain on Christmas morning. But there was no rain. 'Like my luck,' he said as he came out of his lodgings and turned his steps to that corner of Jubilee Avenue from which the Hanbridge-Bursley trams start every half-hour.

Since Jos Wrackgarth had introduced him to his sister at the Hanbridge Oddfellows' Biennial Hop, when he danced two quadrilles with her, he had seen her but once. He had nodded to her, Five Towns fashion, and she had nodded back at him, but with a look that seemed to say 'You needn't nod next time you see me. I can get along well enough without your nods.' A frightening girl! And yet her brother had since told him she seemed 'a bit gone, like' on him. Impossible! He, Albert Grapp, make an impression on the brilliant Miss Wrackgarth! Yet she had sent him a verbal invite to spend Christmas in her own home. And the time had come. He was on his way. Incredible that he should arrive! The tram must surely overturn, or be struck by lightning. And yet no! He arrived safely.

The small servant who opened the door gave him another verbal message from Miss Wrackgarth. It was that he must wipe his feet 'well' on the mat. In obeying this order he experienced a thrill of satisfaction he could not account for. He must have stood shuffling his boots vigorously for a full minute. This, he told himself, was life. He, Albert Grapp, was alive. And the world was full of other men, all alive; and yet, because they were not doing Miss Wrackgarth's bidding, none of them really lived. He was filled with a vague melancholy. But his melancholy pleased him.

In the parlour he found Jos awaiting him. The table was laid for three.

'So you're here, are you?' said the host, using the Five Towns formula. 'Emily's in the kitchen,' he added. 'Happen she'll be here directly.'

'I hope she's tol-lol-lish?' asked Albert.

'She is,' said Jos. 'But don't you go saying that to her. She doesn't care about society airs and graces. You'll make no headway if you aren't blunt.'

'Oh, right you are,' said Albert, with the air of a man who knew his way about.

A moment later Emily joined them, still wearing her kitchen apron. 'So you're here, are you?' she said, but did not shake hands. The servant had followed her in with the tray, and the next few seconds were occupied in the disposal of the beef and trimmings.

The meal began, Emily carving. The main thought of a man less infatuated than Albert Grapp would have been 'This girl can't cook. And she'll never learn to.' The beef, instead of being red and brown, was pink and white. Uneatable beef! And yet he relished it more than anything he had ever tasted. This beef was her own handiwork. Thus it was because she had made it so. . . . He

warily refrained from complimenting her, but the idea of
a second helping obsessed him.

'Happen I could do with a bit more, like,' he said.

Emily hacked off the bit more and jerked it on to the
plate he had held out to her.

'Thanks,' he said; and then, as Emily's lip curled, and
Jos gave him a warning kick under the table, he tried to
look as if he had said nothing.

Only when the second course came on did he suspect
that the meal was a calculated protest against his presence.
This is a Christmas pudding? The litter of fractured
earthenware was hardly held together by the suet and
raisins. All his pride of manhood—and there was plenty
of pride mixed up with Albert Grapp's humility—dictated
a refusal to touch that pudding. Yet he soon found himself touching it, though gingerly, with his spoon and fork.

In the matter of dealing with scruts there are two
schools—the old and the new. The old school pushes
its head well over its plate and drops the scrut straight
from its mouth. The new school emits the scrut into the
fingers of its left hand and therewith deposits it on the
rim of the plate. Albert noticed that Emily was of the new
school. But might she not despise as affectation in him what
came natural to herself? On the other hand, if he showed
himself as a prop of the old school, might she not set her
face the more stringently against him? The chances were
that whichever course he took would be the wrong one.

It was then that he had an inspiration—an idea of the
sort that comes to a man once in his life and finds him,
likely as not, unable to put it into practice. Albert was not
sure he could consummate this idea of his. He had indis-
putably fine teeth—'a proper mouthful of grinders' in
local phrase. But would they stand the strain he was going
to impose on them? He could but try them. Without a
sign of nervousness he raised his spoon, with one scrut
in it, to his mouth. This scrut he put between two of his
left-side molars, bit hard on it, and—eternity of that
moment!—felt it and heard it snap in two. Emily also

heard it. He was conscious that at sound of the percussion she started forward and stared at him. But he did not look at her. Calmly, systematically, with gradually diminishing crackles, he reduced that scrut to powder, and washed the powder down with a sip of beer. While he dealt with the second scrut he talked to Jos about the Borough Council's proposal to erect an electric power station on the site of the old gas-works down Hillport way. He was aware of a slight abrasion inside his left cheek. No matter. He must be more careful. There were six scruts still to be negotiated. He knew that what he was doing was a thing grandiose, unique, epical; a history-making thing; a thing that would outlive marble and the gilded monuments of princes. Yet he kept his head. He did not hurry, nor did he dawdle. Scrut by scrut, he ground slowly but he ground exceeding small. And while he did so he talked wisely and well. He passed from the power-station to a first edition of Leconte de Lisle's *Parnasse Contemporain* that he had picked up for sixpence in Liverpool, and thence to the Midland's proposal to drive a tunnel under the Knype Canal so as to link up the main-line with the Critchworth and Suddleford loop-line. Jos was too amazed to put in a word. Jos sat merely gaping—a gape that merged by imperceptible degrees into a grin. Presently he ceased to watch his guest. He sat watching his sister.

Not once did Albert himself glance in her direction. She was just a dim silhouette on the outskirts of his vision. But there she was, unmoving, and he could feel the fixture of her unseen eyes. The time was at hand when he would have to meet those eyes. Would he flinch? Was he master of himself?

The last scrut was powder. No temporising! He jerked his glass to his mouth. A moment later, holding out his plate to her, he looked Emily full in the eyes. They were Emily's eyes, but not hers alone. They were collective eyes—that was it! They were the eyes of stark, staring womanhood. Her face had been dead white, but now suddenly up from her throat, over her cheeks, through the down between her eyebrows, went a rush of colour, up over her temples, through the very parting of her hair.

'Happen', he said, without a quaver in his voice, 'I'll have a bit more, like.'

She flung her arms forward on the table and buried her face in them. It was a gesture wild and meek. It was the gesture foreseen and yet incredible. It was recondite, inexplicable, and yet obvious. It was the only thing to be done—and yet, by gum, she had done it.

Her brother had risen from his seat and was now at the door. 'Think I'll step round to the Works,' he said, 'and see if they banked up that furnace aright.'

NOTE.—*The author has in preparation a series of volumes dealing with the life of Albert and Emily Grapp.*

ENDEAVOUR
by J*hn G*lsw*rthy

THE DAWN OF CHRISTMAS DAY found London laid out in a shroud of snow. Like a body wasted by diseases that had triumphed over it at last, London lay stark and still now, beneath a sky that was as the closed leaden shell of a coffin. It was what is called an old-fashioned Christmas.

Nothing seemed to be moving except the Thames, whose embanked waters flowed on sullenly in their eternal act of escape to the sea. All along the wan stretch of Cheyne Walk the thin trees stood exanimate, with not a breath of wind to stir the snow that pied their soot-blackened branches. Here and there on the muffled ground lay a sparrow that had been frozen in the night, its little claws sticking up heavenward. But here and there also those tinier adventurers of the London air, smuts, floated vaguely and came to rest on the snow—signs that in the

seeming death of civilisation some housemaids at least
survived, and some fires had been lit.

One of these fires, crackling in the grate of one of those
dining-rooms which look fondly out on the river and
tolerantly across to Battersea, was being watched by the
critical eye of an aged canary. The cage in which this bird
sat was hung in the middle of the bow-window. It contained three perches, and also a pendent hoop. The tray
that was its floor had just been cleaned and sanded. In
the embrasure to the right was a fresh supply of hemp-
seed; in the embrasure to the left the bath-tub had just
been refilled with clear water. Stuck between the bars was
a large sprig of groundsel. Yet, though all was thus in
order, the bird did not eat nor drink, nor did he bathe.
With his back to Battersea, and his head sunk deep between his little sloping shoulders, he watched the fire.
The windows had for a while been opened, as usual, to
air the room for him; and the fire had not yet mitigated
the chill. It was not his custom to bathe at so in-
clement an hour; and his appetite for food and drink,
less keen than it had once been, required to be whetted by
example—he never broke his fast before his master and
mistress broke theirs. Time had been when, for sheer
joy in life, he fluttered from perch to perch, though there
were none to watch him, and even sang roulades, though
there were none to hear. He would not do these things
nowadays save at the fond instigation of Mr and Mrs
Adrian Berridge. The housemaid who ministered to his
cage, the parlourmaid who laid the Berridges' breakfast
table, sometimes tried to incite him to perform for their
own pleasure. But the sense of caste, strong in his protuberant little bosom, steeled him against these advances.

While the breakfast table was being laid, he heard a
faint tap against the window-pane. Turning round, he
perceived on the sill a creature like to himself, but very
different—a creature who, despite the pretensions of a red
waistcoat in the worst possible taste, belonged evidently
to the ranks of the outcast and the disinherited. In

previous winters the sill had been strewn every morning with bread-crumbs. This winter, no bread-crumbs had been vouchsafed; and the canary, though he did not exactly understand why this was so, was glad that so it was. He had felt that his poor relations took advantage of the Berridges' kindness. Two or three of them, as pensioners, might not have been amiss. But they came in swarms, and they gobbled their food in a disgusting fashion, not trifling coquettishly with it as birds should. The reason for this, the canary knew, was that they were hungry; and of that he was sorry. He hated to think how much destitution there was in the world; and he could not help thinking about it when samples of it were thrust under his notice. That was the principal reason why he was glad that the windowsill was strewn no more and seldom visited.

He would much rather not have seen this solitary applicant. The two eyes fixed on his made him feel very uncomfortable. And yet, for fear of seeming to be out-faced, he did not like to look away.

The subdued clangour of the gong, sounded for break-fast, gave him an excuse for turning suddenly round and watching the door of the room.

A few moments later there came to him a faint odour of Harris tweed, followed immediately by the short, some-what stout figure of his master—a man whose mild, fresh, pink, round face seemed to find salvation, as it were, at the last moment, in a neatly-pointed auburn beard.

Adrian Berridge paused on the threshold, as was his wont, with closed eyes and dilated nostrils, enjoying the aroma of complex freshness which the dining-room had at this hour. Pathetically a creature of habit, he liked to savour the various scents, sweet or acrid, that went to symbolise for him the time and the place. Here were the immediate scents of dry toast, of China tea, of napery fresh from the wash, together with that vague, super-subtle scent which boiled eggs give out through their unbroken shells. And as a permanent base to these there was the scent of much-polished Chippendale, and of bees'-waxed parquet, and of Persian rugs. To-day, moreover, crowning the composition, there was the delicate pungency of the holly that topped the Queen Anne mirror and the Mantegna prints.

Coming forward into the room, Mr Berridge greeted the canary. 'Well, Amber, old fellow,' he said, 'a happy Christmas to you!' Affectionately he pushed the tip of a plump white finger between the bars. 'Tweet!' he added.

'Tweet!' answered the bird, hopping to and fro along his perch.

'Quite an old-fashioned Christmas, Amber!' said Mr Berridge turning to scan the weather. At sight of the robin, a little spasm of pain contracted his face. A shine of tears came to his prominent pale eyes, and he turned quickly away. Just at that moment, heralded by a slight fragrance of old lace and of that peculiar, almost unseizable odour that uncut turquoises have, Mrs Berridge appeared.

'What is the matter, Adrian?' she asked quickly. She glanced sideways into the Queen Anne mirror, her hand fluttering, like a pale moth, to her hair, which she always wore braided in a fashion she had derived from Pollaiuolo's St Ursula.

'Nothing, Jacynth—nothing,' he answered with a lightness that carried no conviction; and he made behind his back a gesture to frighten away the robin.

'Amber isn't unwell, is he?' She came quickly to the cage. Amber executed for her a roulade of great sweetness. His voice had not perhaps the fullness for which it had been noted in earlier years; but the art with which he managed it was as exquisite as ever. It was clear to his audience that the veteran artist was hale and hearty.

But Jacynth, relieved on one point, had a misgiving on another. 'This groundsel doesn't look very fresh, does it?' she murmured, withdrawing the sprig from the bars. She rang the bell, and when the servant came in answer to it, said, 'Oh Jenny, will you please bring up another piece of groundsel for Master Amber? I don't think this one is quite fresh.'

This formal way of naming the canary to the servants always jarred on her principles and on those of her husband. They tried to regard their servants as essentially equals of themselves, and lately had given Jenny strict orders to leave off calling them 'Sir' and 'Ma'am', and to call them simply 'Adrian' and 'Jacynth'. But Jenny, after one or two efforts that ended in faint giggles, had reverted to the crude old nomenclature—as much to the relief as to the mortification of the Berridges. They did, it is true, discuss the possibility of redressing the balance by calling the parlourmaid 'Miss'. But, when it came to the point, their lips refused this office. And conversely their lips persisted in the social prefix to the bird's name.

Somehow that anomaly seemed to them symbolic of their lives. Both of them yearned so wistfully to live always in accordance to the nature of things. And this, they felt, ought surely to be the line of least resistance. In the immense difficulties it presented, and in their constant failures to surmount these difficulties, they often wondered whether the nature of things might not be, after all, something other than what they thought it. Again and again it seemed to be in as direct conflict with duty as with inclination; so that they were driven to wonder also whether what they conceived to be duty were not also a mirage—a marsh-light leading them on to disaster.

The fresh groundsel was brought in while Jacynth was pouring out the tea. She rose and took it to the cage; and it was then that she too saw the robin, still fluttering on the sill. With a quick instinct she knew that Adrian had seen it—knew what had brought that look to his face. She went and, bending over him, laid a hand on his shoulder. The disturbance of her touch caused the tweed to give out a tremendous volume of scent, making her feel a little dizzy.

'Adrian,' she faltered, 'mightn't we for once—it is

Christmas Day—mightn't we, just to-day, sprinkle some bread-crumbs?'

He rose from the table, and leaned against the mantel-piece, looking down at the fire. She watched him tensely. At length, 'Oh Jacynth,' he groaned, 'don't—don't tempt me.'

'But surely, dear, surely——'

'Jacynth, don't you remember that long talk we had last winter, after the annual meeting of the Feathered Friends' League, and how we agreed that those sporadic doles could do no real good—must even degrade the birds who received them—and that we had no right to meddle in what ought to be done by collective action of the State?'

'Yes, and—oh my dear, I do still agree, with all my heart. But if the State will do nothing—nothing——'

'It won't, it daren't, go on doing nothing, unless we encourage it to do so. Don't you see, Jacynth, it is just because so many people take it on themselves to feed a few birds here and there that the State feels it can afford to shirk the responsibility?'

'All that is fearfully true. But just now—Adrian, the look in that robin's eyes——'

Berridge covered his own eyes, as though to blot out from his mind the memory of that look. But Jacynth was not silenced. She felt herself dragged on by her sense of duty to savour, and to make her husband savour, the full bitterness that the situation could yield for them both. 'Adrian,' she said, 'a fearful thought came to me. Suppose —suppose it had been Amber!'

Even before he shuddered at the thought, he raised his finger to his lips, glancing round at the cage. It was clear that Amber had not overheard Jacynth's remark, for he threw back his head and uttered one of his blithest trills. Adrian, thus relieved, was free to shudder at the thought just suggested.

'Sometimes,' murmured Jacynth, 'I wonder if we, hold-ing the views we hold, are justified in keeping Amber.'

'Ah, dear, we took him in our individualistic days. We cannot repudiate him now. It wouldn't be fair. Besides, you see, he isn't here on a basis of mere charity. He's not a parasite, but an artist. He gives us of his art.'

'Yes, dear, I know. But you remember our doubts about the position of artists in the community—whether the State ought to sanction them at all.'

'True. But we cannot visit those doubts on our old friend yonder, can we, dear? At the same time, I admit that when—when—Jacynth: if ever anything happens to Amber, we shall perhaps not be justified in keeping another bird.'

'Don't, please don't talk of such things.' She moved to the window. Snow, a delicate white powder, was falling on the coverlet of snow.

Outside, on the sill, the importunate robin lay supine, his little heart beating no more behind the shabby finery of his breast, but his glazing eyes half-open as though even in death he were still questioning. Above him and all around him brooded the genius of infinity, dispassionate, inscrutable, grey.

Jacynth turned and mutely beckoned her husband to the window.

They stood there, these two, gazing silently down.

Presently Jacynth said: 'Adrian, are you sure that we, you and I, for all our theories, and all our efforts, aren't futile?'

'No, dear. Sometimes I am not sure. But—there's a certain comfort in not being sure. To die for what one knows to be true, as many saints have done—that is well. But to live, as many of us do nowadays, in service of what may, for aught we know, be only a half-truth or not true at all—this seems to me nobler still.'

'Because it takes more out of us?'

'Because it takes more out of us.'

Standing between the live bird and the dead, they gazed across the river, over the snow-covered wharves, over the dim, slender chimneys from which no smoke

came, into the grey-black veil of the distance. And it
seemed to them that the genius of infinity did not know
—perhaps did not even care—whether they were futile
or not, nor how much and to what purpose, if to any
purpose, they must go on striving.

THE FEAST
by J*s*ph C*nr*d

THE HUT IN WHICH slept the white man was on a
clearing between the forest and the river. Silence, the
silence murmurous and unquiet of a tropical night,
brooded over the hut that, baked through by the sun,
sweated a vapour beneath the cynical light of the stars.
Mahamo lay rigid and watchful at the hut's mouth. In his
upturned eyes, and along the polished surface of his lean
body black and immobile, the stars were reflected, creat-
ing an illusion of themselves who are illusions.

The roofs of the congested trees, writhing in some kind
of agony private and eternal, made tenebrous and shifty
silhouettes against the sky, like shapes cut out of black
paper by a maniac who pushes them with his thumb this
way and that, irritably, on a concave surface of blue steel.
Resin oozed unseen from the upper branches to the trunks
swathed in creepers that clutched and interlocked with
tendrils venomous, frantic and faint. Down below, by
force of habit, the lush herbage went through the farce
of growth—that farce old and screaming, whose trite end
is decomposition.

Within the hut the form of the white man, corpulent
and pale, was covered with a mosquito-net that was itself
illusory like everything else, only more so. Flying squad-
rons of mosquitos inside its meshes flickered and darted
over him, working hard, but keeping silence so as not to
excite him from sleep. Cohorts of yellow ants disputed
him against cohorts of purple ants, the two kinds slaying

one another in thousands. The battle was undecided when suddenly, with no such warning as it gives in some parts of the world, the sun blazed up over the horizon, turning night into day, and the insects vanished back into their camps.

The white man ground his knuckles into the corners of his eyes, emitting that snore final and querulous of a middle-aged man awakened rudely. With a gesture brusque but flaccid he plucked aside the net and peered around. The bales of cotton cloth, the beads, the brass wire, the bottles of rum, had not been spirited away in the night. So far so good. The faithful servant of his employers was now at liberty to care for his own interests. He regarded himself, passing his hands over his skin.

'Hi! Mahamo!' he shouted. 'I've been eaten up.'

The islander, with one sinuous motion, sprang from the ground, through the mouth of the hut. Then, after a glance, he threw high his hands in thanks to such good and evil spirits as had charge of his concerns. In a tone half of reproach, half of apology, he murmured—

'You white men sometimes say strange things that deceive the heart.'

'Reach me that ammonia bottle, d'you hear?' answered the white man. 'This is a pretty place you've brought me to!' He took a draught. 'Christmas Day, too! Of all the—— But I suppose it seems all right to you, you funny blackamoor, to be here on Christmas Day?'

'We are here on the day appointed, Mr Williams. It is a feast-day of your people?'

Mr Williams had lain back, with closed eyes, on his mat. Nostalgia was doing duty to him for imagination. He was wafted to a bedroom in Marylebone, where in honour of the Day he lay late dozing, with great contentment; outside, a slush of snow in the street, the sound of church-bells; from below a savour of especial cookery. 'Yes,' he said, 'it's a feast-day of my people.'

'Of mine, also,' said the islander humbly.

'Is it though? But they'll do business first?'

'They must first do that.'

'And they'll bring their ivory with them?'

'Every man will bring ivory,' answered the islander, with a smile gleaming and wide.

'How soon'll they be here?'

'Has not the sun risen? They are on their way.'

'Well, I hope they'll hurry. The sooner we're off this cursed island of yours the better. Take all those things out,' Mr Williams added, pointing to the merchandise, 'and arrange them—neatly, mind you!'

In certain circumstances it is right that a man be humoured in trifles. Mahamo, having borne out the merchandise, arranged it very neatly.

While Mr Williams made his toilet, the sun and the forest, careless of the doings of white and black men alike, waged their warfare implacable and daily. The forest from its inmost depths sent forth perpetually its legions of shadows that fell dead in the instant of exposure to the enemy whose rays heroic and absurd its outposts annihilated. There came from those inilluminable depths the equable rumour of myriads of winged things and crawling things newly roused to the task of killing and being killed. Thence detached itself, little by little, an insidious sound of a drum beaten. This sound drew more near.

Mr Williams, issuing from the hut, heard it, and stood gaping towards it.

'Is that them?' he asked.

'That is they,' the islander murmured, moving away towards the edge of the forest.

Sounds of chanting were a now audible accompaniment to the drum.

'What's that they're singing?' asked Mr Williams.

'They sing of their business,' said Mahamo.

'Oh!' Mr Williams was slightly shocked. 'I'd have thought they'd be singing of their feast.'

'It is of their feast they sing.'

It has been stated that Mr Williams was not imaginative. But a few years of life in climates alien and intemperate had disordered his nerves. There was that in the rhythms of the hymn which made bristle his flesh.

Suddenly, when they were very near, the voices ceased, leaving a legacy of silence more sinister than themselves. And now the black spaces between the trees were relieved by bits of white that were the eyeballs and teeth of Mahamo's brethren.

'It was of their feast, it was of you, they sang,' said Mahamo.

'Look here,' cried Mr Williams in his voice of a man not to be trifled with. 'Look here, if you've——'

He was silenced by sight of what seemed to be a young sapling sprung up from the ground within a yard of him —a young sapling tremulous, with a root of steel. Then a thread-like shadow skimmed the air, and another spear came impinging the ground within an inch of his feet.

As he turned in his flight he saw the goods so neatly arranged at his orders, and there flashed through him, even in the thick of the spears, the thought that he would be a grave loss to his employers. This—for Mr Williams was, not less than the goods, of a kind easily replaced— was an illusion. It was the last of Mr Williams' illusions.

From

AROUND THEATRES
(I)

Almond Blossom in Piccadilly Circus
[1901]

An Hypocrisy in Playgoing
[1903]

Mr Shaw's New Dialogues
[1903]

ALMOND BLOSSOM
IN PICCADILLY CIRCUS

OUR OWN ALMOND-TREES HAVE duly shed their blos-
soms, to be blown out of sight by the blasts of our own
spring. But, just where we should least hope to find it,
an exotic specimen has been planted, and blooms there
fairer and more fragrant, assuredly, than any native growth.
There, in Piccadilly Circus, where the chaotic shoddiness
of modern civilisation expresses itself most perfectly;
there, in that giddy congestion of omnibuses, advertisements, glossy restaurants and glossier drinking-bars,
glossy men and glossier women; there, in that immediate
inferno of ours, this gracious almond-tree is in flower. Let
us tend it lovingly. Let us make the most of its brief
season—the brief 'season' for which the players from the
Imperial Court Theatre of Tokio have leased the Criterion.

There seems to be something appropriate in the coming
of these players to the very centre of our vulgarity. For
have not we, in our greedy occidental way, made a very
great point of vulgarising down to our own level the
notion of Japan? The importation of a few fans and
umbrellas and idols set us all agog. Forthwith Brum-
magem could not turn out a big enough supply of cheap
and nasty imitations to keep us happy. The trade began
about twenty years ago, waxing ever faster and more
furious. 'Japanese Stores' sprung up on every side.
Japanese musical comedies were produced, 'Jolly Japs'
peddled around and about. Now at length we have had
our surfeit. We are eager to vulgarise some other national
art. And lo! suddenly in the midst of us, appear these
players from Tokio, to remind us how much nicer the real

358 ALMOND BLOSSOM IN PICCADILLY CIRCUS

thing is, and to warn us against making any more such
spurious imitations as those which we have made of them.
Their warning is likely to be the more effective through
the shock which their presence gives us. In the fullness
of our national pride, we had believed that the old Japan
was no more. We had flattered ourselves that the Japanese
were now as vulgar and occidental as we. And yet here,
classic and unperturbed, untouched by time or by us,
these players stand before us, as though incarnate from
the conventions of Utamaro and Hokusai.

Straight from the prints and drawings of Utamaro and
Hokusai these creatures have come to us. Those terrific
men, bristling with hair, and undulating all over with
muscle and showing their teeth in fixed grins; those pretty
little ladies, with their little sick smiles, drooping this
way or that as though the weight of their great sleek
head-dresses were too much for them—here they all are,
not outlined on flimsy paper, but alive and mobile in the
glory of three dimensions. Here they all are, magically
restored to the very flesh in which the limners saw them.
See! Two of the men have drawn their broadswords and
are planting their feet far apart in the classical attitude
that one knows so well. They are grunting, snorting,
gnashing their teeth. They are athirst for each other's
blood, both loving Katsuragi, the Geisha (whom, by the
way, they do *not* call the jewel of Asia). The swords clash
noisily, and sparks fly from them. The grins and the
grunts become more and more terrible, as the combatants
stamp round and round. And she, the cause of the com-
bat, sways this way and that, distracted, yet with a kind
of weary composure on her face and in every fold of her
red kimono, watching for the moment when she can throw
herself between, to separate and soothe and save them.
Whether she succeed or fail we care not. Merely are we
entranced by the sight of her, by the realisation of the
dreams that the colour-prints wove for us. Again, when
her lover has deserted her and to escape her vengeance
has hidden himself within a Buddhist monastery, we care

not whether by her dancing she shall persuade the monks to admit her within their gates. She dances, and that is enough for us. She divests herself of her kimono. Swathed and rigid, she averts herself from us. Faint, monotonous music is heard, and a crooning voice. Gradually she turns towards us. Her left hand is across her mouth, in her right hand she holds aloft her shut fan. The music is insistent. Still she stands motionless. Suddenly, with a sharp downward fling of the arm she shoots open her fan. The left hand flutters upon the air. She sways, droops forward, and sidles into her dance—a dance of long soft strides, indescribable. Presently she sinks on her knees under an almond-tree, and claps the palms of her hands delicately. Down from the branch falls a light shower of petals. These she sweeps together, imprisons them between her hands, runs away with them, scatters them from her, and, always in some mysterious accord to that mysterious music, chases them round and round.

Some symbolism there is, doubtless, in these evolutions. For us the grace of the kitten suffices. Anon, she does another dance, wearing on her head a hat that is like a pink plate and is tied with a pink riband across her lips. Anon, she is beating a tiny drum as she dances. See with what strange movements of her arms she waves the tiny drum-sticks! She is never still, and yet her every gesture imprints itself on our gaze as though it were the one arrested gesture of a figure in a picture. Nothing is blurred by mobility. Nothing escapes us. It is as though one were not seeing actual life in unrest, but inspecting at leisure a whole series of those instantaneous plates which are contained in a cinematograph, and wondering at the strange secrets revealed in them—those movements which are impalpable and unsuspected because only within the fraction of a second can they be caught. And yet, though we see everything thus separate, we see it also in its general relation to the rest. Though we see those quaintly exquisite postures and gestures which the limners recorded for us, we see also how they were made, and what——

no! what they expressed remains for us a mystery. We, who do not even know the Japanese language, how should we penetrate the mysteries of the Japanese spirit? We, to whom all these men and women look respectively (and delightfully) just like one another, how, in the name of goodness, are we to know what their souls are driving at?

True, 'arguments' of the two plays performed at the Criterion are duly included in the programme. Thus one knows roughly what is going on. One knows that one person is jealous, another frightened, another pleased, and so forth. And, as I have suggested, one doesn't care. So differently are the emotions expressed in Japan that illusion is completely merged for us in curiosity. When an Englishman is indignant because the mother of his betrothed has given her in marriage to another man, he expresses himself ebulliently. Yet when Yendo Morito meets Koromogawa, the mother of Kesa, and learns from her how badly he has been treated, he merely grunts and snarls. That (in the light of the argument) is his way of expressing anguish and rage. Naturally, we are more interested in the situation than touched by it. When he draws his sword and bids Koromogawa prepare for instant death, she does not, as would an Englishwoman, scream or kneel or try to run away; on the contrary, she remains perfectly still, rolls her eyes and grunts.

Such is the form that fear takes in Japan. Again, our sympathy is unaroused, tightly though our attention is held. Such is our experience of every climax in the play. We understand it, from the argument; but we cannot feel it. And between every climax is a long interval, which the argument does but very faintly illuminate. In these intervals we see the figures moving, gesticulating; we hear quaint sounds made by them. The hands wave and the lips curve and the arched eyebrows move up and down and the bodies sway to and fro and everything of course means something, but nothing reveals a hint to us. And we, if we are wise, do not try to penetrate the veil. We do not try to think: we merely look on. For sheer

visual delight, nothing can match this curious performance. All who have eyes to see should see it. The one
fault to be found with it is that the figures are seen
against very elaborate and gaudily-painted backgrounds.
Plain, pale backgrounds were needed to make them 'tell'
worthily of their own quaint perfection.

AN HYPOCRISY
IN PLAYGOING

Eecosstoetchiayoomahnioeevahrachellopestibahntamahnta-
fahnta . . . shall I go on? No? You do not catch my meaning, when I write thus? I am to express myself please, in
plain English? If I wrote the whole of my article as I
have written the beginning of it, you would, actually, refuse to read it? I am astonished. The chances are that
you do not speak Italian, do not understand Italian when
it is spoken. The chances are that Italian spoken from the
stage of a theatre produces for you no more than the
empty, though rather pretty, effect which it produces for
me, and which I have tried to suggest phonetically in
print. And yet the chances are also that you were in the
large British audience which I saw, last Wednesday afternoon, in the Adelphi Theatre—that large, patient, respectful audience, which sat out the performance of 'Hedda
Gabler'. Surely, you are a trifle inconsistent? You will
not tolerate two columns or so of gibberish from me, and
yet you will profess to have passed very enjoyably a
whole afternoon in listening to similar gibberish from
Signora Duse. Suppose that not only my article, but the
whole of this week's *Review* were written in the fashion
which you reject, and suppose that the price of the *Review*
were raised from sixpence to ninepence (proportionately,
to the increased price for seats at the Adelphi when

Signora Duse comes there). To be really consistent, you would have to pay, without a murmur, that ninepence, and to read, from cover to cover, that *Review*, and to enjoy, immensely, that perusal. An impossible feat? Well, just so would it be an impossible feat not to be bored by the Italian version of 'Hedda Gabler'. Why not confess your boredom? Better still, why go to be bored?

All this sounds rather brutal. But it is a brutal thing to object to humbug, and only by brutal means can humbug be combated, and there seems to me no form of humbug sillier and more annoying than the habit of attending plays that are acted in a language whereof one cannot make head nor tail. Of course, I do not resent the mere fact that Signora Duse comes to London. Let that distinguished lady be made most welcome. Only, let the welcome be offered by appropriate people. There are many of them. There is the personnel of the embassy in Grosvenor Square. There are the organ-grinders, too, and the ice-cream men. And there are some other, some English, residents in London who have honourably mastered the charming Italian tongue. Let all this blest minority flock to the Adelphi every time, and fill as much of it as they can. But, for the most part, the people who, instead of staying comfortably at home, insist on flocking and filling are they to whom, as to me, Italian is gibberish and who have not, as have I, even the excuse of a mistaken sense of duty. Perhaps they have some such excuse. Perhaps they really do feel that they are taking a means of edification. 'We needs must praise the highest when we see it'; Duse is (we are assured) the highest; therefore we needs must see her, for our own edification, and go into rhapsodies. Such, perhaps, is the unsound syllogism which these good folk mutter. I suggest, of what spiritual use is it to see the highest if you cannot understand it? Go round to the booksellers and buy Italian grammars, Italian conversation-books, the 'Inferno', and every other possible means to a nodding acquaintance with Italian. Stick to your task; and then, doubtless, when next Signora

Duse comes among us, you will derive not merely that edification which is now your secret objective. I know your rejoinder to that. 'Oh, Duse's personality is so wonderful. Her temperament is so marvellous. And then her art! It doesn't matter whether we know Italian or not. We only have to watch the movements of her hands' (rhapsodies omitted) 'and the changes of her face' (r. o.) 'and the inflections of her voice' (r. o.) 'to understand everything, positively *everything*.' Are you so sure? I take it that you understand more from the performance of an Italian play which you have read in an English translation than from the performance of an Italian play which never has been translated. There are, so to say, degrees in your omniscience. You understand more if you have read the translation lately than if a long period has elapsed since your reading of it. Are you sure that you would not understand still more if the play were acted in English? Of course you are. Nay, and equally of course, you are miserably conscious of all the innumerable things that escape you, that flit faintly past you. You read your English version, feverishly, like a timid candidate for an examination, up to the very last moment before your trial. Perhaps you even smuggle it in with you, for furtive cribbing. But this is a viva voce examination: you have no time for cribbing: you must rely on Signora Duse's voice, hands, face and your own crammed memory. And up to what point has your memory been crammed? You remember the motive of the play, the characters, the sequence of the scenes. Them you recognise on the stage. But do you recognise the masquerading words? Not you. They all flash past you, whirl round you, mocking, not to be caught, not to be challenged and unmasked. You stand sheepishly in their midst, like a solitary stranger strayed into a masked ball. Or to reverse the simile, you lurch this way and that, clutching futile air, like the central figure in blindman's buff. Occasionally you do catch a word or two. These are only the proper names, but they are very welcome. It puts you in pathetic conceit with yourself, for the moment, when from the welter of unmeaning vowels and consonants 'Eilert Lövborg' or 'Hedda Gabler' suddenly detaches itself, like a silver trout 'rising' from a muddy stream. These are your only moments of comfort. For the rest, your irritation at not grasping the details prevents you from taking pleasure in your power to grasp the general effect.

I doubt even whether, in the circumstances, you can have that synthetic power fully and truly. It may be that what I am going to say about Signora Duse as Hedda Gabler is vitiated by incapacity to understand exactly her rendering of the part as a whole. She may be more plausibly like Hedda Gabler than she seems to me. Mark, I do not say that she may have conceived the part more intelligently, more rightly, with greater insight into Ibsen's meaning. And perhaps I should express myself more accurately if I said that Hedda Gabler may be more like Signora Duse than she seems to me. For this actress never stoops to impersonation. I have seen her in many parts, but I have never (you must take my evidence for what is is worth) detected any difference in her. To have seen her once is to have seen her always. She is artistically right or wrong according as whether the part enacted by her can or cannot be merged and fused into her own personality. Can Hedda Gabler be so merged and fused? She is self-centred. Her eyes are turned inward to her own soul. She does not try to fit herself into the general scheme of things. She broods disdainfully aloof. So far so good; for Signora Duse, as we know her, is just such another. (This can be said without offence. The personality of an artist, as shown through his or her art, is not necessarily a reflection, and is often a flat contradiction—a complement—to his or her personality in life.) But Hedda is also a minx, and a ridiculous minx, and not a nice minx. Her revolt from the circumstances of her life is untinged with nobility. She imagines herself to be striving for finer things, but her taste is in fact not good enough for what she gets. One can see that Ibsen hates her, and means us to laugh at her. For that reason she 'wears' much better than those sister-rebels whom Ibsen glorified. She remains as a lively satire on a phase that for serious purposes is out of date. She ought to be played with a sense of humour, with a comedic understanding between the player and the audience. Signora Duse is not the woman to create such an understanding. She cannot, moreover, convey a hint of minxishness: that quality is outside her rubric. Hedda is anything but listless. She is sick of a life which does not tickle her with little ready-made excitements. But she is ever alert to contrive these little excitements for herself. She is the very soul of restless mischief. Signora Duse suggested the weary calm of one who has climbed to a summit high above the gross world. She was as one who sighs, but can afford to smile, being at rest with herself. She was spiritual, statuesque, somnambulistic, what you will, always in direct opposition to eager, snappy, fascinating, nasty little Hedda Gabler. Resignedly she shot the pistol from the window. Resignedly she bent over the book of photographs with the lover who had returned. Resignedly she lured him to drunkenness. Resignedly she committed his MS to the flames. Resignation, as always, was the keynote of her performance. And here, as often elsewhere, it rang false.

However, it was not the only performance of Hedda Gabler. There was another, and, in some ways, a better. While Signora Duse walked through her part, the prompter threw himself into it with a will. A more raucous whisper I never heard than that which preceded the Signora's every sentence. It was like the continuous tearing of very thick silk. I think it worried every one in the theatre, except the Signora herself, who listened placidly to the prompter's every reading, and, as soon as he had finished, reproduced it in her own way. This process made the matinée a rather long one. By a very simple expedient the extra time might have been turned to good account. How much pleasure would have been gained, and

how much hypocrisy saved, if there had been an inter-
preter on the O.P. side, to shout in English what the
prompter was whispering in Italian!

MR SHAW'S
NEW DIALOGUES

ARISTOTLE, OFTEN AS HE sneered at Plato, never called
Plato a dramatist, and did not drag the Platonic dialogues
into his dramatic criticism. Nor did Plato himself profess
to be a dramatist; and it would need a wide stretch of
fancy to think of him dedicating one of his works to
Aristotle as notable expert in dramatic criticism. On the
other hand, here is Mr Bernard Shaw dedicating his new
book to 'my dear Walkley', that pious custodian of the
Aristotelian flame, and arguing, with platonic subtlety,
that this new book contains a play. Odd! For to drama
Mr Shaw and Plato stand in almost exactly the same relation. Plato, through anxiety that his work should be read,
and his message accepted, so far mortified his strongly
Puritan instincts as to give a setting of bright human
colour to his abstract thought. He invented men of flesh
and blood, to talk for him, and put them against realistic
backgrounds. And thus he gained, and still retains, 'a
public'. Only, his method was fraught with nemesis, and
he is generally regarded as a poet—he, who couldn't abide
poets. Essentially, he was no more a poet than he was a
dramatist, or than Mr Shaw is a dramatist. Like him, and
unlike Aristotle, for whom the exercise of thought was
an end in itself, and who, therefore, did not attempt to
bedeck as a decoy the form of his expression, Mr Shaw
is an ardent humanitarian. He wants to save us. So he
gilds the pill richly. He does not, indeed, invent men of
flesh and blood, to talk for him. There, where Plato suc-

ceeded, he fails, I must confess. But he assumes various
disguises, and he ventriloquises, and moves against realistic
backgrounds. In one direction he goes further than Plato.
He weaves more of a story round the interlocutors. Suppose that in the 'Republic', for example, there were
'Socrates (in love with Aspasia)', 'Glaucon (in love with
Xanthippe)', etcetera, and then you have in your mind
a very fair equivalent for what Mr Shaw writes and calls
a play. This peculiar article is, of course, not a play at all.
It is 'as good as a play'—infinitely better, to my peculiar
taste, than any play I have ever read or seen enacted.
But a play it is not. What is a dramatist? Principally, a
man who delights in watching, and can portray, the
world as it is, and the various conflicts of men and
women as they are. Such a man has, besides the joy of
sheer contemplation, joy in the technique of his art—how
to express everything most precisely and perfectly, most
worthily of the splendid theme. He may have a message
to deliver. Or he may have none. *C'est selon.* But the
message is never a tyrannous preoccupation. When the
creative and the critical faculty exist in one man,
the lesser is perforce overshadowed by the greater. Mr
Shaw knows well—how could so keen a critic fail to
detect?—that he is a critic, and not a creator at all. But,
for the purpose which I have explained, he must needs
pretend through Mr Walkley, who won't believe, to an
innocent public which may believe, that his pen runs
away with him. 'Woman projecting herself dramatically
by my hands (a process over which I have no control).'
A touching fib! The only things which Mr Shaw cannot
consciously control in himself are his sense of humour
and his sense of reason. 'The man who listens to Reason
is lost: Reason enslaves all whose minds are not strong
enough to master her.' That is one of many fine and profound aphorisms printed at the end of the book, and
written (one suspects) joyously, as a private antidote to
the dramatic tomfoolery to which Mr Shaw had perforce
condescended. Well! Mr Shaw will never be manumitted

by Reason. She is as inexorable an owner of him as is
Humour, and a less kind owner, in that she does prevent
him from seeing the world as it is, while Humour, not
preventing him from being quite serious, merely prevents
stupid people seeing how serious he is. Mr Shaw is
always trying to prove this or that thesis, and the result is
that his characters (so soon as he differentiates them,
ever so little, from himself) are the merest diagrams.
Having no sense for life, he has, necessarily, no sense for
art. It would be strange, indeed, if he could succeed in
that on which he is always pouring a very sincere contempt. 'For art's sake alone', he declares, 'I would not
face the toil of writing a single sentence.' That is no fib.
Take away his moral purpose and his lust for dialectic,
and Mr Shaw would put neither pen to paper nor mouth
to meeting, and we should be by so much the duller. But
had you taken away from Bunyan or Ibsen or any other
of those great artists whom Mr Shaw, because they had
'something to say', is always throwing so violently at our
heads, they would have yet created, from sheer joy in life
as it was and in art as it could become through their
handling of it. Mr Shaw, using art merely as a means of
making people listen to him, naturally lays hands on the
kind that appeals most quickly to the greatest number of
people. There is something splendid in the contempt with
which he uses as the vehicle for his thesis a conventional
love-chase, with motors and comic brigands thrown in.
He is as eager to be a popular dramatist and as willing to
demean himself in any way that may help him to the goal,
as was (say) the late Mr Pettitt. I hope he will reach the
goal. It is only the theatrical managers who stand between
him and the off-chance of a real popular success. But if
these managers cannot be shaken from their obstinate
timidity, I hope that Mr Shaw, realising that the general
public is as loth to read plays as to read books of un-
diluted philosophy, will cease to dabble in an art which
he abhors. Let him always, by all means, use the form of
dialogue—that form through which, more conveniently

than through any other, every side of a subject can be laid bare to our intelligence. It is, moreover, a form of which Mr Shaw is a master. In swiftness, tenseness and lucidity of dialogue no living writer can touch the hem of Mr Shaw's garment. In *Man and Superman* every phrase rings and flashes. Here, though Mr Shaw will be angry with me, is perfect art. In Mr Shaw as an essayist I cannot take so whole-hearted a delight. Both in construction and in style his essays seem to me more akin to the art of oral debating than of literary exposition. That is because he trained himself to speak before he trained himself to write. And it is, doubtless, by reason of that same priority that he excels in writing words to be spoken by the human voice or to be read as though they were so spoken.

The name of this play's hero is John Tanner, corrupted from Don Juan Tenorio, of whom its bearer is supposed to be the lineal descendant and modern equivalent. But here we have merely one of the devices whereby Mr Shaw seeks to catch the ear that he desires to box. Did not the end justify the means, Mr Shaw's natural honesty would have compelled him to christen his hero Joseph or Anthony. For he utterly flouts the possibility of a Don Juan. Gazing out on the world, he beholds a tremendous battle of sex raging. But it is the Sabine ladies who, more muscular than even Rubens made them, are snatching and shouldering away from out the newly-arisen walls the shrieking gentlemen of Rome. It is the fauns who scud coyly, on tremulous hoofs, through the woodland, not daring a backward-glance at rude and dogged nymphs who are gaining on them every moment. Of course, this sight is an hallucination. There are, it is true, women who take the initiative, and men who shrink from following them. There are, and always have been. Such beings are no new discovery, though their existence is stupidly ignored by the average modern dramatist. But they are notable exceptions to the rule of Nature. True, again, that in civilised society marriage is more important than desirable to a woman than to a man. 'All women,' said one of Disraeli's characters, 'ought to be married, and no men.' The epigram sums up John Tanner's attitude towards life even more wittily than anything that has been put into his mouth by Mr Shaw. John Tanner, pursued and finally bound in matrimony by Miss Ann Whitefield, supplies an excellent motive for a comedy of manners. But to that kind of comedy Mr Shaw will not stoop— not wittingly, at least. From John Tanner he deduces a general law. For him, John Tanner is Man, and Ann Whitefield is Woman—nothing less. He has fallen into the error—a strange error for a man with his views—of confusing the natural sex-instinct with the desire for marriage. Because women desire marriage more strongly than men, therefore, in his opinion, the sex-instinct is communicated from woman to man. I need not labour the point that this conclusion is opposite to the obvious truth of all ages and all countries. Man is the dominant animal. It was unjust of Nature not to make the two sexes equal. Mr Shaw hates injustice, and so, partly to redress the balance by robbing Man of conscious superiority, and partly to lull himself into peace of mind, he projects as real that visionary world of flitting fauns and brutal Sabines. Idealist, he insists that things are as they would be if he had his way. His characters come from out his own yearning heart. Only, we can find no corner for them in ours. We can no more be charmed by them than we can believe in them. Ann Whitefield is a minx. John Tanner is a prig. Prig versus Minx, with the gloves off, and Prig floored in every round—there you have Mr Shaw's customary formula for drama; and he works it out duly in *Man and Superman*. The main difference between this play and the others is that the minx and the prig are conscious not merely of their intellects, but of 'the Life Force'. Of this they regard themselves, with comparative modesty, as the automatic instruments. They are wrong. The Life Force could find no use for them. They are not human enough, not alive enough. That is the main drawback for a dramatist who does not love raw life: he cannot create living human characters.

And yet it is on such characters as John and Ann that Mr Shaw founds his hopes for the future of humanity. If we are very good, we *may* be given the Superman. If we are very scientific, and keep a sharp look out on our instincts, and use them just as our intellects shall prescribe, we *may* produce a race worthy to walk this fair earth. That is the hope with which we are to buoy ourselves up. It is a forlorn one. Man may, in the course of æons, evolve into something better than now he is. But the process will be not less unconscious than long. Reason and instinct have an inveterate habit of cancelling each other. If the world were governed by reason, it would not long be inhabited. Life is a muddle. It seems a brilliant muddle, if you are an optimist; a dull one, if you aren't; but in neither case can you deny that it is the muddlers who keep it going. The thinkers cannot help it at all. They are detached from 'the Life Force'. If they could turn their fellow-creatures into thinkers like themselves, all would be up. Fortunately, or unfortunately, they have not that power. The course of history has often been turned by sentiment, but by thought never. The thinkers are but valuable ornaments. A safe place is assigned to them on the world's mantelpiece, while humanity basks and blinks stupidly on the hearth, warming itself in the glow of the Life Force.

On that mantelpiece Mr Shaw deserves a place of honour. He is a very brilliant ornament. And never have his ornamental qualities shone more brightly than in this latest book. Never has he thought more clearly or more wrongly, and never has he displayed better his genius for dialectic, and never has his humour gushed forth in such sudden natural torrents. This is his masterpiece, so far. Treasure it as the most complete expression of the most distinct personality in current literature. Treasure it, too, as a work of specific art, in line with your Plato and Lucian and Landor.

From

AROUND THEATRES
(II)

Dan Leno
[1904]

Henry Irving
[1905]

'Sarah's' Memoirs
[1907]

DAN LENO

So LITTLE AND FRAIL a lantern could not long harbour so big a flame. Dan Leno was more a spirit than a man. It was inevitable that he, cast into a life so urgent as is the life of a music-hall artist, should die untimely. Before his memory fades into legend, let us try to evaluate his genius. For mourners there is ever a solace in determining what, precisely, they have lost.

Usually, indisputable pre-eminence in any art comes of some great originative force. An artist stands unchallenged above his fellows by reason of some 'new birth' that he has given to his art. Dan Leno, however, was no inaugurator. He did not, like Mr Albert Chevalier, import into the music-hall a new subject-matter, with a new style. He ended, as he had started, well within the classic tradition. True, he shifted the centre of gravity from song to 'patter'. But, for the rest, he did but hand on the torch. His theme was ever the sordidness of the lower middle class, seen from within. He dealt, as his forerunners had dealt, and as his successors are dealing, with the 'two pair-back', the 'pub', the 'general store', the 'peeler', the 'beak', and other such accessories to the life of the all-but-submerged. It was rather a murky torch that he took. Yet, in his hand, how gloriously it blazed, illuminating and warming! All that trite and unlovely material, how new and beautiful it became for us through Dan Leno's genius! Well, where lay the secret of that genius? How came we to be spell-bound?

Partly, without doubt, our delight was in the quality of the things actually said by Dan Leno. No other music-hall artist threw off so many droll sayings—droll in idea as in verbal expression. Partly, again, our delight was in the way that these things were uttered—in the gestures and grimaces and antics that accompanied them; in fact, in Dan Leno's technique. But, above all, our delight was in Dan Leno himself. In every art personality is the paramount thing, and without it artistry goes for little. Especially is this so in the art of acting, where the appeal of personality is so direct. And most especially is it so in the art of acting in a music-hall, where the performer is all by himself upon the stage, with nothing to divert our attention. The moment Dan Leno skipped upon the stage, we were aware that here was a man utterly unlike any one else we had seen. Despite the rusty top hat and broken umbrella and red nose of tradition, here was a creature apart, radiating an ethereal essence all his own. He compelled us not to take our eyes off him, not to miss a word that he said. Not that we needed any compulsion. Dan Leno's was not one of those personalities which dominate us by awe, subjugating us against our will. He was of that other, finer kind: the lovable kind. He had, in a higher degree than any other actor that I have ever seen, the indefinable quality of being sympathetic. I defy any one not to have loved Dan Leno at first sight. The moment he capered on, with that air of wild determination, squirming in every limb with some deep grievance, that must be outpoured, all hearts were his. That face puckered with cares, whether they were the cares of the small shopkeeper, or of the landlady, or of the lodger; that face so tragic, with all the tragedy that is writ on the face of a baby-monkey, yet ever liable to relax its mouth into a sudden wide grin and to screw up its eyes to vanishing point over some little triumph wrested from Fate, the tyrant; that poor little battered personage, so 'put upon', yet so plucky with his squeaking voice and his sweeping gestures; bent but not broken; faint but pursuing; incarnate of the will to live in a world not at all worth living in—surely all hearts went always out to Dan Leno, with warm corners in them reserved to him for ever and ever.

To the last, long after illness had sapped his powers of actual expression and invention, the power of his personality was unchanged, and irresistible. Even had he not been in his heyday a brilliant actor, and a brilliant wag, he would have thrown all his rivals into the shade. Often, even in his heyday, his acting and his waggishness did not carry him very far. Only mediocrity can be trusted to be always at its best. Genius must always have lapses proportionate to its triumphs. A new performance by Dan Leno was almost always a dull thing in itself. He was unable to do himself justice until he had, as it were, collaborated for many nights with the public. He selected and rejected according to how his jokes, and his expression of them, 'went'; and his best things came to him always in the course of an actual performance, to be incorporated in all the subsequent performances. When, at last, the whole thing had been built up, how perfect a whole it was! Not a gesture, not a grimace, not an inflection of the voice, not a wriggle of the body, but had its significance, and drove its significance sharply, grotesquely, home to us all. Never was a more perfect technique in acting. The technique for acting in a music-hall is of a harder, perhaps finer, kind than is needed for acting in a theatre; inasmuch as the artist must make his effects so much more quickly, and without the aid of any but the slightest 'properties' and scenery, and without the aid of any one else on the stage. It seemed miraculous how Dan Leno contrived to make you see before you the imaginary persons with whom he conversed. He never stepped outside himself, never imitated the voices of his interlocutors. He merely repeated, before making his reply, a few words of what they were supposed to have said to him. Yet there they were, as large as life, before us. Having this perfect independence in his art—being thus all-sufficient to himself—Dan Leno was, of course, seen to much greater advantage in a music-hall than at Drury Lane. He was never 'in the picture' at Drury Lane. He could not play into the hands of other persons on the

stage, nor could they play into his. And his art of suggestion or evocation was nullified by them as actualities. Besides, Drury Lane was too big for him. It exactly fitted
Mr Herbert Campbell, with his vast size and his vast
method. But little Dan Leno, with a technique exactly
suited to the size of the average music-hall, had to be
taken, as it were, on trust.

Apart from his personality and his technique, Dan
Leno was, as I have said, a sayer of richly grotesque
things. He had also a keen insight into human nature.
He knew thoroughly, outside and inside, the types that
he impersonated. He was always 'in the character', whatever it might be. And yet if you repeat to any one even
the best things that he said, how disappointing is the
result! How much they depended on the sayer and the
way of saying! I have always thought that the speech
over Yorick's skull would have been much more poignant
if Hamlet had given Horatio some specific example of the
way in which the jester had been wont to set the table on
a roar. We ought to have seen Hamlet convulsed with
laughter over what he told, and Horatio politely trying
to conjure up the ghost of a smile. This would have been
good, not merely as pointing the tragedy of a jester's
death, but also as illustrating the tragic temptation that
besets the jester's contemporaries to keep his memory
green. I suppose we shall, all of us, insist on trying to give
our grand-children some idea of Dan Leno at his best.
We all have our especially cherished recollection of the
patter of this or that song. I think I myself shall ever
remember Dan Leno more vividly and affectionately as
the shoemaker than as anything else. The desperate hope-
fulness with which he adapted his manner to his different
customers! One of his customers was a lady with her
little boy. Dan Leno, skipping forward to meet her, with a
peculiar skip invented specially for his performance,
suddenly paused, stepped back several feet in one stride,
eyeing the lady in wild amazement. He had never seen
such a lovely child. *How* old, did the mother say? Three?

He would have guessed seven at least—'except when I look at you, ma'am, and then I should say he was one at most.' Here Dan Leno bent down, one hand on each knee, and began to talk some unimaginable kind of baby-language. . . . A little pair of red boots with white buttons? Dan Leno skipped towards an imaginary shelf; but, in the middle of his skip, he paused, looked back, as though drawn by some irresistible attraction, and again began to talk to the child. As it turned out, he had no boots of the kind required. He plied the mother with other samples, suggested this and that, faintlier and faintlier, as he bowed her out. For a few moments he stood gazing after her, with blank disappointment, still bowing automatically. Then suddenly he burst out into a volley of deadly criticisms on the child's personal appearance, ceasing as suddenly at the entrance of another customer. . . . I think I see some of my readers—such of them as never saw Dan Leno in this part—raising their eyebrows. Nor do I blame them. Nor do I blame myself for failing to recreate that which no howsoever ingenious literary artist could re-create for you. I can only echo the old heart-cry *'Si ipsum audissetis!'* Some day, no doubt, the phonograph and the bioscope will have been so adjusted to each other that we shall see and hear past actors and singers as well as though they were alive before us. I wish Dan Leno could have been thus immortalised. No actor of our time deserved immortality so well as he.

HENRY IRVING

ONE MOURNS NOT MERELY a great actor, who had been a great manager. Irving was so romantically remarkable a figure in modern life, having such a hold on one's imagination (partly because he left so much to it), that his death is like the loss of a legend. As an actor, and as a

manager, he had his faults; and these faults were obvious.
But as a personality he was flawless—armed at all points
in an impenetrable and darkly-gleaming armour of his
own design. *The Knight from Nowhere* was the title of a
little book of pre-Raphaelite poems that I once read. I
always thought of Irving as the Knight from Nowhere.

That he, throughout his memorable tenancy of the
Lyceum Theatre, did nothing to encourage the better sort
of modern playwright, is a fact for which not he himself
should be blamed. It was the fault of the Lyceum Theatre.
In that vast and yawning gulf the better sort of modern
drama would (for that it consists in the realistic handling
of a few characters in ordinary modern life) have been
drowned and lost utterly. On a huge stage, facing a huge
auditorium, there must be plenty of crowds, bustle, up-
roar. Drama that gives no scope for these things must be
performed in reasonably small places. A more plausible
grievance against Irving, as manager, is that in quest of
bustling romances or melodramas he seemed generally
to alight on hack-work. I think there can be no doubt that
he was lacking in literary sense, and was content with any
play that gave him scope for a great and central display
of his genius in acting. He did not, of course, invent the
'star' system. But he carried it as far as it could be carried.
And the further he carried it, the greater his success. From
an artistic standpoint, I admit that this system is indefensible. But theatres, alas! have box-offices; and the
public cares far more, alack! for a favourite actor than
for dramatic art. Justice, then, blames rather the public
than the favourite actor.

It was as a producer of Shakespeare that Irving was
great in management. He was the first man to give Shakespeare a setting contrived with archaic and æsthetic care
—a setting that should match the pleasure of the eye with
the pleasure of the ear. That was a noble conception.
Many people object, quite honestly, that the pleasure of
the ear is diminished by that of the eye—that spectacle
is a foe to poetry. Of course, spectacle may be overdone.

Irving may sometimes have overdone it; but he always overdid it beautifully. And there was this further excuse for him: he could not, even had the stage been as bare as a desert, have given us the true music and magic of Shakespeare's verse. He could not declaim. That was one of the defects in his art. His voice could not be attuned to the glories of rhythmic cadence. It was a strange, suggestive voice that admirably attuned itself to the subtleties of Irving's conception of whatever part he was playing. It was Irving's subtle conception, always, that we went to see. Here, again, Irving was an innovator. I gather that the actors of his day had been simple, rough-and-ready, orotund fellows who plunged into this or that play, very much as the water-horse plunges through the reeds. They were magnificent, but they had no pretensions to intellect. Irving had these pretensions, and he never failed to justify them. One missed the music of the verse, but was always arrested, stimulated, by the meanings that he made the verse yield to him. These subtle and sometimes profound meanings were not always Shakespeare's own. Now and again, the verse seemed to yield them to Irving only after an intense effort, and with a rather bad grace. All the parts that Irving played were exacting parts, but he had his revenge sometimes, exacting even more from them. This was another defect in his art: he could not impersonate. His voice, face, figure, port, were not transformable. But so fine was the personality to which they belonged that none cried shame when this or that part had to submit to be crushed by it. Intransformable, he was —multiradiant, though. He had, in acting, a keen sense of humour—of sardonic, grotesque, fantastic humour. He had an incomparable power for eeriness—for stirring a dim sense of mystery; and not less masterly was he in evoking a sharp sense of horror. His dignity was magnificent in purely philosophic or priestly gentleness, or in the gaunt aloofness of philosopher or king. He could be benign with a tinge of malevolence, and arrogant with an

under-current of sweetness. As philosopher or king, poet
or prelate, he was matchless. One felt that if Charles the
Martyr, Dante, Wolsey, were not precisely as he was, so
much the worse for Wolsey, Dante, Charles the Martyr.
On the other hand, less august types, such as men of
action and men of passion, were outside his range, and
suffered badly when he dragged them within it. Macbeth
had a philosophic side, which enabled Macbeth to come
fairly well out of the ordeal. But Romeo's suicide in the
vault of Capulet could only be regarded as a merciful
release. Unfortunately, though I saw and can remember
Irving as Romeo, I never saw him as Hamlet. This is one
of the regrets of my life. I can imagine the gentleness
(with a faint strain of cruelty), the aloofness, the grace
and force of intellect, in virtue of which that performance
must have been a very masterpiece of interpretation. I
can imagine, too, the mystery with which Irving must
have involved, rightly, the figure of Hamlet, making it
loom through the mist mightily, as a world-type, not as a
mere individual—making it loom as it loomed in the soul
of Shakespeare himself—not merely causing it to strut
agreeably, littly, as in the average production. Above all,
I can imagine how much of sheer beauty this interpretation must have had. Though, as I have said, Irving could
not do justice to the sound of blank-verse, his prime
appeal was always to the sense of beauty. It was not, I
admit, to a sense of obvious beauty. It was to a sense of
strange, delicate, almost mystical and unearthly beauty.
To those who possessed not, nor could acquire, this sense,
Irving appeared always in a rather ridiculous light. 'Why
does he walk like this? Why does he talk like that?' But,
for any one equipped to appreciate him, his gait and his
utterance were not less dear than his face—were part of a
harmony that was as fine as it was strange. And, though
the cruder members of the audience could not fall under
the spell of this harmony, they were never irreverent until
they reached their homes. Never once at the Lyceum did

I hear a titter. Irving's presence dominated even those who could not be enchanted by it. His magnetism was intense, and unceasing. What exactly magnetism is, I do not know. It may be an exhalation of the soul, or it may be a purely physical thing—an effusion of certain rays which will one day be discovered, and named after their discoverer—Professor Jenkinson, perhaps: the Jenkinson Rays. I only know that Irving possessed this gift of magnetism in a supreme degree. And I conjecture that to it, rather than to the quality of his genius, which was a thing to be really appreciated only by the few, was due the unparalleled sway that he had over the many.

In private life he was not less magnetic than on the stage. The obituarists seem hardly to do justice to the intensely interesting personality of Irving in private life. He has been depicted by them merely as a benevolent gentleman who was always doing this or that obscure person a good turn. Certainly, Irving was benevolent, and all sorts of people profited by his generosity. But these two facts are poor substitutes for the impression that Irving made on those who were brought into contact with him. He was always courteous and gracious, and everybody was fascinated by him; but I think there were few who did not also fear him. Always in the company of his friends and acquaintances—doubtless, not in that of his most intimate friends—there was an air of sardonic reserve behind his cordiality. He seemed always to be watching, and watching from a slight altitude. As when, on the first or last night of a play, he made his speech before the curtain, and concluded by calling himself the public's 'respectful—devoted—loving—servant', with special emphasis on the word 'servant', he seemed always so like to some mighty cardinal stooping to wash the feet of pilgrims at the altar-steps, so, when in private life people had the honour of meeting Irving, his exquisite manner of welcome stirred fear as well as love in their hearts. Irving, I think, wished to be feared as well as

loved. He was 'a good fellow'; but he was also a man of
genius, who had achieved pre-eminence in his art, and,
thereby, eminence in the national life; and, naturally, he
was not going to let the 'good fellow' in him rob him of
the respect that was his due. Also, I think, the process of
making himself feared appealed to something elfish in
his nature. Remember, he was a comedian, as well as a
tragedian. Tragic acting on the stage is, necessarily, an
assumption; but comedy comes out of the actor's own
soul. Surely, to be ever 'grand seigneur', to be ever
pontifically gracious in what he said and in his manner
of saying it, and to watch the effect that he made, was all
wine to the comedic soul of Irving. He enjoyed the dignity
of his position, but enjoyed even more, I conjecture, the
fun of it. I formed the theory, once and for all, one morning in the year 1895—the morning of the day appointed
for various gentlemen to be knighted at Windsor Castle. I
was crossing the road, opposite the Marble Arch, when a
brougham passed me. It contained Irving, evidently on
his way to Paddington. Irving, in his most prelatical
mood, had always a touch—a trace here and there—of
the old Bohemian. But as I caught sight of him on this
occasion—a great occasion, naturally, in his career; though
to me it had seemed rather a bathos, this superimposition
of a smug Hanoverian knighthood on the Knight from
Nowhere—he was the old Bohemian, and nothing else.
His hat was tilted at more than its usual angle, and his
long cigar seemed longer than ever; and on his face was a
look of such ruminant, sly fun as I have never seen
equalled. I had but a moment's glimpse of him; but that
was enough to show me the soul of a comedian revelling
in the part he was about to play—of a comedic philosopher revelling in a foolish world. I was sure that when
he alighted on the platform of Paddington his bearing
would be more than ever grave and stately, with even the
usual touch of Bohemianism obliterated now in honour
of the honour that was to befall him.

Apart from his genuine kindness, and his grace and magnetism, it was this sense that he was always playing a part—that he preserved always, for almost every one, a certain barrier of mystery—that made Irving so fascinating a figure. That day, when I saw him on his way to Windsor, and tried to imagine just what impression he would make on Queen Victoria, I found myself thinking of the impression made there by Disraeli; and I fancied that the two impressions might be rather similar. Both men were courtiers, yet incongruous in a court. And both had a certain dandyism—the arrangement of their hair and the fashion of their clothes carefully thought out in reference to their appearance and their temperament. And both, it seemed to me, had something of dandyism in the wider, philosophic sense of the word—were men whose whole life was ordered with a certain ceremonial, as courtly functions are ordered. 'Brodribb', certainly, was an English name; but surely Irving had some strong strain of foreign blood: neither his appearance nor the quality of his genius was that of an Englishman. Possibly, like Disraeli, he had Spanish blood. Anyhow, his was an exotic mind, like Disraeli's, dominating its drab environment partly by its strength and partly by its strangeness. Both men were romantic to the core, ever conceiving large and grandiose ideas, which they executed with a fond eye to pageantry. And, above all, both men preserved in the glare of fame that quality of mystery which is not essential to genius, but which is the safest insurance against oblivion. It has been truly said that Irving would have been eminent in any walk of life. Had Disraeli the Younger drifted from literature to the foot-lights, and had Henry Brodribb strayed from the schoolroom into politics, I daresay that neither our political nor our theatrical history would be very different from what it is —except in the matter of dates.

'SARAH'S' MEMOIRS*

I WISH I HAD read this book before I left London. In a
very small and simple village on the coast of Italy I find
it over-exciting. Gray and gentle are the olive-trees
around me; and the Mediterranean mildly laps the shore,
with never a puff of wind for the fishermen, whose
mothers and wives and daughters sit plying their bobbins
all day long in the shade of the piazza. In mellow under-
tones they are gossiping, these women at their work, all
day long, and day after day. Gossiping of what, in this
place where nothing perceptibly happens? The stranger
here loses his sense of life. A trance softly envelops him.
Imagine a somnambulist awakening to find himself peering
down into the crater of a volcano, and you will realise
how startling Mme Sarah Bernhardt's book has been to
me.

Hers is a volcanic nature, as we know, and hers has
been a volcanic career; and nothing of this volcanicism is
lost in her description of it. It has been doubted whether
she really wrote the book herself. The vividness of the
narration, the sure sense of what was worth telling and what
was not, the sharp, salt vivacity of the style (which not
even the slip-shod English of the translator can obscure)
—all these virtues have to some pedants seemed incompatible with authenticity. I admit that it is disquieting
to find an amateur plunging triumphantly into an art
which we others, having laboriously graduated in it,
like to regard as a close concern of our own.
When Sarah threw her energies into the art of sculpture, and acquitted herself very well, the professional
sculptors were very much surprised and vexed. A similar

* *Memoirs of Sarah Bernhardt*. London: Heinemann. 1907.

disquiet was produced by her paintings. Let writers console themselves with the reflection that to Sarah all things are possible. There is no use in pretending that she did not write this book herself. Paris contains, of course, many accomplished hacks who would gladly have done the job for her, and would have done it quite nicely. But none of them could have imparted to the book the peculiar fire and salt that it has—the rushing spontaneity that stamps it, for every discriminating reader, as Sarah's own.

Her life may be said to have been an almost unbroken series of 'scenes' from the moment when, at the age of three, she fell into the fire. 'The screams of my foster-father, who could not move, brought in some neighbours. I was thrown, all smoking, into a large pail of fresh milk. ... I have been told since that nothing was so painful to witness and yet so charming as my mother's despair.' The average little girl would not resent being removed from a boarding school by an aunt. She would not 'roll about on the ground, uttering the most heart-rending cries.' But that is what little Sarah did; and 'the struggle lasted two hours, and while I was being dressed I escaped twice into the garden and attempted to climb the trees and to throw myself into the pond. ... I was so feverish that my life was said to be in danger.' On another occasion she swallowed the contents of a large ink-pot, after her mother had made her take some medicine; and 'I cried to mamma, "It is you who have killed me!"' The desire for death—death as a means of scoring off some one, or as an emotional experience—was frequent both in her childhood and in her maturity. When she was appearing at 'Zaïre', M. Perrin, her manager, offended her in some way, and she was 'determined to faint, determined to vomit blood, determined to die, in order to enrage Perrin.' An old governess, Mlle de Brabender, lay dying, and 'her face lighted up at the supreme moment with such a holy look that I suddenly longed to die.' Fainting was the next best thing to dying, and Sarah, throughout her early career, was continually fainting, with or without provocation. It is a wonder that so much emotional energy as she had to express in swoons, in floods of tears, in torrents of invective, did not utterly wear out her very frail body. Somehow her body fed and thrived on her spirit. The tragedian in her cured the invalid. Doubtless, if she had not been by nature a tragedian, and if all her outbursts of emotion had come straight from her human heart, she could not have survived. It is clear that even in her most terrific moments one half of her soul was in the position of spectator, applauding vigorously. This artistic detachment is curiously illustrated by the tone she takes about herself throughout her memoirs. The test of a good autobiography is the writer's power to envisage himself. Sarah envisages herself ever with perfect clearness and composure. She does not, in retrospect, applaud herself except when applause is deserved. She is never tired of laughing at herself with the utmost good humour, or of scolding herself with exemplary sternness. Of her sudden dash into Spain she says: 'I had got it into my head that my Fate willed it, that I must obey my star, and a hundred other ideas, each one more foolish than the other.' And such criticisms abound throughout the volume. It is very seldom that her sense of humour fails her, very seldom that she does not see herself from without as clearly as from within. She seems surprised that people were surprised at her sleeping in a coffin; and it still seems strange to her that a menagerie in a back-garden of Chester Square should excite unfavourable comment. Of this menagerie she gives an engaging description. 'The cheetah, beside himself with joy, sprang like a tiger out of his cage, wild with liberty. He rushed at the trees and made straight for the dogs, who all four began to howl with terror. The parrot was excited, and uttered shrill cries; and the monkey, shaking his cage about, gnashed his teeth to distraction.' Sarah's 'uncontrollable laughter', mingled with that of Gustav Doré and other visitors, strengthened the symphony. M. Got called next day to remind Sarah of the dignity of the Comédie Française; whereupon she again had the cheetah released, with not less delectable results. Can we wonder that there were comments in the newspapers of both nations? Sarah can. 'Injustice has always roused me to revolt, and injustice was certainly having its fling. I could not', says she, 'do a thing that was not watched and blamed.'

Now and again she pauses in her narrative to make remarks at large—to develop some theory of artistic criticism, or to handle some large social problem. And in these disquisitions she is always delightfully herself. She is a shrewd and trenchant critic of art, and in her ideas about humanity she is ever radiantly on the side of the angels, radiant with a love of mercy and a hatred of oppression. Capital punishment she abominates as 'a relic of cowardly barbarism'. 'Every human being has a moment when his heart is easily touched, when the tears of grief will flow; and those tears may fecundate a generous thought which might lead to repentance. I would not for the whole world be one of those who condemn a man to death. And yet many of them are good, upright men, who when they return to their families are affectionate to their wives, and reprove their children for breaking a doll's head.' That is the end of one paragraph. The next paragraph is: 'I have seen four executions, one in London, one in Spain, and two in Paris.' Was Sarah dragged to see them by force, as an awful punishment for lapses in the respect due to the dignity of the Comédie Française? She appears to have gone of her own accord. Indeed, she waited all night on the balcony of a first-floor flat in the Rue Merlin to see the execution of Vaillant, the anarchist, whom she had known personally and had liked. After the knife had fallen, she mingled with the crowd, and was 'sick at heart and desperate. There was not a word of gratitude to this man, not a murmur of vengeance or revolt.' She 'felt inclined to cry out "Brutes that you are! kneel down and kiss the stones that the blood of this poor madman has stained for your sakes, for you, because he believed in you!"' The wonder is that she did not actually cry these words out. Her reticence must have cost her a tremendous effort. Be sure that she really was horrified, at the time, by the crowd's indifference. Be sure that she really does altogether hate capital punishment. Be sure, too, that she had a genuine admiration for the character of the man whom she was at such pains to see slaughtered. You, gentle reader, might not care to visit an execution—especially not that of a personal friend. But then, you see, you are not a great tragedian. Emotion for emotion's sake is not the law of your being. It is because that is so immutably, so over-whelmingly, the law of Sarah's being that we have in Sarah—yes, even now, for all the tricks she plays with her art—the greatest of living tragedians. If ever I com-mitted a murder, I should not at all resent her coming to my hanging. I should bow from the scaffold with all the deference due to the genius that has so often thrilled me beyond measure. And never has it thrilled me more than through this unusual medium, in this unusual place.

ACKNOWLEDGMENTS

Grateful acknowledgment is made to the Beer-bohm Estate and to the following publishers for the use of copyright material: Rupert Hart-Davis Ltd ('Almond Blossom in Picca-dilly Circus', 'An Hypocrisy in Playgoing', 'Mr Shaw's New Dialogues', 'Dan Leno', 'Henry Irving', '"Sarah's" Memoirs'); William Heinemann Ltd ('Enoch Soames', 'James Pethel', '"Savonarola" Brown', 'Felix Argallo and Walter Ledgett', 'The Humour of the Public', 'The Naming of Streets', '"The Ragged Regiment"', 'No. 2. The Pines', 'Hosts and Guests', 'Going Out for a Walk', '"A Clergyman"', 'The Crime', 'William and Mary', '"How Shall I Word It?"', 'Laughter', 'The Mote in the Middle Distance', 'P.C., X, 36', 'Some Damnable Errors About Christmas', 'Scruts', 'Endeav-our', 'The Feast', *Zuleika Dobson*).